DAGONET ABROAD

DAGONET ABROAD

GEORGE R. SIMS

PREFACE

IF 'Dagonet Abroad' is found to be mainly a record of personal adventure, my excuse must be that I have always endeavoured to attend to my own business and leave other people's alone. I have described the cities and peoples of Europe entirely from my own personal observation. In no instance have I described a country without visiting it. I trust that this admission will not in any way injure my reputation as a traveller, or as a journalist.

GEO. R. SIMS.
LONDON,
September 1, 1895.

CHAPTER I.

IN BORDEAUX.

I AM in Bordeaux in February, and in a hotel; which hotel I am not quite sure. Over the top of the front door it is called 'Hôtel de la Paix,' on the left side of the door it is called 'Hôtel des Princes,' on the right side of the door it is called 'Hôtel de Paris.' It is three single hotels rolled into one; but its variety of nomenclature is slightly confusing. It is nice to be in so many hotels all at once, but I hope they won't all send me in a separate bill. The key to the enigma is this: Many hotels in Bordeaux have failed, or given up business. The landlord of *my* hotel has bought the goodwill of each, and stuck its title up over his own front door.

It is early in the morning and bitterly cold when I arrive, but as the day advances it gets aired. The sun comes out in the heavens and slowly gathers strength. By noon the streets are bathed in a warm glow. Bordeaux has changed from the frozen North to the sunny South. It is no longer Siberian; it is Indian. The pavements that were frozen with the cold in the early morning are now baking with the heat. I fling off my ulster, and I light a cigarette and stroll forth, airily clad, to bask and revel in the golden sunlight.

At the corner of the street I come upon a great crowd dressed in black. They are waiting for a funeral. Presently a modest little open hearse draws up. It is drawn by two horses covered from head to tail in rusty black clothing. Two men in faded bottle-green coats jump off, and go into a house. Presently they return with a poor, cheap, common coffin. They place it on the hearse, and throw a faded, rusty-looking pall over it. Then one of the men returns to the house, and comes back with a big wreath of yellow immortelles. On this is executed in black beads the legend, 'To Raoul Laval; from his friends of the Bureau.'

I mix with the crowd. I inquire who was this Raoul Laval who is starting on his journey to the great Terminus. 'An employé, monsieur, in the great shop yonder,' is the answer. 'So this is the funeral of a little clerk in a big shop,' I say to myself. 'Why, then, this big crowd?' The hearse starts. Then, to my astonishment, I behold this great crowd form behind the hearse—old men and women, young men and maidens, two and two, until the line of procession reaches as far as the eye can see. The hearse is a black dot far away, and still the mourners fall in and follow the little clerk to his grave. There are four gentlemen who hold the tasselled cords of the pall. These are the proprietors of the great emporium. Then come the relatives—Raoul's mother and his wife—then all the gentlemen in the office, then the gentlemen behind the counter and the smart shopgirls and the humble little workgirls, the porters and the packers, and the needlewomen, and the coachmen who drive out the carts, and the boys who deliver the parcels. Every living soul, great and small, rich and poor, all who earn their daily bread in that big drapery house where Raoul Laval was a humble clerk, have turned out to-day to do him honour and to see him home.

Slowly the long line of mourners (I count 760) passes on its way up the broad street until it is out of sight. I am left alone looking after it. Not quite alone, for an old man, who leans upon a stick and is bent with age, stands beside me, and shades his time-dulled eyes from the fierce sun, and peers through the distance to get the last glimpse of the fast-vanishing cortége. 'It is an honour to him, poor fellow!' I say to the patriarch, as we turn away together; 'a great honour for the whole firm to have followed him like this.' 'Yes, monsieur,' he answers, 'it is an honour; but he deserves it. He has been a faithful servant to the firm for twenty years, and everybody respected him. We shall all miss him now he is gone.' 'Ah! you are of the firm, too?' 'Yes, sir; I am the concierge. Poor Monsieur Raoul! Always a kind word for everybody, he had; and always at his post, monsieur—always at his post. The firm has lost a brave fellow—God rest his soul!'

Our ways divided; the old concierge went back to the shop, and I strolled on to the busy quay, teeming with colour and movement and life. But though I looked on the great river with its forest of masts, and listened to the babble of the thousand labourers on the quay as they loaded and unloaded the mighty ships, my thoughts were with the little clerk of the big drapery shop who was having so grand a funeral.

Yes, a grand funeral. The horses were broken-kneed, the coffin was cheap and common, the pall was threadbare and faded; but that great crowd of genuine mourners was something that a monarch might have envied. For every man and woman, every boy and girl in that long line of witnesses to his worth, loved and respected the man. Happy Raoul Laval! Lucky little clerk to have managed your life so well! How many of us whose names are known to fame—how many of us who fret and fume, and wear our hearts out in the battle for renown—would fall back into the ranks, and toil on quietly as you did to gain such love and respect and sympathy when our work is done, and we are put to bed to rest through the long dark night that must be passed ere we awaken to that brighter day which no living eyes may see!

Bordeaux is big and clean, and strikes one as a healthy town. The streets are wide and well kept, and parks and open spaces are plentiful. The people of Bordeaux have a healthy, happy, prosperous look. They walk briskly, instead of slouching about like the people of Marseilles. In fact, Bordeaux is the exact opposite of Marseilles. If you particularly wanted to see what cholera was like, and had to pick out a town where there was a fine chance of getting it, you couldn't do better than try Marseilles. If you wanted to escape from the epidemic, and get to a town where there was the least probability of its following you, you couldn't do better than settle in Bordeaux. I can't put the difference between the two towns in a more striking way than that.

The French equivalent of 'carrying coals to Newcastle' is 'carrying wine to Bordeaux.' You haven't been in Bordeaux five minutes before the presence of an enormous wine trade makes itself felt. Wine stares at you and confronts you everywhere. The wine lists in the hotels are huge volumes. Hundreds of varieties of wines, red and white, are elaborately set out. First you have the names of the 'cru's,' then the year, the price, the proprietors, and the place where the wine was bottled. You can read down a whole page of red wines, the cheapest of which is 25 francs a bottle, and the dearest 100 francs. These wine lists, which are handed to you in every hotel and restaurant, are magnificently bound in morocco and lettered in gold, and it is set forth that the 'cellars' from which you are drinking belong to a house founded so many years after the Flood, and that it has 'a speciality for the grand wines of Bordeaux, bottled at the châteaux, with the mark of their authentic origin on the corks, capsules, and labels.'

If ever one drinks genuine 'Bordeaux,' it ought to be at Bordeaux. At Yarmouth one does not suspect the freshness of the bloater; in Devonshire one blindly accepts the cream; at Banbury nothing can shake one's faith in the cake; and at Whitstable one does not say to the waiter at one's hotel, as he hands you the oysters, 'Waiter, are these *really* natives?' At Bordeaux I was prepared to gulp down even the *vin ordinaire* with the sublime faith of a Christian martyr; but, lounging on the great quays of Bordeaux, my faith sustained a shock from which it will never recover, and this is how it happened:

I am of a curious and inquiring turn of mind. When I saw great ships being unloaded, and casks of wine being piled high upon the quays, I said to my companion, 'Albert Edward, mon ami' (Albert Edward are the Christian names of my travelling companion), 'tell me is not this strange? Behold, here are vessels which are actually carrying wine to Bordeaux! Go and gather information.' My companion departed, and presently returned armed—nay, actually bristling—with facts.

The wine which we saw was wine imported from Spain. Enormous quantities of common Spanish wines are brought periodically from Spain to Bordeaux, and are there mixed with the 'wines of the country.' This discovery was a great blow to me; but I had a still greater blow when I found tremendous cargoes of all sorts of chemicals being unloaded, and I learnt that these also were imported for the purpose of manufacturing Bordeaux wines. Of course, the high-priced old wines are above suspicion; but I don't think I shall ever recover my faith in the *vin ordinaire*, after seeing that tremendous importation of Spanish wines and chemicals.

The fact is that Bordeaux has for a long time past been unable to meet the tremendous demands for its wines. The phylloxera has further increased the difficulty by ravaging the vineyards. So Nature having failed, Art steps in to supply the deficiency.

For the terrible spread of the phylloxera the growers were probably themselves originally to blame. They had been interfering with nature. The farmers in some countries have come to grief again and again from the same cause. Their crops have been destroyed by insects because they (the farmers) slaughtered all the small birds who would have kept the insects down. Everything in nature has its uses, and is meant to keep things in proportion. The world only prospers so long as we eat one another. Directly we upset the equilibrium of nature, we must pay the penalty. Half the diseases and epidemics which ravage the world are caused by the selfishness of man in endeavouring to work that willing horse, Nature, to death.

My hotel is exactly opposite the Grand Theatre of Bordeaux. The theatre is a magnificent building, and worthy of any capital. It stands alone in the centre of an immense square. This theatre was in 1871 the seat of the French Government, and here the Chamber of Deputies sat. It is very nice to live opposite a grand theatre, because you can pop across the road after dinner, and there you are, don't you know.

While I was in Bordeaux a grand opera company had possession of the theatre, and it was for this reason that I presently found out that there are also *dis*advantages in living in a hotel opposite a grand theatre. I had just settled down to my work, when I was startled by female shrieks in the next room to me. I imagined that a murder was being committed, and I rushed to the keyhole. But the shrieks suddenly became melodious, and then merged into shakes and cadenzas and trills, and general vocal gymnastics of the high Italian style. It was the prima donna of the opera company practising for the evening. She practised all the morning and all the afternoon, and it was past seven in the evening before she left off.

It was very interesting at first to hear all those lovely top notes gratis, but when a lady in the room on the other side of me commenced the same diversion in a rich contralto, and the gentleman in a room on the other side of my corridor began to sing in a basso profundo, and a gentleman up above me, who was the leading violinist, began tuning his fiddle, and a gentleman somewhere else in the hotel practised a solo on the trombone, being engaged for a private party after the opera, I began to gather together my writing materials, and rang the bell for the waiter, and inquired if he could direct me to a hotel, a little way out of town, at which the members of an opera company were not likely to put up.

The soprano lady in the next room to me was Mdlle. Isaak, and she travelled with a nice old mama and a dear old papa. Mama and papa accompanied her everywhere, and when they were in their own room they sat and applauded her shakes and runs vigorously with their feet and their hands. They all three came down and dined opposite me in the restaurant, and even between the courses Mdlle. Isaak hummed a little aria from the opera, and papa kept time with his fork on his wine-glass.

I had grand opera all day, and long after midnight I was suddenly aroused from my slumber by a terrific operatic duet in the next room. The tenor had returned to supper with the soprano family, and he and the lady were obliging mamma and papa with the duet they were going to sing together on the morrow. When they had finished I rose stealthily, and crept to the keyhole and hissed through it like a hundred discontented first-nighters. I would have paid my hotel bill twice over to have seen the faces of mamma and papa when that unwelcome sound burst upon their startled ears.

I have told you what beautiful sunshine we had at Bordeaux, and how nice and warm it was in the daytime. As long as the sun kept out it was lovely; but oh, when the sun went down! They gave me a beautiful, large, lofty room at the hotel, with doors and windows all over it. After dinner I went up to it to try and write, and then I found that Siberia had come again. I put great logs of wood upon the fire, and blew them with the bellows till the flames roared up the chimney; but still I shivered in the icy blasts that blew through every crevice. I put on my ulster, I dragged the blankets from the bed, I ran races round the room, and practised the Indian clubs with a heavy portmanteau in each hand; but still I felt my blood congealing, and the horrors of the early morning came back again. In this dilemma my companion's Soudan experiences stood us in good stead. (He was with Gordon in the expedition of '76-'77.) He took our walking-sticks and umbrellas, and with these and the blankets and the rugs he rigged up a nice, comfortable tent in front of the fire. Sitting in this tent in our big room we at last got warm, and my fingers were able to hold a pen.

People who have not travelled find it difficult to believe how cold it can be at night in places which are hot during the day. Houses in these places are arranged to keep out the warmth, and in consequence they let in the cold. A Russian gentleman who was shivering in Rome said to me one evening: 'Ah, in my country we *see* the cold; in Italy we *feel* it.' It is a fact that in a really cold country you can always keep yourself warm, while in a warm country you find it extremely difficult to prevent yourself feeling cold.

I think we saw everything in Bordeaux except the Zoological Gardens, and we didn't see these for a reason. At the hotel they gave me a local guide-book, which duly set forth the wonders of the town. A whole page was devoted to the Zoological Gardens. Here, the book informed the traveller, were to be seen lions and tigers and elephants, all sorts of dogs and monkeys and serpents and rare birds. Moreover, on Sunday afternoons, it stated, there was always a grand concert and a children's ball. 'Ah!' said I to myself, 'this is the thing for Sunday afternoon. Let us away to the lions and tigers and the children's ball.' We hailed a chariot which was on the rank—a regular Lord Mayor's coach, with room for twenty inside, and magnificently decorated. True, it was about one hundred years old, and it dropped little bits of itself as it rattled over the stones. The coachman was eighty if he was a day, and he sat on the huge box-seat with his feet in great sabots stuffed full of hay. We were able in this immense vehicle to take driving and walking exercise together, for we walked round and round it inside arm-in-arm, while two bony and broken-kneed horses staggered along the streets with it. We told our coachman to take us to the Zoological Gardens. He said nothing, but drove on with us.

In about a quarter of an hour he put us down at the Jardins Publiques, and we entered. Beautiful hothouses, a fine museum, nice lawns and ponds, but no animals. We re-entered the dilapidated Lord Mayor's coach, and said that was not what we wanted. We desired the gardens with the animals and the children's ball. Good! Off we drove again.

Presently the old coachman, by a series of feeble gymnastic exertions, dropped himself off the box and came to the carriage-door. 'Pardon, but would the gentlemen like to see the Museum of Paintings?' We said we would do anything to oblige so venerable a man; and he took us to the picture gallery. Then we started once more, impressing upon our aged Jehu that the real object of our promenade *en voiture* was the local Zoo. This time he drove us for nearly three-quarters of an hour, and at last pulled up in a lonely suburb opposite a stone wall, and, landing himself by easy stages to the earth, came hat in hand to the door and begged us to descend.

We descended. He then personally conducted us to a gap in the wall which was boarded up. In one board there was a little hole. 'Behold, gentlemen,' he said; 'if you will give yourselves the trouble to look through that little hole you will see the ground which is being converted into a new public park. It will be finished in two years.' We looked through and beheld a waste of brick and mortar and plank-strewn ground—and nothing more. 'But this is not the garden with the animals and the children's ball!' I exclaimed, after catching a violent cold in my eye from the wind which blew through the little hole in the hoarding; 'a truce to practical joking, mon vieux! To the Zoological Gardens at once, or I will swear at you.' The old man bowed and smiled and grinned, and begged a thousand pardons. He would gladly conduct us to such a place, but he did not know where to find it.

Then I abused him. I told him his conduct was disgraceful—that he had no right to be a coachman in Bordeaux if he did not know the way to its most famous place of public resort. He replied that he had never heard of such a place. Then I called a police-officer, and interrogated him. He, too, knew of no wild animals in Bordeaux, and of no gardens such as I described. We interrogated every passer-by, including a postman. The latter told us that perhaps we meant Paris—there was a garden like that there. In despair we gave up the expedition, and returned in the Lord Mayor's coach to our hotel.

There we triumphantly produced the local guide-book and read it aloud to the coachman, the concierge, the waiters, and the landlord. It made no impression. One and all declared on their honour, as citizens of Bordeaux, that no such place existed in the town. *And they were right.* I ascertained the fact by finding an old man who had lived seventy years in Bordeaux, and he told me that when he was a boy there was such a place, but it had disappeared this fifty years. And my guide-book is dated 1885! The editor is a good citizen. He refuses to allow the attractions of his native town to disappear from his pages. He wishes to paint his city to the greatest advantage. He is right from his point of view; but a guide-book which includes exhibitions which have been closed for fifty years—whose very sites have been built over—is not the best companion for a traveller who hires a carriage by the hour in order to drive about and see 'everything.'

I didn't trust to that guide-book any more. I quitted Bordeaux on Monday for Bayonne, *en route* for Biarritz. If you go to Biarritz direct, you must leave by a train at seven in the morning. I don't love early rising, so I determined to take a later train to Bayonne, from which place you can get on to Biarritz at any time. The distance is 124 miles, and the train does it in seven hours. It was slow, but I did not regret the journey.

CHAPTER II.

IN THE BASQUE COUNTRY.

BAYONNE, as all good little girls and boys who take prizes at school for geography and history are aware, is a fortified town commanding the passes of the West Pyrenees, and is a high road to Spain. It was here that the citadel which formed the key to an entrenched camp of Marshal Soult was invested by a portion of the army of the Duke of Wellington in 1814. The whole neighbourhood teems with memories of the halcyon days of the British arms. One comes to many a spot immortalized by a story which makes the Briton's heart beat faster with patriotic pride. The arms of England may still be seen upon the vault of the cathedral, and in the cemetery lies many a gallant officer and brave soldier of the Coldstream Guards who fell in the sortie of April 14, 1814. It was here—— But for further particulars look up your history. The dead past can bury its dead; my business is with the present.

I had a terrible fright coming from Bordeaux to Bayonne. The railway runs for a portion of the way through the Landes, a vast tract of heaths and ash-coloured sands and brackish streams. The inhabitants of this strange district lead hard and terrible lives. Food is scarce, and, what is worse, they can get very little water that is fit to drink, most of Sir Wilfrid Lawson's favourite beverage that finds its way to the Landes being salt and nauseous. I reached the Landes after the moon had risen. Owing to a little accident on the line, we were detained at a wayside station for half an hour. I lit a pipe, and strolled outside and made my way down a kind of road that skirted a wild, uncultivated heath. The road was very lonely, and everything looked weird in the moonlight. I was alone, for my companion had sacrificed comfort to a tight boot, and declined to walk. All of a sudden I saw a gigantic shadow thrown on the ground in front of me. I looked up and beheld a man twelve or fourteen feet high stalking towards me with strides that covered ten feet of ground at a time. On, on the giant came at a terrific pace, and the great beads of perspiration broke out upon my brow. He was a wild-looking giant, with long black hair, and a huge sheepskin covered his body. His legs were the longest and the thinnest I had ever seen in my life. I didn't believe he was human. I made up my mind he was a creature from the fable world, and that I was about to be carried away to his haunt, wherever it may be, and devoured. I thought of Jack and the Beanstalk, and I expected the creature every moment to say, 'Fee, fo, fum!' and refer to the fact that the blood of an Englishman had saluted his olfactory organs. Just as I was going to drop on my knees and shriek for mercy, the giant suddenly halted, put a big pole which he carried in his hand behind his back, and stood stock-still in the moonlight, a living, breathing tripod.

I held my breath, and waited for the dénouement. The giant raised his cap, and asked me, in excellent French, if I could tell him what the time was. Then I took a calmer view of him, and suddenly it dawned upon me that my giant was no giant at all, but merely a shepherd of the Landes mounted upon enormous stilts.

I am not the first traveller who has been startled by such an apparition. The inhabitants of this district walk upon stilts from childhood to old age. They would not be able to get over the sandy ground studded with prickly heather in ordinary boots and shoes. They stride over hedges and ditches in this way at a pace which no horse can keep up with, and while they are watching their flocks they stick a long pole in the ground, and, resting their backs against it, stop in this position for hours knitting stockings. The spectacle to the unaccustomed eye is one of the most startling that can be conceived. I told my stilted friend the time, and, wishing him good-night, walked back to the station; but it was a long time before I got over the 'turn' which his sudden apparition in the moonlight had given me.

In Bayonne I spent the Mardi Gras and had my 'carnival.' The people of the South know how to be merry and enjoy themselves, and they can disguise themselves humorously and in good taste. All night long the quaint streets were crowded with hundreds of masquerading revellers, and the fun was fast and furious. Many of the costumes were Spanish, and really fine pieces of colouring. The ladies were particularly charming, though I fancy some of them must have suffered the next day with rheumatism in the lower limbs, for the roads were damp and muddy, and the wind blew keenly. Wet roads and keen winds are hardly suited to extra short skirts and pink fleshings and dainty little shoes and head-dresses of gauzy lace.

They certainly were not rheumatic on the night of the Mardi Gras, for I procured a box at the theatre and watched the grand carnival ball at its height during the small hours. The masked ball at the Paris Opera House is a grander sight for variety and richness of costume, and the crowd of revellers is greater, but no ball that I have ever witnessed came near to this little Bayonne celebration in mirth and unforced gaiety and rollicking good humour. Heavens, how the natives danced! How they whirled round and round, and capered and kicked their legs up, and laughed and shouted, and threw themselves heart and soul into the maddest of mad quadrilles! I left the theatre at four in the morning, and the Bayonne lads and lasses, masked, disguised, and brilliantly costumed, were hard at it still; and when I got outside into the cool air of the early morning there were still dozens of masqueraders, male and female, promenading the public square arm-in-arm, with never a cloak or a wrap about them, yet not a single cough or sneeze broke in upon the merry laughter that floated on the cool and humid air. I hurried towards my hotel with my overcoat buttoned to my chin, and on my way I passed a little sylph in an airy pink ballet costume, seated on a stone bench, and listening to the old, old story from the lips of a youthful Spanish matador; and the little sylph in pink gauze had taken great care not to sit upon the delicate texture of her skirts. I could understand that the tender passion had warmed her heart, but it must have also spread a glow all over to enable her to listen to the vows of her swain in that costume and on that seat without a single chatter of the teeth.

From Bayonne, before going to Biarritz, I determined to push further into the interior of the Basque country, and see for myself this strange race of people as they are in their mountain homes. Many of the inhabitants of Bayonne are Basque, and all the servants in the hotels. From coachmen, waitresses (there are very few waiters in Basque hotels), peasants, and fishermen, I gleaned a good deal of useful information before starting; but years of study might be devoted to this extraordinary people, the aborigines of Western Europe, who have seen Celts, Carthaginians, Romans, Goths, Vandals, and Saracens pass away like shadows, and still linger on themselves, retaining their old traditions and superstitions and their old language, which is like no other European tongue. Of their habits and customs, and of their homes, I shall have something to say presently; but I cannot resist giving here a specimen of this extraordinary Basque language, which one hears to-day freely talked, not only in the mountains and the valleys, but in the busy streets of the big towns.

The following paragraph I take from a dialogue between two Basque peasants, which is printed in a Basque paper. An election in the department was fixed for February 27, and it is concerning the merits of the Conservative and the Republican candidate that Batichta and Piarres are engaged in animated converse:

'BATICHTA ETA PIARRES.—Canden igande arratsaldean, bezperetaric lekhora, ikhus, en gintuen Batichta eta Piarres, bi etcheco jaun adiskide handiac, bici bicia mintzo pilota plaza hegal batean. Huna, gero entzun dugunaz, car cerasaten.'

The linguist will see how utterly unlike any European tongue these words are. There is a suggestion of Arabic now and then, and a slight resemblance to a few Finnish and Spanish words; but, as a whole, it is absolutely original. Here is the translation: 'Last Sunday, in the afternoon, on coming from vespers, we noticed two landowners—Batichta and Piarres—two good friends. They spoke very excitedly at the corner of the Jeu de Paume ground, and here is what they said——' Then follows a long political conversation.

The Basques are strongly anti-Republican. Hundreds of young men are leaving their villages and going to South America to avoid serving in the army of the Republic. Their fathers would rather let their children go from them to the great land beyond the seas than see them fighting for a Government which they detest. The Basque population swarms in such places as Ecuador, Uruguay, the Brazils, Chili, and the Spanish-speaking portions of South America. Many of them return in after-years, rich and prosperous, to their native mountain homes, and build magnificent châteaux on the site of the old paternal cottages. When they return they are called 'Americans'; and this rather bothered me, as one day, near Cambo, I had grand villa after villa pointed out to me as the residence of an 'American.' By cross-questioning my guides I arrived at the truth. The 'Americans' were wealthy Basques who had made fortunes 'across the seas,' and come home to be great men among their poorer compatriots. There is a good deal of South America dotted about the Basque country. You come upon the 'Auberge de

Monte Video,' and the 'Hôtel de Buenos Ayres,' and the 'Auberge de Rio Janeiro.' My coachman's sister has married and gone to Peru. My chambermaid's brother is making money in Chili. An old fisherman who told me all the legends of St. Jean de Luz has two sons at Monte Video. Half the cottagers one talks to have friends and relatives in South America. South America is the El Dorado of the young Basque's dreams. But when he has made his pile, he likes to come back to the old home, and spend it among his people.

With all these travellers among them, you would think the Basque peasantry would cease to be strongly conservative, that their ideas would broaden, and their exclusiveness would be broken down. But it is not so. They hate railways, and they hate the foreigners to come and disturb their peaceful ways. At Cambo the other day I fell in with a group of small landowners who were discussing the new railway schemes, and they were purple with passion that such an idea should have been mooted.

This conservative spirit among the Basque population is tremendously worked upon at election time. It will be interesting to all who study French politics (and who does not nowadays?) to see the sort of language which a local Conservative candidate indulges in at the expense of the Republic. Listen to this:

FOR GOD AND FOR FRANCE.

Electors of the Basses Pyrénées,—The struggle begins; the banners are unfolded. On which side should good Catholics and simple and honest folks range themselves? Under the banner of the Republic?

No; for it is this Republic whose dead weight lies upon our unhappy country, and crushes out its life.

Who suppressed the catechism and prayers in our public schools?

Who has driven God from the army?

Who has driven the priest from the bedside of the sick and of the dying?

Who established the anti-Christian and immoral law of divorce?

Who, not content with paganizing France, has robbed her of her fortune and her glory?

Who for the last ten years has augmented by milliards the debt of France?

Who dishonours the armies of France by making them the Armies of the Republic?

Who has left us in all Europe without a single alliance?

Who has led us to the very brink of war, from which God preserve us?

The Republic!

Will you vote for the Republic?

No; you will vote for God and for France—

And for the Conservative candidate.

This inflammatory address is placarded throughout the Basque villages of the department concerned in the election. Crowds of the peasants stand round the walls and read it sympathetically.

Everything is bright and pretty and quaint and picturesque in the Basque country. The men, clean shaven and with fine Saracen faces, in their dark blue berets and red waistbands; the women, with their red, or blue, or black, or yellow toques; the half-Spanish, half-Swiss houses; the carts drawn by yoked oxen; the waggons and diligences with their long string of Spanish mules; the crosses and signs upon the doorways; the Eastern custom of carrying gracefully water-jars upon the head; the tall wooden crosses on every hill and highway—all these things, thrown into relief by a background of glorious scenery, make an impression upon the traveller which does not soon pass away.

The waitress in my hotel, who is at once waitress, *femme de chambre*, and everything that is useful, is a wonder in her way. Of Spanish Basque origin, she has travelled with families during her early life, and she speaks Spanish, French, German, and Italian, as well as her native Basque. She likes the English, she tells me, and is very proud of the fact that she one day waited on the Prince of Wales when he came incognito to breakfast at the Hôtel St. Martin, at Cambo (a beautiful Basque village about twelve miles from Bayonne). No one knew the Prince, and he and his companions made a good breakfast, and then went about and talked with the villagers, and inspected the farms, and smoked their cigars out on the terrace of the hotel, which overlooks a landscape not to be matched in Switzerland. The Prince talked to my waitress, and asked her what this was in Basque and what that was, and questioned her as to the habits and customs of the country.

To all intents and purposes the royal party were simply English tourists, when suddenly a grand carriage drove up to the hotel. A French duke and another gentleman alighted, and, bowing themselves into the presence of the Prince, invited him to a grand breakfast at Biarritz; and a third gentleman arrived almost immediately with an invitation from the English consul. 'Thanks,' said the Prince, laughing; 'I have breakfasted excellently, and I'm going to spend the day here. Let me enjoy myself in this delightful spot, like good fellows, and go back and say you couldn't find me.'

My *femme de chambre* ran on for a quarter of an hour eulogizing the Prince. She has the five-franc piece which he gave her when he paid his bill, and it is to go to her family when she dies as a precious legacy. She believes in royalty tremendously, for the royal family of Portugal, she tells me, always stop at this hotel, and they laugh and talk with her always like old friends. 'Ah,' she says, 'your royal folks when they travel are simple and easily pleased, and they make no fuss. It is your people of small rank who are proud and cold and want so much attention. There is a little German countess who comes here in the season *en route* for Biarritz, and she travels with a dog and two servants, and she must have the whole of the first-floor reserved for her, and she will take nothing from the servants of the hotel. Her dog even will not notice us, but walks past us with his tail in the air.'

I let my *femme de chambre* chatter on. She tells me stories of the Empress Eugénie in the old Biarritz days, and tears come into her eyes as she speaks of the dead Prince Imperial. They worship the memory of the imperial family of France all round this district, and have many a pleasant tale to tell of the young lady who lived so much among them in the days before the love of an emperor raised her to the throne. When she has quite finished her royal and imperial anecdotes, I cross-question her as to Basque habits and customs and superstitions. My head is full of the beautiful Basque legends and ghost stories which I have lately picked up, and I ask her if it is true that the people still believe in them. Then she informs me that her venerable father and mother are Basque peasants, and that they themselves believe in witchcraft and sorcery, and all the spells of the Evil One, and all the bad spirits that haunt the mountains and the woods. Her papa has, in fact, just moved out of his house on account of sorcery. He lost last year six cows, and he was so convinced that they had been bewitched, and that a spell had been worked upon his house, that he quitted it, and built another close by. He then sent for the priest to come and bless it, and after that he painted up a big white cross on the front door to keep the evil spirits from entering therein. 'Superstitious!' she says. 'Ah, mon cher monsieur, I have travelled and seen the world, and I know better; but when I go to my native village and say I do not believe in witches and charms and the evil spirits of the night, the peasants cross themselves, and my old father and mother weep and curse themselves for allowing me to leave home and become "une fille perdue."'

Wandering about the Basque villages, I have gleaned a few of their superstitions. No man, woman, or child among them will be out of doors after midnight, for they all believe that wicked spirits are abroad, and that terrible misfortune will befall anyone who meets them. On certain feast days they light a great fire, and the whole family kneels and prays round the burning wood until it is all reduced to ashes. These ashes are then carefully collected and scattered on the fields to make them fruitful. If any man neglects to propitiate the spirits by strewing these ashes, his crops will fail.

One afternoon I come to a little auberge on the slope of a lonely mountain on the Spanish side. A great white cross is roughly chalked on the door, and outside sits an old woman talking with the landlord and his wife. They are listening with rapt attention, and cross themselves again and again. Presently the old crone goes away, and I sit on the bench and call for something 'for the good of the house,' and gradually get the landlord to tell us what the old lady was talking to him about. Then he tells us that last night the old crone saw the 'arguiduna' in the village graveyard—the 'arguiduna' of her son whom she buried a month since. The 'arguiduna' is the soul of a dead person when it takes the shape of a will-o'-the-wisp. This strange light came from her son's grave, and stopped close to her. As she moved away it followed her, and accompanied her to the old home. On the threshold she stood still, and her son's soul in its fiery form circled three times round her, and then slowly went up, up, up into the skies till it was lost among the stars. 'And now,' says the innkeeper, 'the old mother is happy, for she has been in great trouble about her boy, for he had been wild and had done many evil things, and she feared it might not be well with his soul. Now that she has seen the "arguiduna" go up like that to the skies, she knows that his sins have been forgiven him, and that he is with the blessed. She will weep for him no more.'

People who live in great cities, where ideas rush at railway speed, and where the bustle and noise of modern life destroy romance and drive fancy from the field, find it difficult to believe that such a superstition as this can be implicitly believed by a whole race of people living in civilized countries in the nineteenth century; but these Basque people believe to this day in all the legends and fables which their ancestors believed a thousand years ago. With them nothing has changed, and to-day they have their Arguiduna; their Maitgarri, or Fairy of the Lakes; the Lamia, a weird being inhabiting the wave-washed coasts; the Jauna, or Spirits of the Wood; and the Sorguinas, the Spirits of the Plains. In these and a hundred other spirits, evil and good, in witches, sorcerers, and devils, the Basque people of to-day believe as firmly and as devoutly as they did in the dark ages. Their daily life, their habits and customs, are all shaped by these superstitions, and their priests, unable to combat them, now tacitly admit them, and even bless many of the charms which they use against the spirits of darkness. And these people live many of them within walking distance of a railway-station, and Liberal candidates address them and canvass for their votes at election time.

Cambo is a lovely Basque village, about twelve miles from Bayonne. Imagine a sweet Swiss valley shut in by an amphitheatre of olive-green and purple hills! Through the valley winds a broad stream of silver water. Fair white houses, and châlets with bright red roofs, throw back the rays of a glorious sun that bathes the scene in golden light. Above is a sky of cloudless blue. Far as the eye can reach all is luxuriance and beauty. As one gazes upon the perfect landscape from the broad stone terrace of the Hôtel St. Martin, a great peace steals into one's soul, and the cares and troubles of the outer world are for a time forgotten. On the slope of the hill which faces this glorious scene stands a quaint Basque village. The people live by the land, which yields a bounteous harvest. They keep the simple manners and customs of bygone centuries; they have been here, undisturbed by the rattle of traffic and the snort of the railway engine, ever since the place came into existence; and now, if you please, the French are going to desecrate their village with a railway. There is to be a station at Cambo. The inhabitants are furious; the landowners have refused to sell their land, and the Government replies that if they persist it will be taken from them by force.

My sympathies are with Cambo. A railway will destroy the poetry of the place. All the Basque people ask is to be allowed to live quietly in their homes. They don't want to be hustled by a crowd of townsfolk, whose ways are not their ways, and who speak a foreign language. Even the rich 'Americans,' whose splendid châteaux dot the hills, are crying out. They are Basque to the backbone, and they don't want excursionists gaping about their grounds, and driving over them in their winding, tree-shaded roadways.

But I must not go Basque-mad, and imagine everyone is as interested in the people as I am. Let us return to modern civilization, and go to Biarritz. My coachman drives me there from Bayonne. He is a beautiful creature, my coachman. He wears the old postilion jacket and hat. He is trimmed with scarlet and silver lace, and my arithmetic stops short in an attempt to add up his buttons. His little jacket alone costs £5; his waistcoat costs £1; his hat costs 15s.; and his horses have bells all over them, so that we make merry music as we dash along the roads, and the whip cracks joyously, and the dogs bark a concert in our rear, and the children pursue us at full speed, yelling for coppers; and that's how we go to Biarritz.

CHAPTER III.

FROM BIARRITZ TO BURGOS.

BIARRITZ disappoints one at first, and then grows upon one. It is like a jumble of Ilfracombe, Westgate-on-Sea, the Land's End, Ostend, and Broadstairs. The sea dashes in gloriously, and makes tremendous breaches in coast and cliff. The hotels are as grand as money can make them, and on the Parade, in all their glory, I came suddenly upon Mary Ann and Susan, two English nursemaids, in the usual hats and feathers, and the usual imitation fur-trimmed jackets, and the usual fingers through the gloves, wheeling unmistakable English perambulators, full of unmistakable English babies; and when, later on, I came upon Eliza Jane sitting down and reading the *London Journal* while *her* perambulator was gently working itself, baby and all, over the parade on to the beach, I actually looked up and down and round about for the Life Guardsman.

The French *bonnes* and the Basque nurses, so clean, so neatly dressed, must have been considerably astonished when Mary Ann and Eliza Jane first came from Clapham to the Bay of Biscay. Even now they eye their ostrich feathers, their brooches, and their fur-trimmed jackets with awe. I earnestly trust the awe is not mixed with admiration. It would be a very terrible thing if the neat and picturesque French *bonne*, corrupted by the English example, suddenly broke out into hats and feathers, and bad boots and rusty finger-twisted gloves. The downfall of France would then be assured. Whichever way I turn, the British nursemaid meets me and defies me. I sit down to contemplate a grand effect of wave-washed rock, and a female voice behind me shouts to Master Tommy not to go too near the edge; I climb the cliffs and gaze at the distant coast of Spain, and a little imp in a sailor costume, with a broken spade and a sand-grimed bucket, assaults me with, 'Please, sir, can you tell me the time?' I find a lovely romantic spot right out on the extreme ledge of an overhanging rock, and, on turning round to look back at the town, I see a young woman behind me nursing a baby and reading the *Family Herald*. When I rise and fly to the streets for refuge, when I gaze into the shop windows at the fans and tambourines of Spain, the English nursemaid still pursues me. A perambulator is wheeled across my heels, and the wheeleress says, 'Beg yer pardon, sir; I 'ope I didn't 'urt you!'

Ye gods! Is it for this I have travelled many hundreds of miles? Is it for this I have been saturating myself with the language and the legends of the Basques? I go to an hotel and order my lunch. At the next table to me are a young gentleman and a young lady. The young gentleman says, 'Are you coming to the lawn-tennis ground this afternoon?' and the young lady replies, 'No; Jack's going to drive me to St. Jean de Luz in his dogcart.' It is all English—everywhere English, and nothing but English. The stationers' shops are full of English valentines and English books; the grocers' shops display English jams and English pickles; the chemists' shops have their windows stocked with English patent medicines, and English pills and English plaisters; and, as I live, when I turn to make a mad dash for the railway-station, two little boys come along arm-in-arm, and as they walk they whistle 'Grandfather's Clock'!

Oh, for the lost illusions of my youth! Oh, for the Biarritz of my dreams! I am at Margate; I am at Brighton; I am at Eastbourne; I am anywhere and everywhere on the coast of England; but I can't possibly be on the Biscayan shores, and almost within hail of the Spanish coast! Sadly I enter the train, and return to Bayonne and a foreign land. I like England *in* England; but to come to Biarritz and find everything British, to be abroad and to be run down by London nursemaids, and to have 'Grandfather's Clock' all over again, is worse than earthquakes to me.

After the shock of the English nursemaids wore off, I appreciated Biarritz at its true value, and I ceased to wonder that it had such a large winter colony of English. All along this coast there are huge hotels, which are kept open in the winter solely on account of the English. At St. Jean de Luz, a lovely little seaside spot, I saw a whole dozen of English Mary Janes and Sarah Anns sitting on the Parade in the warm sunshine, and talking, I suppose, of the lovers they had left in dear old England far away. While I was in the post-office, an English nursemaid came in and sat down at the table, and put the stamps lovingly on a letter she had in her hand, and I was curious enough to look over her shoulder and read the address. It was 'Private John Smith, The Barracks, Chelsea.' How I wished I could see under the envelope! I should like to read a description of life on the Basque coasts from the pen of a true-born British nursemaid, reared in all the insular prejudices and antipathies.

If I had to choose the spot where I would spend my winter, it would not be Biarritz or St. Jean de Luz, but San Sebastian, the Spanish watering-place, where in the season the Spanish aristocracy are so numerous you can walk on their heads. I should want a chapter to do justice to this glorious spot, so I must pass it by with just a nod of friendly recognition, and continue my journey—a journey which was nearly being interrupted in a manner which, much as I desire novel experiences, I am heartily glad that I was spared.

My original idea was to return from Bayonne to Bordeaux, and then take the Pacific mail steamer for Lisbon, working from thence to Seville and Granada, and then to Madrid, and so up through Spain into France and home again. I had even gone so far as to send to the shipping office for the tickets. My messenger returned with the information that the ship would be the *Valparaiso*, but that we could not have berths until the agent received a telegram from Liverpool telling him if there were any vacant. On the day before we were to return to Bordeaux, we received a letter from the agent saying we could have berths. We packed up. We were on the point of starting to Bordeaux, when, sitting in my armchair after dinner, I fell asleep and had a dream. I dreamt that I was shipwrecked. I felt the water closing over my head. I struck out and tried to swim, but the great waves struck me and threw me back. I clung to spars; I shouted for help. I went through a whole catalogue of agonies; and, just as a big shark was opening his mouth to swallow me, I woke up with a start. 'It is time to go,' said Albert Edward. 'The omnibus is at the door. Shall I send the luggage down?' 'No,' I exclaimed, starting up and rubbing my eyes. 'No; a hundred times no! I've had a dream, and nothing will tempt me to make that sea-trip now.' A few days after, in the reading-room of our hotel in Madrid, I picked up a newspaper, and saw that the *Valparaiso*, the ship by which we should have sailed but for that dream, had been wrecked in Vigo Bay, and that all the passengers' luggage had been lost.

I am always anxious for adventures which will furnish material for my books, but I very much prefer to rely upon my imagination for my shipwrecks. A good many people have described earthquakes without being in them, and I am sure I can give a good account of 'an awful night at sea' without being taken off in a small boat and losing my luggage.

Instead of going by sea, we went by land, and the next day found us in the sleeping-car *en route* from Bayonne to Burgos, our first halting-place on our way to Madrid. The French authorities arrange this journey admirably. You arrive at Hendaye, the French frontier, at five minutes past twelve, and here you have half an hour for luncheon. The train then goes on, and reaches Irun in five minutes, where the Spanish authorities, not to be outdone in politeness, give you an hour. It is a battle between France and Spain which shall have the buffet money. Seeing that you have an hour at Irun, I can in no other way account for the absurdity of giving you half an hour at Hendaye. A run of two and a quarter miles in an hour and a half is surely the best on record for a special express train like the Paris-Madrid mail bound on a journey of 968 miles.

At Irun we entered on Spanish territory, Spanish customs, and Spanish manners. We received the utmost courtesy at the station and in the Custom House, and everywhere along the line. And we did it all with a well-filled case of halfpenny cigars. No official in the world is so polite or appreciates politeness so much as a Spanish one. The French are artificially polite, the Spaniards are naturally so. Hats are raised everywhere, faces are wreathed in smiles, bows are low and stately. To the chiefs of stations, to Custom House officers, after a few words of courteous inquiry, we offered a cigar. If we had offered gold and precious stones our gift could not have been received with greater sweetness and recognition. And for those few cigars we were treated everywhere like princes. Gold-braided caps-in-hand, stationmasters wished us a pleasant journey, and guards came and mounted on the steps and peeped in and inquired as to our comfort. At the end of the journey I really felt ashamed that we had received so much for so little. On the return journey we are going to fill that cigar-case with penny ones.

The run through the Pyrenees in the blazing sunshine was magnificent. When the train stopped, high up upon the great mountains, we got out and let our faces bronze, inhaled the splendid mountain air, and contrasted the scene around us (it was Sunday afternoon) with the aspect of Tottenham Court Road and Camden Town. We pitied the people in London, and we wondered if they were having a fog and crouching over their fires with the gas alight, and we made up our minds, when we were rich enough to retire, to come and end our days in the sunshine of the Pyrenees. The difficulty must be *to* end your days there. Unless you go up to the top of a precipice, and throw yourself deliberately over, it is difficult to see what can kill you in such a splendidly healthy, bracing air—in a land of perpetual life-giving sunshine.

The guard of our train was a very wonderful man, I have heard of a sailor who had a wife in every port, but we almost came to the conclusion that our guard had a wife at every station. Whenever the train stopped there was a young woman waiting, who was instantly kissed on both cheeks by our guard. Some of the ladies he kissed had little boys and girls with them, and he kissed the children too. It was to us a matter of much speculation as to what this constantly-recurring lady waiting to be kissed by our guard could mean. It remains a mystery to this hour. Perhaps he was one of a very large family, and his sisters and his cousins and his aunts had scattered and settled all along the line.

At Miranda we had 'buffet' again. It was a wonderful meal—real Spanish cookery, everything done in oil; but it was by no means bad. The wonderful thing about it was the way in which the passengers got through a meal of ten courses in fifteen minutes by the clock. It was one plate down and another up. The waiters actually galloped round the table piling plates full of soup, fish, entrée, joint, fowl, salad, pastry, cheese, and fruit before the astonished passengers. Heavens, how we ate! How we finished one plate and pushed it aside and seized the full one by our side! No changing knives and forks. It was just one wild waltz from dish to dish, and when the bell rang and we rushed out to the train we carried oranges and apples and figs and dates and biscuits in our hands. I had an indigestion five minutes afterwards which has lasted up to now, and which bids fair to remain with me until the end of my chequered career.

The rest of the journey was performed in the dark. The only bit of colour was made by our gens d'armes, who, with loaded rifles, accompanied the train, and were changed at each station. All trains in Spain carry two of these men—'Civil Guards' they are called—to protect the passengers in case of attack. These men, a picked body, without fear and without reproach, have cleared Spain of brigands. They are to Spain what the Irish constabulary was once to Ireland. They are unbribable, and have only one idea—duty. They are empowered to shoot at their own discretion, and they are trusted not to make a mistake. There is no arresting with them. A man taken red-handed, they put a bullet into. Spanish justice is slow—a man sent for trial knows there are a hundred ways of getting acquitted, and failing that of escaping from prison. So the Spanish Civil Guard executes its own justice in a speedy and summary manner. Murderers and brigands they kill first and try afterwards. These men have made Spain safe for the traveller for the first time for many hundreds of years.

Our halting-place was Burgos. Here we left the train, and began our first experience of Spanish towns and Spanish hotel life. We had been reading up our guide-books, and we alighted with doubt and dread. We were told that the hotels were bad, and that the people were difficult to deal with. But we had a little knowledge of the language, and we had determined to conform literally to Spanish customs and to observe the forms of Spanish etiquette, and so we hoped to fare better than the bulk of English travellers who, in print and out of it, have made such a parade of the drawbacks to a sojourn in Spain.

These Spanish customs are most interesting. They *must* be observed by anyone who wants to get on with the people. The usual British idea of looking upon natives as 'a lot of foreigners' won't do here. If you insist upon being English and doing as you would in England you will have a very bad time among a people who are the proudest and the most sensitive in Europe. Cast your British prejudices to the wind, and try to be Spanish, and you will carry home with you pleasant memories which will last you all your life. We decided to be Spanish down to the ground, to treat every man as a grandee, and to praise everything we saw with all the adjectives we could find the Spanish for in our dictionary.

In the first place, we commenced to practise worshipping each other's hats. The hat in Spain is elevated almost to the position of an idol. When anyone comes to see you, you place his hat in an armchair all to itself. You take it from him at the door. With loving care you bear it across the room, and then, with many flowery speeches, you deposit the sacred tile gently on the right-hand chair of honour. All Spanish sitting-rooms are arranged for this ceremony. They contain no furniture, as a rule, but a sofa, a console table, and some chairs, and this gives them a bare appearance, which is not decreased by the entire absence of a fireplace.

The sofa in the Spanish room is put against the wall in the right-hand corner. In front of it on each side are two chairs, one an armchair, and the other an ordinary one. The sofa and the four chairs are so arranged as to form three sides of a square. The sofa is for you and your guests, the armchairs are for their hats, and the smaller chairs for ornament. This 'reception of the hat' sounds like an exaggeration, but it is a ceremony which is observed with the greatest punctiliousness all through Spain. My companion and I practised it in our sitting-room for hours. First he knocked at the door and pretended to be a Spanish hidalgo, and I received him, took his hat and conducted it, walking backwards, to the armchair. Then I recited verses in its honour, kissed its brim, and bestowed titles upon it. Then he received me and *my* hat, and we buttered each other up in our best Spanish and bowed to each other till our backs ached. We very soon got perfect in the art of receiving gentlemen visitors, and, of course, that was all we wanted, as we were not likely to have any lady visitors.

When you go to a lady's house there are terrible ceremonies to be gone through. When you rise to leave you are bound to say, 'A los piés de usted' (this last word is always written thus, 'V.' simply, in Spanish), 'señora.' 'My lady, I place myself at your feet.' Then the lady says, 'Beso á V.' (usted that V. means) 'la mano, caballero.' 'I kiss your hand, sir.' 'Vaya V. con Dios que V. lo pase bien.' 'May you depart with God and continue well.' Then you have to answer to that, 'Quede V. con Dios.' 'May you remain with God.' And so you go, your hat being handed to you as if it were a new-born baby.

The salutations and greetings and farewells among the common people are many of them very poetical. When I left my first Spanish hotel, the waiter and the chambermaid came out with the landlord to see us off. My companion and I laid ourselves figuratively at the chambermaid's feet; we invoked all the blessings of Heaven on the landlord's head, and, in accordance with Spanish etiquette, we expressed a hope that the waiter might remain with God. The group returned our adieux, and the little chambermaid made us a sweet reverence in the Andalusian manner (she was of Seville, was our 'chica'), and said, 'Good-bye, your lordships; may we all meet again some day in God's big parlour.' Now, I think that was very pretty—don't you?

'Chica' means sweetheart. It is another pretty custom in Spanish inns to call the waitress 'chica.' It sounds odd at first to English ears—'Sweetheart, bring me a glass of beer;' 'Sweetheart, a cup of chocolate;' 'Sweetheart, do you call these boots blacked, or have you given them to the dog to lick?' When an inn is full, and everybody is shouting for his 'sweetheart,' the Englishman unused to the form of address, but knowing a little of the language, wonders what it means. But he soon drops into the habit, and addresses the dark-eyed Spanish muchacha as 'chica,' too.

Spain is saturated with Moorish manners and customs. The Eastern custom of clapping the hands, instead of calling the waiter or attendant, prevails everywhere. You never hear a sound of 'Waiter!' in a café, only here and there two sharp short claps of the hand. The effect is pleasing, and it saves your throat considerably.

But I am keeping you waiting a long time before taking you to see Burgos, and I have told you nothing about hotel life.

The first things that strike you as you enter an old Spanish town at night are the dark and mysterious-looking men gliding along in the dark shadows, cloaked to the eyes. Nearly all Spaniards still wear the old 'capa,' or long black mantle, and the folds of this are so arranged as to completely muffle the face, leaving only the eyes visible. The Castilians muffle like this in the hottest weather. They dread a breath of fresh air. But it makes them look awfully like murderers, and it gave us quite a creepy sensation as we plodded through old, decaying Burgos, late at night, and came suddenly on men muffled in black to the eyes at the street corners. But having occasion to ask one to direct us to the hotel, he instantly flung his cloak from his face and disclosed his features. This is another Spanish custom. If you keep your cloak over your face when you stop anyone, or when you address anyone, you are at once supposed to be a bad character, or an assassin, and the man talking to you clasps his knife or his revolver, and gets ready for you.

We reached the hotel in Burgos in safety, and walked upstairs, and found a gentleman smoking a cigarette in an easy-chair, who rose and bowed, and told us to choose what rooms we liked and to make ourselves at home, and God be with us; and then he sat down and lit another cigarette. We chose our rooms, then went down and bargained with the gentleman for so much a day. All hotels in Spain lodge and feed you at so much a day, and you have to make the contract on arrival. There are no extras when once you have agreed to the price. We arranged at 50 reals a day each (a real is 2½d.). For this we had our rooms and the following meals: The desayuno in the bedroom, a cup of chocolate and a piece of sour bread; the almuerzo, or lunch, at eleven; the comida, or dinner, at seven. The Spanish lunch begins generally with eggs cooked in various fashions, then a roast, *then the fish*, very highly flavoured, then salad and the sweets and dessert. The fish is always served after meat. The dishes for dinner are few, but curious, and the cooking is excellent for those with cosmopolitan palates. The dishes cooked in oil are not deserving the opprobrium heaped upon them by bigoted British guide-book writers. The Spaniards do not over-eat like the French, and the meals are not long ones. But between every course at *table d'hôte* Spaniards smoke a cigarette. It is an excellent idea for filling in the waits; but English ladies don't like it. There were no ladies and no English at our first *table d'hôte*, so we adopted the custom of the country.

Burgos is a grand old city, famous in history for many things, but for nothing so much as being the city of the Cid. You know who the great Cid was, or you ought to, so I won't tell you. We saw his bones, and the bones of Ximena, his wife—the real bones and the real skulls, in a real coffin, in a room in the Prefecture hung with banners and patriotic emblems. Of course we saw the cathedral and the ancient gates and the old Palace of the Inquisition, now fallen to ruins. We stood and smoked cigarettes in the grass-grown courtyard, where many a hero had been done to death, where the hideous tortures devised by human fiends were carried out in the blasphemed name of God, and we leaned against old crumbling pillars that had looked down upon scenes of the most unutterable human anguish. All is but as a dream now, yet the old stones and pillars remain to this day, and cry out against the infamy of that dark and cruel era in the blood-stained annals of Spain. The rooms around, which look down upon the courtyard, are let to the poor at a shilling or two a month. The Palace of the Inquisition is now a slum, and from the windows where monarchs and grandees and Grand Inquisitors looked down hang the yellow rags of beggars and the blue sheets of poor labourers drying in the sun.

Burgos at night is the absolutely dullest place I ever saw in my life, and that is saying a good deal. Some Spanish gentlemen who had made friends with us at the hotel took us to a café, and we spent the evening in getting all the information out of them that we could. The theatre was shut, there was no music-hall, no entertainment of any kind. There is no trade in Burgos, and how the people live is a mystery. But for the military the place would be a city of the dead. And yet it is the capital of proud Castile, and was at one time the residence of kings. At ten at night I have the quiet deserted town almost to myself. I want to tire myself out and make myself sleep if I can, for my old enemy insomnia dogs my footsteps still. I smoke a cigarette under the shadow of the great cathedral. I cross the bridge of the dried-up Arlanzon (all the rivers of Spain have been emptied in consequence of the rapidly-increasing export of Spanish wines), and I linger by the ruins of the house of the mighty Cid. Everywhere I am alone save for some cloaked and muffled figure that steals past me now and then, stealthily and silently as a man bent on a mission of midnight assassination.

I am not afraid. Albert Edward is always close by me with a sword-stick, a revolver, and a pair of fists that, though they have not much skill, would be extremely useful in splitting pavingstones or breaking heads; and, better than all, the old Sereno, or night-watchman, who, with his lantern, his pointed staff, and his whistle, paces every street. The Sereno has plenty of work at night in a Spanish town. In addition to his duties as a watchman, he calls the hours. Quaint and weird upon the night air floats the old watchman's cry, 'Ten o'clock at night, and all's well!' 'Las diez y sereno!' It is from this last word, which means 'All serene!' that the watchman takes his name of 'Sereno.'

He sees a good deal of the night side of (Spanish) nature, does the old Sereno. He passes my lady's balcony at midnight, and sees the cloaked lover underneath twanging his guitar. He sees the lights in the rooms in the small hours when the watchers of the sick keep their long vigils, and he is the first to tumble over the bodies of the wounded and the murdered at the street corners. Then his whistle rings out clear and shrill over the silence, and the police come up and bear the body away. Assassinations are still common enough in Spain. Every street-corner is famous for somebody who was done to death at it. The lower classes and many of the middle classes still carry the murderous 'navaja,' and justice rarely overtakes the midnight assassin. Some of the murders are political, but most of them are 'all on account of Eliza.' The Spanish men are furiously jealous, and the Spanish women are terrible flirts. The national custom of concealing your features entirely at night lends itself splendidly to the use of the knife at dark street-corners.

We left Burgos by the night mail for Madrid. At the hotel they gave us an omnibus. The roof was so low that we had to crawl in on our hands and knees and lie flat on the cushions till we got to the station. There we were the only passengers, but the station-master (another halfpenny cigar did it) took us to his own private room and gave us armchairs in front of his private fire while we waited. He took our hats and placed them in royal state on more armchairs, and when the train arrived he personally conducted us to it, recommended us to the guard, and, bestowing on us all the titles of the noblest grandees of Old Castile, expressed a devout desire that he, too, might have the honour of renewing our acquaintance in God's big parlour.

CHAPTER IV.

MADRID—BULL FIGHTS, THEATRES, CAFÉS, AND COCIDO.

THE journey from Burgos to Madrid takes ten hours by the express. There is only one good train a day to anywhere in Spain. When it doesn't start at eight at night it starts at eight in the morning. This is a dreadful nuisance to people who object equally to travelling all night and to getting up at six in the morning. All trains, except the one express, are fearfully slow. You can take twenty-two hours to do a hundred miles on some of the lines.

The Spaniards have a couplet which runs thus:—'El aire de Madrid es tan sotil Que mata à un hombre y no apaga un candil.' This, in plain English, means that the subtle air of Madrid, which won't extinguish a candle, will put out a man's life. For two or three days in Madrid I was up in the stirrups. I think I have been ill in all the principal towns of the United Kingdom and the Continent; but in Madrid, for the first time for many years, I felt absolutely well. The dry, exhilarating air suited me admirably. I did an endless round of sightseeing by day, I went to three or four theatres at night, and I stopped in the magnificent cafés until the waiters began to pile the chairs on the tables and put on their hats and cloaks to go home to their families. And when I got back to my hotel I sat up in my room and wrote till the small hours. With all this exertion, I was able to get up early the next morning, with a beautiful complexion and a perfect temper.

But with my first bull-fight a change came o'er the spirit of my dream. On Sunday all Madrid crowded to the great open arena, 'La Plaza de Toros.' On Monday all Madrid was coughing and sneezing, and I outcoughed and outsneezed them all. The stone seats of the bull-ring and the boxes open to all the winds of heaven are dear to the hearts of doctors and undertakers. The sun beats down upon an excited multitude, and it is not till nearly sunset that the last bull dies. Then out the great populace pours, and takes a chill at the most dangerous hour of the day. I caught a champion cold at the bull-fight, and it was no consolation to me that everywhere I went during the next two or three days there was a chorus of coughs, and that all my neighbours were as miserable as myself. At the theatre on Monday evening the play I witnessed was absolutely performed in dumb show. The actors strove in vain to make themselves audible over the perpetual hacking and barking of an audience in the agonies of asthma, the inconveniences of influenza, the convulsions of catarrh, and the breath-battle of bronchitis.

The arrangements at Spanish theatrical performances are unique. They must be seen to be believed. But before I come to the theatres I have to get through the bull-fight, and before I come to the bull-fight I should like to say a word or two about the illustrious gentlemen who get their living by it, and who are commonly called toreros. This term includes the espadas, the picadors, and the banderilleros, whose various parts in the performance will presently be made clear to you.

The profession of bull-fighter is in Spain the royal road to fortune. There are half a dozen men, not yet middle-aged, who have become millionaires by killing bulls, and their names are idolized wherever the Spanish language is spoken. Their society is courted by the highest nobles in the land, and they are *au mieux* with many a fair and aristocratic dame. The leading matadors ('espadas' is the technical name) receive for a single afternoon's show sums varying from £200 to £500. They star in the provinces on sharing terms, and when you take into account the fact that a good 'house' at a bull-fight means between two and three thousand pounds, you can imagine what these starring engagements are worth. After they have conquered Spain they go to South America, and there some of them make sums which would cause even Sir Henry Irving and Madame Sarah Bernhardt to open their eyes to their fullest extent.

Mazzantini, who at the time of my visit was starring in Havannah, was the idol of the hour. Long telegrams were published in the principal Spanish papers announcing his magnificent receptions, and describing in 'the language of the ring' his feats with the bulls. Some time ago Mazzantini, who as a bull-fighter makes £20,000 a year, was a porter on the Great Northern Railway of Spain. He was strong and handsome and full of pluck, and he said to himself, 'I want to make money. In Spain there are only two ways—to be a tenor or a bull-fighter. I can't sing, but I know I could kill a bull.' He began as one of the gang of assistants at small shows; he soon acquired skill, and to-day whenever he travels his is a royal progress; his diamonds are the envy of prima donnas, he has his town mansion and his shooting-box and his villa at the seaside, and the reigning belles of Society send him love-letters. Frascuelo, who has now retired, being rich beyond the dreams of avarice, was nearly being made a marquis by King Amadeus.

To read of these riches and honours, to see the receptions given to these princes of the ring by all grades of society, you would think that a bull-fight was a magnificent spectacle, and the matadors were men of splendid bravery and consummate skill.

You had better sit a Corrida de Toros out with me from beginning to end, and then you will be able to form your own judgment. There is one thing, however, you must do first, and that is, get rid entirely of your English views with regard to cruelty to animals. You will see plenty of that; but if you argue with a Spaniard about it he will tell you that you are quite as cruel to animals, only in another way, in England. You will reply that in your sports where the death of an animal is involved the animal has 'a chance.' In bull-fighting the animals have none.

But if you are wise, you will not argue at all. You will take a bull-fight as it is, and come away thankful that it is not the national sport of England. There have been many attempts to revive it in the South of France, and the French would, I fancy, take kindly to it, if it were once made legal, and could be carried out with all the pomp and splendour of Spain.

All Englishmen do not dislike bull-fighting. Many Englishmen who live in Spain follow it enthusiastically; and a young Irish gentleman of fortune at one time took to the bull-ring professionally, and attained a certain amount of distinction.

Madrid is covered with red bills announcing a bull-fight for Sunday. The bills are curious reading and interesting to the student of the language of Cervantes. Here is one of them:

PLAZA DE TOROS DE MADRID

CORRIDA EXTRAORDINARIA

QUE SE VERIFICARÁ (SI EL TIEMPO NO LO IMPIDE)

EL DOMINGO 6 DE MARZO DE 1887

PRESIDIRÀ LA PLAZA LA AUTORIDAD COMPETENTE

ORDEN DE LA FUNCIÓN

1.º CUATRO TOROS de puntas, defectuosos, de las ganaderías y con las divisas siguientes: DOS, con azul turquí, de la acreditada de Don Manuel Bañuelos y Salcedo, de Colmenar Viejo, y DOS, con blanca, de la de Don Alejandro Arroyo (antes Mazpule), de Miraflores de la Sierra.

LIDIADORES

Picadores.—Francisco Parente (*El Artillero*), Francisco Coca, Antonio Bejarano (*El Cano*) y Mariano Ledesma (*El Morenito*), sin que en el case de inutilizarse los cuatro pueda exigirse que salgan otros.

ESPADAS

Rafael Guerra (Guerrita), de Córdoba
Julio Aparici (Fabrilo), de Valencia

Banderilleros.—Miguel Almendro, Rafael Rodriguez (*Mojino*), José Martínez (*Pito*), Rafael Sánchez (*Bebe*), Rafael Llorens y Miguel Burguet (*Pajalarga*).

Sobresaliente de espada.—Miguel Almendro.

Puntillero.—Antonio Guerra.

Y 2.º CUATRO NOVILLOS EMBOLADOS para los aficionados que gusten bajar al redondel á capearlos.

* * * *

La corrida empezará á las TRES Y MEDIA en punto
Las puertas de la Plaza se abrirán dos horas antes

* * * *

Se observarán con todo rigor las prevenciones vigentes para esta clase de espectáculos.

* * * *

La banda de música de Baleares tocará antes de empezar la corrida y en los intermedios.

* * * *

PRECIOS DE LAS LOCALIDADES

		PESETAS.
Tendidos—	Barreras	3
	Contrabarreras y delanteras	2.50
	Asiento sin numeracion	1.50
Gradas—	Delanteras	3
	Filas 1.ª, 2.ª, 3.ª, 4.ª y Tabloncillos	1.25
Andanadas—	Delanteras	3
	Filas 1.ª, 2.ª, 3.ª, 4.ª y Tabloncillos	1
Meseta del Toril—	Delanteras	3
	1.ª y 2.ª filas	1.50
Entrada para palco—		2

Toda ocalidad que exceda de una peseta pagará diez centimos de impuesto.

ADVERTENCIAS

Los billetes se venderán en el Despacho establecido en la calle de Sevilla, el *Viernes* 4 del corriente, de una á cinco de la tarde, el *Sábado* 5 de diez de la mañana hasta las cinco de la tarde, y el *Domingo* 6, día de la corrida, de neuve de la mañana á tres y media de la tarde, y en los de la Plaza de Toros desde la una y media en adelante.

Después de tomados los billetes no se admitirán en los Despachos sino en el caso de que se suspenda la función antes de comenzada; no se darán *contraseñas de salida* y los **ninos que no sean de pecho necesitan billete**.

No se correrán más torros ni novillos que los anunciados.

No se permitirá estar entre barreras sino á los precisos operarios, ni bajar de los tendidos hasta que el último toro esté enganchado al tiro de mulas.

Se prohibe bajar á torear los novillos embolados á los niños y ancianos, á fin de evitar desgracias, así como que lleven palos, pinchos ú otros objetos con que puedan perjudicar al ganado.

Four bulls are to be killed, each four years old. Their names are Bailador, Cigarrero, Manquito, and Primoroso. The 'stars' on this occasion are the two espadas, Guerrita and Fabrilio. The first man is a famous matador; the second a beginner. Having made the acquaintance of a retired bull-fighter—an affable, gray-haired old gentleman, who still wears the chignon and pigtail, which are *de rigueur*, and by which you can always tell a bull-fighter in the crowd—I ask him to accompany me, and explain the points of the performance. He readily consents, and he secures me a private box next to the box of the president—the gentleman, generally a member of the Town Council, who is the official master of the ceremonies, judge, referee, and several other things rolled into one. I ought to mention that, the arena being open to the sky, one-half of the spectators have to sit with the blazing sun in their faces. This causes one side to be dearer than the other. There are two prices—the sol and the sombra. Seats in the shade are 50 per cent. the dearer. When I enter my box in the great arena, the spectacle is a magnificent one. Sixteen thousand people are crowded into the building, and a fourth of them are women. There are elegantly-dressed ladies in the boxes, and in the cheaper seats are gaily-attired women and girls of the lower class. Many of the women have brought their babies with them to see the show. Everybody is on the tiptoe of expectation. As we enter our box, my friend the bull-fighter has a friendly greeting from the mob. In the next box is a duke—a grandee of Spain of the first class—and a general renowned in war. Both of them lean over and shake hands effusively with my friend the bull-killer. Presently the president and his suite enter the official box. Then a trumpet sounds, and two alguazils, dressed in black velvet suits and plumed hats, ride into the ring on gaily-caparisoned steeds. They wheel round, face the president, and bow. The president then bids them summon the bull-fighters. Off go the alguazils across the ring with the message. The gates of the barrier are flung open, and a grand procession enters, and marches across the arena to salute the president. This is the prettiest part of the show. The costumes of the twenty or thirty toreros are brilliant and beautiful. Silver and gold, and yellow and crimson and blue are their jackets and breeches; their hats, of black velvet, are most picturesque; and their mantles, worn in a peculiar fashion, are such as the courtiers of a king might be proud to wear on gala days. Terrific applause breaks from the huge crowd of spectators as popular favourites advance with the band. About six of the men are mounted on wretched, broken-down horses. These men carry long lances, and are the picadors. You will see what they do presently.

The procession having saluted the president, the members of it scatter themselves about the arena, and prepare for business. Another trumpet sounds. The alguazil, in black velvet, rides up again and salutes the president. The president from his box flings him the key of the cells where the bulls are imprisoned, and he catches it in his hat. He hands the key to a torero, who opens the door of a kind of stable opposite, called the toril, and, out of the darkness into the light, out of the silence into the roar of thousands of voices, rushes an infuriated bull, full of life and spirit and courage—a magnificent beast, with terrible horns, already goaded to fierceness by sharp spikes which have been run into him in his prison.

He enters the arena alone. Everybody except the picadors leaps the barriers, and lets him have a run to himself. We are all on the tiptoe of expectation to see how the bull will behave. We can judge by his manner at first what sort of sport he will give. Now several of the toreros, mantle in hand, take their places, and begin to bait the bull to make him lively, and then the first act of the tragedy begins. Unfortunately for the foreigner who *wants* to see sport in a bull-fight, the first act is the most disgusting and dastardly. The picadors—the men with lances, mounted on wretched horses—have it to themselves. The picador, sitting bolt upright on his horse, charges the bull, and digs the spear into him just to tickle him up. The picador then prepares to receive the return charge of the bull. He turns his horse broadside to the bull (the poor horses have their eyes bandaged on one side), and calmly allows the infuriated beast to plunge its sharp horns right into the side of the steed. No attempt is made to save the horse. It is only used by the picador as a barrier between himself and the bull's horns.

If the bull catches the horse fairly underneath, the sight is a hideous one. The wretched animal staggers and falls over, the life blood pouring from it. The audience shouts with delight. The men with the cloaks rush and turn the bull from the prostrate heap, and then pick the picador up. He always falls cleverly, and his legs, being encased in iron, are rarely hurt either by the bull's horns or the falling horse. If the horse is only wounded, it is beaten on to its legs again with sticks, and the wound is stuffed with tow. It is remounted, beaten, and dragged up to the bull to be gored again. On the day of my visit, I saw a horse with its entrails hanging out actually dragged up, cruelly beaten, and remounted. This was considered glorious sport by the Spaniards. As they rode that poor disembowelled beast round the arena again, the spectacle was so hideous that I went to the corner of my box. 'When that horse is dead, tell me, and I'll look again,' I said to my friend the bull-fighter. He laughed, but the next minute he leaned across to the president and said something. The president smiled and raised his hat to me, and then called down an order to one of the ring attendants. A moment afterwards the picador dismounted, and the staggering, bleeding horse was mercifully killed with a blow of the 'puntilla.' I saved one poor beast a few moments' agony, at any rate, that day.

I saw four bulls killed, and the bulls between them killed seven horses. It was always a great relief to me when the bugle sounded, and the horses still living were led out of the ring. Each bull has so many minutes to live, and goes through three acts. The first with the picadors, the second with the banderilleros, and the third with the espada or matador. A bugle sounds the 'time' which terminates each act of the tragedy. I was always glad when the first act was over and the horses were done with. But my delight at seeing one or two go out alive was considerably modified when I was informed that the poor beasts would be kept half-starved until the following Sunday, and then brought out to be gored again. Many of the horses I saw were only fit for the knacker, but they had been good in their time. Some of them still retained fine action, and had probably, in the days of their strength, drawn the carriage of some aristocratic dame now looking down upon the ruthless slaughter. The horses are in no way necessary for the bull-fight. It is wanton cruelty to bring them in to be gored; but that is a part of the show which the Spaniards love best. When a bull has killed five or six horses, as sometimes happens, and there is a delay in bringing in others, the people go mad, and yell at the president, 'More horses! more horses!'

After the picadors have ridden out, the banderilleros commence on the bull. Their feat is a dangerous one. They have to go up to him and stick long darts, ornamented with coloured paper, into his neck. Both darts must be stuck to a nicety side by side. The banderillero must wait till the bull comes full tilt at him, stick the darts in, and slip aside. This is a feat requiring perfect aim, a quick eye, and a steady foot. While this is going on the toreros continue to draw the bull now this way and now that with their mantles. When, maddened by the darts hanging into his bleeding neck, he dashes at them, they have to run for their lives, and leap the barrier. By this time the poor beast has been baited and worried and chased and chivied until he is fairly tired. Now the bugle sounds for the last act, and all is intense excitement.

The espada advances to the president's box, takes off his hat, and says 'Señor President, here is to you, to your family, and all Spaniards.' He then says that he will kill the bull. All the assistants retire. The espada takes a long Toledo sword and his red cloth, and advances to the bull. Man and beast are alone in the great ring. Intelligence and skill are pitted for the first time in the contest against brute force and passion. But daring, graceful, and clever as the matadors are, the chances are a thousand to one in their favour. The bull—poor beast—always runs at the cloth and not at the man. The matador's real danger is a slip when running from the bull. But the toreros, or assistants, are all watching, and at the slightest symptom of danger they rush at the bull and turn him, or envelop his head with their cloaks. Fight he never so bravely, the bull is doomed. He must be killed—that is the rule of the game.

There are a score of names for the different passes and feints and tricks the matador performs with the bull for a few minutes, until he raises his sword in token that he intends to kill it. He baits the bull now this way and now that with the red cloth until he gets the animal to run fairly at him. Then he thrusts the long sword just between the left shoulder and the blade. If the thrust is true and well delivered, the bull falls on his knees. His proud head is raised in defiance for a moment, and then he falls over on his side dead. When the blow does not kill him, the butchery is completed by one of the toreros with the 'puntilla.' There are many ways in which the espada receives the last charge of the bull. Some are dangerous, and are only practised by the great masters of the art. Some of the matadors will even dispense with the red cloth, called in the parlance of the ring 'muleta,' and defy the bull with folded arms. These feats call forth deafening applause.

When the bull is dead, a team of gaily-bedecked mules enters, and drags out first the dead horses, and then the dead bull. The sand is raked over the pools and tracks of blood, and another bull is turned into the arena to go through the same performance. The second bull that I saw was furious at first, but was baited at last into absolute terror. Long before it came to the turn of the matador the poor brute was bellowing piteously, and trying to leap the barriers and escape. At last he got behind a dead horse, and, making a rampart of it, gored its carcass again and again. It took the whole staff five minutes to get him out into the arena to be killed.

After the bull-fight proper was over, I witnessed a curious spectacle. As the last of the four bulls fell to the ground dead, hundreds of the spectators leaped over the barriers into the arena and took off their cloaks. Then a young bull with knobs on its horns was turned loose among them for them to bait. Hundreds of lads became amateur toreros, and practised the art on the harmless animal. He knocked down a dozen and tossed one or two, to the intense amusement of the spectators. I left young Madrid thus amusing itself, and came out of the Plaza de Toros a wiser man as to bull-fights and a much sadder one. If I live fifty years in Spain, I never want to see such another cruel 'game of blood.'

The bull-ring is *the* amusement of Spain, but the theatre is well patronized. I always study the theatres of foreign countries when I get a chance, and the Spanish theatre is one of the most curious I have seen. The Opera or Teatro Real is the principal, and is patronized by the aristocracy. Gayarré is the star there at present. The Teatro Español is devoted to the legitimate drama. The other theatres which play operettas, farces, and topical reviews are the Apolo, the Princesa, the Variedades, the Lara, the Eslava (so called after a priest who left the money to build it), and the Novedades. I will deal with this latter class first.

At nearly all Spanish theatres the performance commences at half-past eight, and is divided into four parts, each of which is called a 'funcion.' You pay for each of these—so much for entrance and so much for your seat. Thus, when you go to the Apolo, the performance commences at half-past eight with 'La Gran Via.' This is over at a quarter-past nine, and out you all go. A new audience now comes in and sees the first act of 'Cadiz,' an operetta, which terminates at ten. Out you all go again, and a fresh audience comes in and sees the second act of 'Cadiz,' which is over at a quarter to eleven. Out we all go again, and a fourth audience fills the theatre for another performance of 'La Gran Via,' which terminates about half-past eleven.

There is a prison scene in 'La Gran Via.' Several Vias are represented. One of them is called the 'Via de la Liberdad,' and it shows the side of a prison wall.

Some time before I arrived in Spain there had been a military revolt, and six sergeants who had taken a prominent part in the insurrection were confined in a State prison on the charge of high treason, but—owing to the notoriously lax discipline of Spanish prisons—the sergeants very shortly afterwards managed to make their escape, and eventually they succeeded in crossing the Pyrenees into France.

The escape of the sergeants is a standing joke among Spaniards of every shade of political opinion, and the scene in which the six sergeants are seen scudding along the prison wall, called the 'Via de la Liberdad,' is always received with tremendous roars of laughter, and it is probably the main cause of the great success of 'La Fiesta de la Gran Via.'

One day a governor of a gaol who went to a bull-fight was astonished to see several of his prisoners who were under sentence of death enjoying themselves at the spectacle. There is always a golden key to a Spanish prison, and you can generally get a day or a night out if you are on good terms with the officials, and give your word of honour that you will come back again. I dare say a good many people will credit me with giving an extra throw to the hatchet, a stronger pull than usual at the long-bow; but the truth of my prison story is amply borne out by a sensational crime which has startled all Spain, shaken the Puerta del Sol to its foundation, brought lumps of the Generaliffe rolling down the Alhambra hill, caused the Alcazar of Seville to contemplate suicide in the Guadalquivir, and shaken up the coffins of the Kings of Spain in the gloomy Pantheon of the Escorial.

One night an old lady was found murdered in Madrid. She had been first killed, and then saturated with petroleum and set on fire, but the fire had gone out before it had done its work, and the wounds which had caused death were visible. I need not repeat all the incidents, but after suspicion falling on various persons, the crime has at last been brought home to the old lady's son, who was supposed at the time the murder was committed to be a prisoner in close confinement in the Madrid gaol.

Here is a shilling shocker with a vengeance. The young gentleman had, it was proved, actually got out of prison with the connivance of the authorities, spent the night at liberty, and returned early in the morning very much the worse for liquor. Yet not a word was said by the officials of the place who knew the facts, because they knew it would get them into hot water. The story reads like an invention of the romancer, but it is only a series of facts. Spain still remains one of the most remarkable countries in Europe, and its manners and customs are more worthy of the 'Arabian Nights' than modern history.

It was at one of the minor theatres that I heard one of the performers imitate an actor with a peculiar voice and mannerism. The audience recognised the imitation, and encored it again and again. 'Ah,' said I to myself, 'Spain has its Henry Irving. I must find him out.' I made my inquiries, and the result was that I booked a stall to sit out a four-act Spanish drama at the Teatro Español written by one of the great dramatists of to-day, Don José Echegaray, and entitled 'Haroldo el Normando.' When the principal actor, Rafael Calvo, stepped upon the stage and gave off his first speech, I recognised the original of the caricature in a moment, and I knew by the reception and the bursts of applause that I was seeing Spain's favourite tragedian. Calvo's acting and declamation were splendid, but his voice was disagreeable; his gestures were natural, but his mannerisms were marked enough to enable me to give a good imitation of him after one visit to the theatre.

Calvo, who is only a little over thirty, is not a handsome man, but he is very intense and powerful, and is the great exponent of the modern *natural* school. His great rival is Antonio Vico, who is of the old and stilted school. Vico also has a bad voice, a defect from which many of the Spanish actors suffer.

At many points in the play the ladies wept and the gentlemen used their pocket-handkerchiefs. The mounting and dresses were beneath contempt, and there was not a line of comedy or a laugh from beginning to end of the play.

The audience was not a large one, considering the size and sumptuous embellishments of the theatre. I inquired of a Spanish friend why the legitimate drama was not better patronized. He told me that there was never a great house when Echegaray was the author. Ladies were afraid of him. His plays were so dreadfully miserable, they cried for a week after seeing them. He would spring scenes of horror on his audience without a moment's preparation. Suddenly the scene would change, and you would see a mother weeping over two dead children on the stage. Nothing that could harrow the feelings was spared, and the author persisted in leaving everybody miserable at the end. After a new play by Echegaray everyone in Madrid asks, 'Well, how many deaths are there in it?' He is a grand writer, full of nervous force and poetic thought, but his plays make people so wretched that those who do not enjoy the luxury of a good cry stop away. Everybody says, 'What a splendid writer!' The newspapers laud him to the skies. The critics point to him as a man who maintains the prestige of Spanish dramatic literature. But the Spanish people, like the English people, decline to take out their theatrical amusement in essays and sermons delivered from the stage. They go to the theatre to be amused, not to study literature, and so, in spite of the abuse of the critics, who are some of them authors themselves of neglected ten-act tragedies in blank verse, the Spaniards flock to operettas, farces, comedies, reviews, medleys, pieces of any sort so long as they are laughable or interesting, and they leave the legitimate drama and the plays of misery by Señor Echegaray to the amateur and professional critics, who think, because they choose to sit at a theatre as in a church, that there should be no more cakes and ale.

But to return to the Spanish custom of taking a play at an act a night. Of course you may wish to see a play through in one evening. In this case you buy tickets for the second and third 'funcion,' and keep your seat. A man comes round between each act and collects the tickets for the next. Say you want to see the whole four 'funcions' out, you purchase four tickets. The ticket is a slip of paper—half of it is for your numbered seat, another half your entrance ticket. You must buy four entrance tickets and four tickets for your seat to entitle you to sit out the whole performance. The tickets are different colours, so that the checktakers may recognise at once for which funcion they are issued. The first audience comes in with green tickets, the second with pink, the third with white, and the fourth with yellow. The great draws at the present moment at three of the theatres are local reviews in rhyme, and full of topical allusions. The singing and dancing are good, and the points are taken up all over the house in a manner which would gladden the hearts of our burlesque writers. 'La Fiesta de la Gran Via,' which is being played at the Eslava, has beaten all previous records. I assisted at the 41,500th performance! Where are our long runs after that?

The piece is played twice a night, and on Sundays and fête days, of which there are scores in Spain, four times—twice at the morning and twice at the evening performance.

The anti-Conservative demonstrations in Madrid and other Spanish towns, which have been lately of such a violent character as to make some people think we were on the eve of another Spanish revolution, are really volcanic in their origin. The Spaniards are not a very demonstrative people. As a rule, if you offered them a perpetual pension they wouldn't utter a shout or wave a hat. But every now and then, suddenly and unexpectedly, without any previous warning, Castilian pride and Moorish stolidity give way to the wildest excitement and the most utter disregard of the conventionalities of life. Be the offending party a Cabinet Minister, a bishop, or a bull, the Spaniard has but one cry, 'Muerta!'—death! It does not mean all that it says. It is the language of the bull-ring carried into public life, and that is all. The bull-ring enriches Spanish language as the racecourse enriches the English.

Madrid is very much like a volcano on the eve of an eruption. Day and night there is a seething mass of cloaked gentry promenading the streets and squares in the eager hope of something turning up. The Puerta del Sol is as much alive at two in the morning as our Mansion House corner is at two in the afternoon. When the Spaniards go to bed is a mystery. Special editions of the evening papers come out in Madrid at 1 a.m., and small boys of the street-Arab type yell their 'Speshal 'Dishuns' under your window till three, and if anything is on, until four. This all-night shouting and the ceaseless traffic no one who has the misfortune to sleep in a room looking on to the Puerta del Sol will ever forget. And the reason that Madrid is on the alert all night is that it is waiting, like Mr. Micawber, for something to turn up. When something does turn up to justify a row, the Madrileños make the most of it, and they yell 'Muerta!' just as a London mob would yell 'Let him have it!' 'Muerta!' is cried when the spectators in the bull-ring have had enough of the bull, and want him got rid of. 'Muerta!' shouted concerning a politician, a prelate, or a prince, means 'Let him take his hook!'

That expression, by-the-by, though it looks like English slang, is quite a classical utterance. Its origin lies among the Roman gladiatorial games. A gladiator took his hook when the pole with a hook at the end of it was used to drag his dying or dead body from the arena.

The window of my sitting-room looks out upon the world-famed Puerta del Sol. Night and day a mighty, ever-changing crowd passes before me. Night and day the plashing fountain plays in the middle of the great public square. Night and day trains and 'buses and mule-drawn waggons and beautiful landaus and phaetons and broughams and mail-coaches drawn by horses not to be surpassed in Hyde Park dash here and there. Night and day the hum of the idle, sauntering crowd rises and falls, and makes music to my ears.

Madrid is not a city. It is only a town. But such a town!—such streets! such shops! such horses! such carriages! such drives! such promenades! and over all the everlasting gaiety and insouciance of a people whose grand motto in all things mundane is this, 'We have only one life—let us make the best of it and worry about nothing.' Your true Spaniard never hurries and never worries and never frets. He inherits the dignity and the fatalism of the Moors, who have left their mark not only on the architecture of the cities, but upon the character of the citizens. If anything is a little beyond him, he folds his hands, smokes a cigarette, and waits for the dénouement.

Quietly and calmly, with a Spanish guide who walked everywhere so leisurely that I had to keep walking round and round him in order not to leave him miles behind, I saw everything that was to be seen in Madrid. I saw the royal palaces, I saw the bed—ay, and the mattress and bolster—on which King Alfonso died. I saw the royal stables and the royal carriages, I got a desperate fit of the blues in the Escorial—the eighth wonder of the world, the morbid outcome of a morbid mind; the last home of Spanish kings—that glowing palace on a barren rock, in which the monkish Philip died a hideous death of lingering agony, loathsome to himself and all around him, and in his last hours smitten by a gnawing terror that, after all, the royal road to heaven might not be over the dead bodies of countless victims slain 'to the greater glory of God.' I drove in the Prado, and saw grandees of Spain by the gross. I met the sisters of the King and 'el Rey Chico,' 'the King Baby,' with his royal mamma, all out for a drive, and I had all the scandals poured into my ear as great and titled ladies passed in their magnificent equipages.

Some years ago the ladies of Madrid took to driving high-stepping horses in mail phaetons, and even tooling showy teams through the principal thoroughfares. In the crowded traffic this was the cause of frequent accidents. The alcalde (clever man!) made it a regulation that no lady under thirty should drive, except in the Park. You may go all over Madrid now, and you don't meet a single lady holding the reins. They are all under the regulation age.

Next to the bull-fights and the theatres, the things in which I have taken the greatest interest in Spain are the dances and the funerals. Both of these are so curious that I shall leave them until I have travelled with the reader a little further afield. One thing struck me in Madrid as it has struck me everywhere in Spain, and that is the way in which the Germans are monopolizing the trade of the country. Every hotel is crammed with German commercial travellers, and the shops are filled with German goods. The Germans I meet are excellent linguists. They speak Spanish fluently, and many of them can carry on a conversation in English and French as well. The Germans have displayed an enterprise in getting the trade of Europe into their hands which is truly remarkable. Their dealers and manufacturers visit the different countries, study the popular taste, and then produce articles which are as national as possible in character. For instance, half the fans and mantillas which are sold in Madrid and the large provincial towns are of German make. And yet they are absolutely Spanish. Many other things are of German make, and thousands of French and English tourists who carry away with them boxes full of specimen Spanish goods to present to their friends are really taking home things which have been imported from the Fatherland. As to cigars, the Germans supply three-fourths of the genuine Havannahs, even in Spanish seaports at which ships from Havannah constantly touch.

France and England also do a large trade with Spain in manufactured goods. But they supply only the articles which are purely French and English. It has been reserved for Germany to supply, not only German, but *Spanish* goods to Spain.

The cafés in Madrid are enormous and gorgeous in the extreme. The climate does not allow the guests to sit out of doors, but the saloons inside are so vast that in some of them a regiment might go through its manœuvres. The cafés are thronged night and day. Here the revolutions are hatched, here governments are overthrown. Chocolate is the great Spanish drink, but of an evening quite half the people have tea.

And such tea! It is a pale lemon colour when you pour it out, and consists principally of hot water. I noticed several ladies and gentlemen flavoured it with a small glass of rum. The tea I had in one of the grand cafés was rum without being flavoured. In fact, it was the rummest tea I ever tasted in my life.

One evening, hot and thirsty after seeing four 'funcions' at four different theatres, I was wondering what I could drink, when I saw a café in the Calle de Azenal that had a large advertisement outside, 'English refreshments.' I rushed to the door to read the list of English refreshments that was displayed on a card outside. I only read the top line, and that was enough.

This was the top line: 'Zurzaparilla!' One travels and learns. I never knew before that sarsaparilla was the national drink of the Briton.

I stayed at an excellent French hotel in Madrid, but I got tired of the French *table d'hôte*. I wanted to eat as the Spaniards eat. One evening I persuaded a Spanish gentleman to take me to a real Spanish middle-class restaurant, and let me taste the fare of the country. The Spanish are a frugal and moderate race. Two or three dishes and dessert—that is their dinner. There is no long bill of fare as among the French.

The restaurant was a quiet room on the ground-floor of a modest-looking house. There were one or two families and several single gentlemen dining. The women wore handkerchiefs on their heads and shawls over their shoulders. People dropped in, had a soup and a dish of meat, an orange and some nuts, and went away satisfied. Our bill of fare was more extravagant, but it created a sensation. The landlord and all the waiters came in turns to look at the extraordinary Englishmen who had such gigantic appetites.

Here is the exact menu. We began with olives and pickled pimientos and guindelias and chilis. These were the *hors d'œuvres*. Then cigarettes. Then we had an ordinary thin soup, followed by cigarettes; then came the great national dish, called cocido. If you have a good dish of cocido (pronounced cothido, because of the Spanish lisp given to the c before certain vowels) you have a good deal for your dinner. It is a savoury stew of chicken, potatoes, sausage, bacon, and white beans, all boiled up with pieces of beef. In most Spanish families this is the everyday dish. Of course the poorer classes have to leave out some of the ingredients, except on festive occasions. In Andalusia the peasants will sit round a huge panful of their version of this article. It is made according to their means, and often vegetables are plentiful, but the pieces of meat few and far between, and each man ladles it out by spoonfuls into his mouth. Plates are dispensed with.

The foreigner who is suddenly confronted with a huge dish of cocido and politely requested to help himself is in some difficulty. He takes a spoonful at hazard. The waiter still stands at his elbow. 'The señor has only taken beans.' Again you make a dash with the spoon and secure something else. The waiter stares, but does not move away. 'The señor has only taken sausage.' The señor, confused, requests the waiter to assist him; and then the process, though slow, is interesting. A spoonful of beans on the plate; then, selected with the greatest care; a piece of chicken; then a patient search for a slice of sausage buried under a mound of cabbage; then the cabbage itself; then a minute devoted to a voyage of discovery in search of the nicest piece of beef; then an exploration in search of a succulent morsel of bacon; then a spoonful of the potatoes; and then, over all, an extra spoonful of the beautiful gravy. I timed my waiter, and he took six minutes and a half to help me to cocido. When the dish passes down a *table d'hôte* it takes about an hour to go round. It is for this reason that the Spaniards help themselves all together at the same time from the common dish.

The cocido was excellent. Well cooked, it is a dinner for a king. I intend to introduce it into England upon my return. But I am afraid it will give rise to a good deal of ill-feeling in families. Somebody will get all the slices of the sausage, and then there will be recriminations and angry words. We have neither the patience nor the politeness of the Spaniards; and cocido is a dish that requires a good deal of both.

The next item after cigarettes was a Spanish salad. This salad is prepared in a peculiar way, and spread out upon bread into which the oil and vinegar have been allowed to soak. This, too, was excellent. Then more cigarettes; then a cheese made of honey and cream, and several other ingredients which require to be taken on trust; and then, after more cigarettes, some 'angel's hair,' which is really a preparation of orange-rind very thinly shredded. More cigarettes; then an orange, raisins of Malaga, and almonds and Barcelona nuts, dried and salted, and delicious. I am so enchanted with these 'almindras' that I have made all my boxes overweight with them. The wines with this feast were Valdepeñas—a red wine made from grapes grown on the rocky plains around Madrid—and Jerez, which, of course, is sherry. I have been to Jerez lately, and, having seen the extent of the vineyards, I beg to add that, though Jerez is, of course, sherry, it does not follow that all sherry is Jerez—very, very far from it—often thousands of miles from it. And we wound up with more cigarettes.

To finish the evening in a real Spanish way, after going to a rather low Spanish café to see the real Spanish dancing, we had, before retiring to rest, 'Dos chocolates con pica-tostes'; and that, if you please, is two cups of thick chocolate, with square fingers of bread beautifully fried in olive-oil. And we weren't ill.

CHAPTER V.

SEVILLE.

I SPENT a pleasant week in Madrid, and I then went on to Seville. On three days a week there is an express train which does the journey of 350 miles in fifteen hours. This is fortunate, because the ordinary trains take twenty-four, and even this is fast in comparison with the trains on less frequented lines. The express journey was not without its interesting features. We stopped now and again for fifteen minutes or half an hour. When we stopped, everybody got out of the train and went into the buffet—passengers, guards, engine-drivers, porters, and all. We all sat down together, and ate and drank together; and then we all smoked cigarettes together round the fire. When it was time to start, we got up, stretched ourselves, and leisurely strolled back to the train, the guards and the engine-driver and the stoker being generally the last to turn out. It was very friendly and very nice; but as these stoppages of half an hour occur about every twenty minutes, the English traveller, unaccustomed to spend a day and a night in conversing with the engine-driver in a station waiting-room, begins to get impatient.

Our 'civil guards,' of course, went with us, their moustaches fiercely twisted and their rifles loaded. We still want this sort of protection on long railway journeys over lonely plains in Spain, because the brigands are not quite done away with yet. Only last year they stopped and robbed a train. The way in which the robbery is carried out is this: The brigands signal to the engine-driver to stop, and he does so, being generally 'in' with the brigands. Then these gentlemen, called in Spanish 'Salteadores de caminos,' or road jumpers, approach the carriage, raise their hats to the passengers, and, in the most polite language, request them to give up their money and jewels. The 'guardias civiles' are stopped from firing at the robbers by the affrighted passengers, as the rascals have previously explained that if they are fired at, they will shoot at the passengers in return.

The chief of the brigands last year addressed the passengers in these terms:

'LADIES AND GENTLEMEN,—Please deliver up your money and valuables of every description. We do not wish to put you to the indignity of a search, but shall rely upon your honour. But as soon as you tell us you have given up everything we shall search one passenger of each class. If upon either we find a single coin or a single valuable, we shall shoot one passenger in each compartment. Ladies and gentlemen, do not hurry yourselves. Our time is yours.'

You can imagine that, under these circumstances, there is very little kept back. The passengers beg and pray of each other to conceal nothing. As soon as a complete surrender has been made, the brigands raise their hats again, and bid the passengers farewell in these words, 'Vaya ustedes con Dios!'—'May you go with God!'—and, as the train moves off, they add, with beautiful and simple piety, 'And may we all meet again some day in God's big parlour!'

These dignified and solemn Spanish salutations are universal among the people, and are never omitted. Your beggar in Spain is a gentleman, and you address him always in formal and courteous language. 'Brother,' you say, when he importunes you, 'may God put it into your heart to deprive me of the pleasure of your society!' To your waiter, to the servant, to the boy who blacks your boots, your language must never be curt. At the *table d'hôte* in Spain, high-born gentlemen and the officers talk as much with the waiter as they do with each other. He joins in the general conversation; and I have heard an ex-Spanish Minister gravely discussing the political situation with the waiter who was handing round the dishes.

Sometimes the guests agreed with the waiter, and sometimes with the ex-Minister.

A word about the accommodation for travellers in second-rate Spanish towns off the beaten track before I hurry away from the gayest and brightest capital in all Europe, and go on to Seville. English travellers are frightened from visiting many small Spanish towns by tales of bad accommodation, vile cooking, and uncivilized ways. My personal experience proves the contrary. In many places off the beaten track I was excellently housed and fed, and every Spaniard with whom I came in contact put himself out of his way to make my path one of roses. But I didn't walk about rooms with my hat on; I didn't cross the high altar in churches without bowing my knee; and I didn't turn my nose up at all the dishes, and say 'Faugh!' and I didn't call the servants and the proprietor 'd.f.'s' because they didn't understand English. The English who come abroad do much to bring about the incivility with which they are sometimes treated. The off-hand, imperious, insular manner is not understood in a country where the beggars address each other as 'Your excellency' and 'Your lordship.' Instead of finding fault with everything Spanish, praise everything, say you like everything, and flatter instead of abusing your hosts, and you will find the Spaniards, from the highest to the lowest, vying with each other as to which can show you the greatest courtesy.

The courtesy of the servants in Spanish hotels is wonderful. Every waiter, every chambermaid, rises when you pass, and bows and remains standing till you are out of sight. Your coachman remains bareheaded while you get into your carriage. In country places all the drivers you meet on the road raise their hats and wish you all that is good.

In the best hotels a staff of servants sit on sofas on each landing waiting to attend to the summons of the guests. If you walk up and down your corridor for half an hour, every time you pass that sofa the servants will rise and remain standing till you have passed.

In little out-of-the-way towns at *table d'hôte*, if a lady comes into the room all the gentlemen at the table rise and bow to her, and remain standing until she is seated. When the *table d'hôte* is over, the men as they rise bow to those who still remain seated, and, in courtly phraseology, lay themselves at the feet of the company.

At one *table d'hôte* in a little town I was astonished to see a gentleman sit down in his hat and cloak, and keep them on. I made inquiries, and found that he was a Castilian grandee, and it was his privilege to remain covered. The hat in Spain is the seat of dignity. That is why you give your visitor's hat the armchair of honour when he calls upon you.

Seville is a place one longs to see until one has seen it, and then one wonders why one wanted to see it so much. It is beautiful. I am a Philistine, a Goth, a Vandal, a dreadful creature generally, but I am always willing to admit beauty where it exists. I don't prostrate myself and worship simply because I am told it is the proper thing to do, but anything that I like I become enthusiastic over. I can't become enthusiastic over Seville. It is quaint and old and picturesque and pretty and lordly and interesting, and all that sort of thing, but you soon get tired of it. The climate has something to do with this, perhaps. The energy goes out of you in Seville. You saunter and put your hands in your pockets, and so in time the very laziness of the life begins to bore you. If I hadn't heard so much about Seville it is quite possible I should have been enchanted with it. But I have heard its praises sung on the top note all my life, and so I was disappointed.

The people and the patios are the most interesting things in Seville. Artists have painted the men and women of Andalusia in their national costumes for countless ages, so that everyone is familiar with them. Comic operas and ballets by the score have shown us the dark-eyed lasses, with the coquettish comb and the mantilla, and the bright flowers in their hair, casting melting glances from behind a fan. And the songs about the Guadalquivir would bind up into a very big volume. Every Englishman is therefore prepared beforehand for Seville. I was. I got out at the station, and got into an omnibus that rattled my bones over awful stones, and jerked me up in the air, and threw me down on the floor, and reduced me to a living pulp; and, as soon as I was something between a jam and a jelly, I began to look about me.

Seville is built on the regular Moorish system. Narrow streets and houses close together to keep out the fierce heat of the sun. We go full speed through streets that leave only half an inch on each side of the bus. Foot passengers dash into doorways to shelter until we have passed. We come to streets so narrow that the horses could not pass through, let alone the bus; and so we dive up here and dive down there, and describe a circle, in order to arrive at our hotel. There are certain streets that carriages go up, and certain streets that they come down. Nothing could pass! And there are no footways. An unskilful driver who goes an inch to the right or the left chips a piece out of his vehicle by knocking it against a house.

But one thing strikes the first comer and rivets his attention. Every house, small and large, has a lovely gate of ironwork as delicate as lace, through which one sees a beautiful inner patio or marble courtyard filled with waving trees and beautiful plants. Often in the centre a splendid fountain plays. Seville is an old city of the Moors. Their handiwork is everywhere. In these houses that one passes the Moors lived their Eastern life before they were driven out by the reconquest of Spain, and so beautiful is the climate, so clear the atmosphere, that everything stands to-day just as it stood hundreds of years ago. The Moor is everywhere in this part of Spain. The people still dance the Moorish dances and sing the Moorish songs, and the blood of the Moors still lingers in their veins, the features of the Moors still survive, and make the faces that one meets full of Eastern grace and beauty.

The country all round Seville is a garden of Eden. The orange-trees, the palm-trees, and the almond-trees are everywhere. The hedges are the prickly pear and the cactus. The landscape is African in its luxuriance, and the golden sunshine floods the land with glory. But the roads! Oh, ye gods, the roads! They ought to be impossible roads; but we drove over them. They are in ruts a foot deep; they are in holes in which a man might hide himself. They have not been swept for centuries. The mud that was in heaps in the days of the Moors remains in heaps still. The dogs and cats who died by the roadside in the days of the Moors have not yet been buried. Once when I was in Seville it rained all night. The next day we drove through a sea of liquid mud. Even the roadways in front of the palaces of the rich are in great holes and full of ponds. Carriages break down, horses break their legs, visitors disappear down holes in the roadway. The Sevillians regret the circumstances; they repair the carriages, buy new horses, make new friends, but they never repair the roads. Some day the only way of getting about Seville will be by balloon. Even now it is the safest way. So much has been done for Seville by the past Moors; the present burgesses might at least keep the roads in repair.

The Guadalquivir! Another of my lost illusions. Poets have sung it from a distance—the poet who walks upon its bank holds his nose. The Guadalquivir, out of the poetry books and the songs and the romances, is a commonplace, dirty stream, about as romantic as the Thames at Barking Creek, and not so clean.

The people and the patios and the climate make Seville, and the Santa Semaña—the Holy Week!—brings thousands and thousands of people to the marmalade city. It is a week of magnificent processions—a week of such pomp and circumstance and magnificence and show as to be indescribable. All the winter long people come to Seville because it is said to be a beautiful place. During the month of the Santa Semaña they cram into Seville to see a sight which no other town in the world can show.

English swarm in Seville. At the Hotel of the Tower of Babel we sit down 180 to *table d'hôte*. The eighty are English and American. We speak all languages at this hotel. All day long it is a babel of French, English, Italian, Spanish, German, Russian, Swedish, Dutch, and Portuguese. We have magnificent entertainments at dinner-time. One evening a band of fifty 'Estudiantina' play and sing and dance for our amusement. Another evening we have professors of the guitar who serenade us. But this great caravansera of foreigners spoils Seville for me. I might be at a big hotel anywhere except in Spain. Everything is thoroughly un-Spanish. All around one hears English and French, and people dress and give themselves airs, and bring the customs and manners of London and Paris and St. Petersburg to Seville, and so spoil it. It knocks the romance out of the place to hear at every street corner, 'Hullo, old fellow; how are you?' and 'Oh, Jane, did you see that funny old lady?' or 'Bai Jove, what a doosid pretty girl in that balcony!' There are so many places in Spain which are ugly and purely Spanish, that one feels annoyed to come to a place which is pretty but cosmopolitan.

The great tobacco factory at Seville is one of the first sights the stranger is taken to see. It requires a certain amount of courage for a bashful man to run the gauntlet of 6,500 young ladies. Everybody in Spain smokes cigarettes. Little boys begin at the age of eight, and from that time the cigarette is rarely absent from a Spaniard's lips. Many of them die smoking. The consumption of cigarettes is naturally enormous, and the bulk are manufactured in Seville. The Government factory gives daily employment to about 7,000 people, and of these only a hundred or two are men.

When you enter the enormous rooms crowded with girls dressed in bright colours, the *coup d'œil* is striking in the extreme. In one immense low-vaulted room there are 1,500 girls. They sit in endless rows—about twenty girls to a row—on either side of the room, all at little tables, all rolling cigarettes. There is a blaze and blur of colour, a babel of tongues. Every girl has a gay handkerchief about her neck—every girl has a bright flower stuck in her hair. All along the walls hang the gay outdoor dresses of the little cigarette-makers. As I walk, blushing and nervous, down an endless avenue of flashing eyes, I grow almost giddy. It is a sea of women's faces, an undulating ocean of flower-decked heads. One has to pick one's way carefully down the central avenue, for it is blockaded all along the line with cradles. The married cigarette-makers are allowed to bring their babies with them to the factory. They rock the cradle with one foot, while their busy fingers roll the cigarette.

'Silence!' is called by the forewoman as the visitor passes down the lines, but there is a 'chut-chut' every second from some dark-eyed wench who points to a cradle and holds out her hand. It is the habit of visitors to bestow occasional coppers on the babies, and so all the young mothers are on the alert for the visitors' charity.

The girls earn good wages. At many of the tables whole families are working together. But the hours are long, and the atmosphere awful. The damp, warm odour of the tobacco in the long, low-roofed rooms is in itself almost stupefying. But there is no ventilation, and the atmosphere is absolutely indescribable. Many of the girls smoke cigarettes at their work. I was very glad to light one myself long before I had done the round of the factory.

I have said that cigarette-smoking is universal in Spain. Nowhere does the habit strike the foreigner more forcibly than at a funeral. Funerals in Spain are conducted in a manner which is in the highest degree original. When you die you are got rid of as soon as possible. The Spaniards have the same horror of death surroundings as the Italians, but they go a great deal further. As quickly as possible—sometimes within an hour—the body is placed in an elaborate coffin made of metal, and painted to imitate marble. Some of these 'caskets' are smothered in gilt ornaments of a most elaborate character. All sizes are kept ready at the great funeral establishments. The coffins open lengthways. The lid is on hinges, and is locked with a key. The poorer people are buried in wooden coffins, covered with various designs in coloured ribbons. Children's coffins are made in white and blue, and are decorated like a bon-bon box. Coffins of this description are sold almost everywhere in the South. You see them hanging up outside the shops by dozens.

I went over the premises of one of the biggest undertaking concerns in Spain. It is a public company, and is called 'La Funeraria.' I never saw such magnificence in my life. Some of the funeral cars are built in the style of the great gilt and glass cars which figure in a circus procession through a country town. The drivers and footmen are dressed in gorgeous liveries that make you blink to look at them. Some of the liveries that I was shown cost over £200 each. They positively blazed with gold. A grand first-class funeral, with a retinue of footmen and officials, is a perfect Lord Mayor's show in itself.

As a rule, the corpse, even when so magnificently conducted to its last home, is unattended by any relatives. Spaniards finish with their dead when the church ceremony is over. Few corpses are accompanied to the cemetery except by the undertaker's men. But in ordinary cases the coffin is placed in a yellow, open car, and driven up to the cemetery by a gentleman in a short jacket and peaked cap. The driver smokes his cigarette and cracks his whip as he hums his favourite tune. I have seen dozens of these ordinary funerals in Spain, and they have always filled me with amazement. The ridiculous always lives next door to the sublime. The grotesque and the horrible are first cousins. More than once I have with difficulty restrained myself from smiling at a Spanish interment, so utterly out of keeping with English notions of decorum has the final ceremony been.

I will describe two interments that I witnessed in one day at the great cemetery at Seville. Four little barefooted boys arrive at the cemetery gates. Between them they carry a little blue and white coffin. They jog along, chatting and laughing, up the long avenue of trees. Presently they see something which attracts their attention—a bird in a tree. Down they drop the coffin by the roadside, and off they scamper across the grass to the tree. They pick up stones and begin to throw them at the bird. In the process they quarrel about something, and two of the boys have a fight. In the meantime the coffin lies in the roadway. I walk up to it, and through the glass let into the lid I see the dead child's face. It has been dead perhaps twelve hours, so the features are unchanged, and it appears to be calmly sleeping. Several people pass me; no one takes any notice of the coffin in the road. One old gentleman nearly tumbles over it, and swears. It is evidently nothing unusual.

Presently these ragged boys, having arranged their little difference, return, and pick up the coffin. Two of them have lighted cigarettes. They carry their burthen right across the cemetery to a little house, where two or three men with brass numbers on their caps are smoking cigarettes. Here they show a paper, and one of the men, picking up a spade, tells the boys to follow him. Off they go, jogging the coffin now this way and now that, and I follow them.

We come to a long line of brick vaults. Some are empty; some are filled up to the top with what I presume to be mould. The gravedigger turns over the loose earth with his spade, and strikes a coffin here and there. The vault is too full. He moves on to another bricked square, pushes his spade in, and says there is just room. He digs a little hole and lays the coffin flush with the top of the brickwork. Then he throws a few spadefuls of earth over it from a mound close by, and the ceremony is finished. There are thousands of these bricked squares in the cemetery, and each contains a score of coffins. There is no stone over the top, only the loose brown earth. Some of them are so full that the earth has to be piled up to cover the coffin, and thus the coffin is actually above ground.

This system of burying in bricked squares saves a lot of trouble. The graves are always ready, and the dead can be brought to the cemetery and put away at once. There is no necessity to order or select beforehand. To understand this system you must see a Spanish cemetery. No written words can convey a correct impression of its general peculiarities.

The next funeral arrives as I am leaving the cemetery. A car, driven by a man smoking a cigarette, comes up. It is followed by a cab, from which alights an old gentleman, also smoking a cigarette. The car pulls up at the gate of the 'depository,' a little house in the grounds arranged for the reception of people who have died too late to be buried that day. The guardian of this house, cigarette in mouth, flings open the doors, speaks to the gentleman, and then calls for somebody to come. A man with a cigarette in his mouth now approaches. He and the car-driver lift out the coffin and carry it into the house and lay it on the trestles. They then light a candle at the head and foot, and come out and shut the door. Off drives the car, the man lighting another cigarette, and the gentleman to whom the corpse belongs strolls across the cemetery with the gravedigger to choose 'his place.' The gravedigger turns up a little earth in one brick square, and then in another. 'Too full,' says the gentleman, puffing his cigarette. He goes from square to square, and pokes at the loose earth with his stick. At last he settles on a square which is only half full. 'That will do,' he says, and then he returns to his cab and drives away.

I make inquiries of the keeper of the 'depository.' The body inside the coffin is the gentleman's wife. She died last night. She will be buried to-morrow morning. 'Will the gentleman return to see her buried?' 'Oh, no; he has finished. He has left her here. The rest concerns us!' We find it difficult to understand this leaving the dead to be buried without ceremony, and without a friendly watcher; but the Spaniards think nothing of it. They bid their dead good-bye with the last prayer. The interment is no ceremony at all to them. The dead are hurried out of the house as soon as possible. Sometimes they are sent to the undertaker's 'depository' within a couple of hours of their decease, and the friends see no more of them. This, with the Southern horror of a corpse, one can understand. But the cigarette-smoking of hearse-drivers, cemetery attendants, and gravediggers while handling the coffin, strikes the foreign looker-on as, to say the least of it, lacking in ordinary respect for the dead.

In many parts of Spain the death ceremonies are peculiar. The corpse is elaborately dressed in its best, and has its hair beautifully done, and a pair of new boots put on its feet. It is then got rid of as soon as possible, and all the furniture in the room is taken out and sold, or given away. Everything that can remind the family of the deceased is removed. A notice of the death is not only inserted in the newspapers, but in some cases placarded on the walls; and you are requested to go to such and such a church on such and such a day, when a mass will be said for the repose of the dead person's soul.

Among the poor there is a very free-and-easy way of getting their dead buried. One day, outside a great cemetery, I came upon three common coffins lying on the ground near the gate. Seeing that the coffins were occupied, I started back in horror, and asked what, in Heaven's name, such an exhibition meant. 'Oh,' said my Spanish friend, 'they are poor people who cannot afford to be buried yet. There is a little fee to be paid. Someone will come by presently, and pay for the coffins to be put away as an act of charity.'

Unburied coffins are bad enough, but what do you think of dead children hung up outside the cemetery gates, waiting for some kind soul to pay for them to be put into the earth? The sight is not uncommon in the South of Spain, where every form and shape of beggary is rampant. Sometimes the friends of a small corpse, instead of asking charity, will smuggle it into the cemetery hidden under a cloak; and, when no one is looking, drop it into one of the big square graves I have told you about, and kick a little loose earth over it. There are plenty of uncoffined dead under the loose earth in the great cemetery of Seville.

Burials alive are far more common in hot countries, where the burial takes place within twenty-four hours after death, than they are in England, where one gets, as a rule, a week's grace. In Spain the body is frequently removed to the undertaker's shop a few hours after death. In one of the largest of these establishments in Madrid, some years ago, an extraordinary sight was witnessed. A gentleman was brought in his 'casket' one afternoon, and placed in the room set apart for that branch of the business. The proprietor lived over his premises, and on this especial evening was giving a grand ball. When the ball was at its height, a gentleman in full evening dress suddenly joined the company. He danced with the wife of the undertaker, and he danced with the undertaker's daughter, and seemed to be thoroughly enjoying himself.

The undertaker thought he knew his face, but did not like to be rude and ask him his name; but by-and-by all the guests departed, and the strange gentleman was the only one left. 'Shall I send for a cab for you?' said the host at last. 'No thank you,' replied the gentleman; 'I'm staying in the house.' 'Staying in the house!' exclaimed the undertaker; 'who are you, sir?' 'What, don't you know me? I'm the corpse that was brought in this afternoon.' The undertaker, horrified, rushed to the mortuary-room and found the coffin empty. His wife and daughter had been dancing with a corpse. An explanation, of course, followed. The gentleman, who had only been in a trance, had suddenly recovered, and hearing music and revelry above, and having a keen sense of humour, had got out of his coffin (the Spanish coffin closes with a lid, which is only locked just previous to interment) and joined the festive party. He was quite presentable, as in Spain the dead are generally buried in full evening dress.

Writing about funerals in Spain reminds me of a curious ceremony in connection with the burial of Spanish kings. The Pantheon in the Escorial is their last home. Here they lie in splendid marble sarcophagi in great niches, and you can walk about and see them all. Alfonso's sarcophagus is empty as yet. The late King's body lies on a table in an adjoining chamber—a chamber called El Pudridero, which is really a place where the royal bodies are left to undergo the natural process of decay which at last fits them to be placed in the ornamental arrangement in the Pantheon. The ceremony to which I referred above took place at the late King's funeral. The body was brought in great state from Madrid to the Escorial, a distance of thirty miles. The 'intendant' of the royal palace was in charge of it. When the procession reached that gate of the Escorial which is only opened to admit a dead sovereign, the procession halted. The 'intendant' then went to the coffin and opened it, and exclaimed in a loud voice, 'Don Alfonso!' then again still louder, 'Don Alfonso!' and again, 'Don Alfonso!' He then turned to the officials, and said, 'Don Alfonso does not answer; he is dead!' The coffin was locked again, and the King passed on to his last home.

A note or two before I leave Seville. When I arrived in Seville, before seeing the sights, I went to a barber's shop to have my head shampooed and to be shaved, and to be generally put straight after fifteen hours in the train. I asked my 'Figaro' if he was the Barber of Seville. He shook his head deprecatingly, and said, 'No; but he was one of them.' I explained to him that I wanted to know if he was the immortal Barber of Seville—that it was a mild joke. He said there were so many barbers in Seville. He had never heard of Count Almaviva, but he knew a Rosina. She was working in the great tobacco factory of Seville, and was very pretty. I lost my patience. I cried, 'Great heavens, man! you are a barber of Seville, and you never heard of the Barber of Seville who is in an opera known all over the world?' The man thought for a little while, and then exclaimed, 'Ah! I know what you mean now. They show a shop to tourists where a barber once lived who did something. But I didn't know it was true about him. The guides here make so many stories for the tourists!'

I left the Barber of Seville sad and downcast. I had expected that all the time he was shaving me he would be singing the best-known airs of the opera. And he didn't even know who Figaro was!

One more disillusion awaited me in Seville. One morning the waiter brought me for my breakfast some marmalade. 'Ah!' I exclaimed, 'Seville—Seville oranges! Of course, the marmalade here is excellent.' 'Yes, señor,' replied the waiter; 'it is considered a great delicacy in Seville, because we cannot get it here. This is the best Scotch marmalade from London!'

The Andalusian dances are quite as interesting as the funerals. To see the dances in perfection you have, when there is no *fête* or country festival on, to go to the cafés chantants, and these establishments in Spain are only frequented by a low class of people. My companion and I put our dignity in our pockets and went to the cafés, but we had a slight difficulty in explaining to the young ladies of the establishments that we were there to see them dance, and not to drink bottles of Malaga and talk Spanish to them. The dancing of the Andalusian girls is well worth putting up with a little bad company to see. There is a good deal of the Oriental movement of the hips and arms in it; in fact, both the song and the dance of the South are Moorish, but there is also a grace and a coquettishness of a purely Spanish character. When a man and woman dance together with the castanets, and dance well, there is no prettier sight to be seen.

The men are all good dancers. The great dancer of Seville at the present moment is a butcher, one José Fernandez, surnamed 'El Chibo' (the little lamb). He has a fine shop on the Plaza, and is very well to do. Unfortunately he could not dance for me because he had been having a political discussion with a friend, and had received by way of argument two bullets in the chest, and so was confined to the hospital. 'El Chibo' is also one of the leading figures in the great procession of the Holy Week. He takes the character of a Roman general. For this occasion he has had made, at his own expense, a new and beautiful costume, for which he has paid the trifling sum of 15,000 pesetas—say, £600. You may guess that 'El Chibo,' the dancing butcher of Seville, is not a poor man.

The gipsy dancing of Granada is different from the Andalusian dancing. As it was not convenient for me to climb up the Alhambra Hill at night and sit in a gipsy cave, I had the gipsy dancers brought down to a house in the town by their captain, and paid for a private performance. The guide-books say that it is a 'disgusting exhibition.' It isn't exactly the sort of thing a girl would take her mother to see; but 'Honi soit qui mal y pense.' The gipsies dance 'Old Africa' and their other dances without any thought of evil. They are not refined, and many of the 'figures' are coarse and suggestive, but the general effect is striking, and dramatic, and picturesque. After the real Moorish dances of Africa and the Spanish dances of Andalusia, these gipsy dances of Granada are not worth going much out of one's way to see. But the gipsies themselves are interesting, and the old gipsy captain plays the guitar like an angel. I tried to carry on a conversation in Romany with them, and I found that, taking into account the difference of the Spanish and the English pronunciation of the same word, they understood me very well indeed. I stayed with the gipsies and their captain till eleven on Saturday night, and on Sunday, at their special invitation, I went up the hills and spent an hour in their home—a cave burrowed right into the mountain, and fitted up in an exceedingly primitive style. The chief of the party I spent Sunday with is nearly seventy-six, and a hale and hearty old Gitano still. He told me that many years ago he danced with his wife before the Prince of Wales, and he asked me if he was King of England yet, if he was married, and how many children he had. I gave him the desired information, and then he asked me, if I saw the Prince of Wales when I went back to England, to give his best respects to his Royal Highness. I promised that I would, should the opportunity occur. I regret to say that up to the present moment it has not.

CHAPTER VI.

GRANADA AND THE ALHAMBRA AND CORDOBA.

THE journey from Seville to Granada is a fearful affair. The distance is only 179 miles, but it takes all day. Directly you come into the province of Granada the train is besieged with beggars. At every station ragged boys leap up on the steps of the carriages and whine for alms. When you arrive at the terminus, beggars by dozens pounce upon you. You get into an omnibus to go to the town (I selected a real Spanish hotel to escape from the English), and you are rattled over stones so huge that they throw the omnibus up several feet from the ground. Suddenly you stop. You look out and find yourself in the centre of a dirty, half-lighted square. You are in the middle of the roadway. Round you dance dozens of weird forms with bare legs and arms, clad in ragged cloaks. The door is opened, and you are requested to descend. You look in vain for a hotel, and before you can ask a question your luggage is thrown off the roof into the mud. The dozen beggars scream and shout and gesticulate. One seizes your rugs, another your portmanteau, another your bag. In vain you protest and shriek to the bus-driver. In self-defence you rush after the procession of beggars who have seized your property. Then you see that they are wading through the mud on to a pavement, and that there is a hotel in the distance. The roads of Granada are so constructed that a deep ditch separates the road from the pavement. This causes everybody in a carriage to be set down in the middle of the roadway.

I followed the beggars who had seized my luggage, and found myself presently in the hotel. Here the beggars grouped themselves round me until I had been given a number, and then up they filed barefooted and dirty to my sleeping apartment. The hotel people didn't say anything; so I presumed it was usual for the porterage of the hotel to be performed in this way. A handful of coppers relieved me of my attendants, and I counted my packages and found them all safe; but it will be a long time before I forget being turned out on a dark night in the middle of a dark square, and having all my belongings seized and carried off by the beggars of Granada.

Granada is the Alhambra! But for the Alhambra, Granada would be left to the gipsies and the mendicants. But the Alhambra makes the town the Mecca of all travelling Christians. To behold the palace on the hill, the 'red fortress,' the last stronghold of the Moors, it is worth while enduring a good deal more than the persecutions of the most degraded population in all Spain. As one wanders through these world-renowned ruins and gazes in admiration and awe at the glorious handiwork of a race that was swept out of Spain hundreds of years ago, one pinches one's self to see if it is a dream or a reality. One walks upon enchanted ground. Here the genii have been at work. It is too utterly prosaic to imagine that this fairy palace was built by mortal hands. For my own part, I don't believe it. I am as sure as I am of anything that one day a gentleman out of 'The Arabian Nights' was sojourning in Granada and he rubbed a ring, or muttered an incantation, and a djin appeared, and, after a short conversation, the palace and fortress of the Alhambra rose from the ground. I don't dispute the fact that it was afterwards inhabited by mortals, that here 'King Boabdil' and his brave garrison were starved out, and yielded the keys to the Christian conquerors, and so passed away for ever. The splendid marble tombs of Ferdinand and Isabella stand in the Royal Chapel of Granada, and relics of the last defeat of the Moors are everywhere around. Even the banner that the Christians bore as they entered the gates of the Alhambra on January 2, 1492, still hangs, faded and tattered, in a glass case in the chapel. And near it are the crown and sceptre of their most Catholic Majesties; and in a little corner, all by itself, is a golden casket, once the property of a gentleman named Columbus, who has been handed down to posterity in connection with a yarn about cracking eggs to make them stand upright, and is also the hero of other American stories. All these things are solid and substantial realities; but the Alhambra itself is the airy fabric of a vision, an artist's fantasy, a poet's dream, a——

I am checked in my rhapsody by the remembrance of what I heard as I wandered through these halls of heavenly beauty, and floated back along the centuries until I was a Moor myself, and formed one of the proud Sultan's glittering train, and lived in the Alhambra in all its pristine glory of Moorish arch and marble pillar, its masonry of transparent lace-work, its softened hues of red and blue lit up with glowing gold, its glistening Oriental tiles, its pomp, its splendour, its majesty and might. And while I dreamed, and stood aside in the beautiful Court of Lions to let the veiled beauties of the harem pass with their escort of negro guards, a voice broke in upon my dreams, and brought me with an earthquake shock back from the dead centuries to the pulsing, breathing 'time by the clock'—and this is what the voice said: 'H'm! it *is* rather like the place in Leicester Square, isn't it?'

With a cry of horror I looked up and beheld an ulster and a billycock and a red guide-book. And presently one of the officials of the Alhambra approached the ulster and the billycock, and showed it a book of photographs of other ulsters and billycocks, taken on the spot, leaning against the pillars of the Alhambra. Would the gentleman and his friend like to be taken in the Alhambra? They would—and they were. I fled from the scene of desecration. Ulsters and billycocks, with their hands in their pockets, leaning against the marble pillars of the Alhambra! O Moors, that wrought this fairy fabric, beautiful for ever, and to be hallowed until all taste is dead, and barbarians—not from Barbary, but from Europe—have made the world a rubbish-heap of the vulgar, the gross, and the commonplace, if your disembodied spirits ever visit your lost kingdom in the pale glimpses of the moon, what must you think of these billycocks and ulsters, and of the people who wear them, and loll in mustard-coloured tourists' suits against your dainty walls, and are taken like that and duly exhibited to other billycocks and ulsters in a soot-begrimed hole called London, that I don't suppose any Moor ever heard of, and pointed to with pride as 'Me and Jack taken in the Alhambra—don't you know!'

I saw everything in Granada as quickly as I could, for the town is cold and the people are uncouth, and have a habit of looking upon the foreigner as their legitimate prey. Extortion, robbery, cheating, and imposition are rampant. To get about at all one must strew the ground with pesetas. Difficulties are made specially by the guides, in order that the silver key may be produced as often as possible. Being in a hurry to get away, I took a little man and bade him take me everywhere at once. But I told him if he took me to see a Murillo I would put my navaja into him. (I have seen 7,482 Murillos, all genuine, in Spain, and I am getting a little tired of them.) My little man took me everywhere; but every five minutes he turned round and exclaimed, 'Aqui es costumbre dar una propina,' which meant, 'Here it is customary to give a tip.' That wretched little man made me give pesetas to gardeners, servants, coachmen, doorkeepers, officials, watchmen, porters, and every person, male and female, who happened to be in the places or grounds I visited. And I know as well as possible that he afterwards returned and went 'whacks' with the lot. I protested once or twice, and tried to make him ashamed of himself, but he swore by all the saints that it *was* 'costumbre.' He admitted that it was an imposition, but he insisted that the people were paid no wages, and so had to live on what visitors gave them. When I had finished with him, however, I read him a long moral lecture, and gave him to understand that he must not take all the people who were not born in Granada for idiots. I'm afraid my protests were in vain. The motto of Granada will still remain, 'Aqui es costumbre to fleece the foreigner.'

That which filled me with the greatest astonishment in Granada, after the Alhambra, was the way in which all the dogs of the town attended mass in the cathedral. Quite half the ladies who came in and knelt down brought dogs with them. The dogs didn't sit still, but went on excursions into the different chapels, and visited the altars, and certainly, when there, their actions could not be interpreted as showing reverence or respect. I stood petrified to the spot when I saw a big retriever who came in with an old lady deliberately ascend the steps of the high altar, and sniff at the calves of the officiating priests. Nobody took any notice, except a little acolyte, who pulled the dog's tail and then patted his head. Several cats being also in the sacred edifice, there were times when some of the dogs left off sniffing around and joined in a merry scamper after a startled tom, who fled and leapt for refuge on to some upper portion of an altar, and looked down and spat at his enemies. I have been in a good many cathedrals, but I never saw dogs enjoy so much liberty in one before. The people of Granada are exceptionally devout, which made me wonder all the more at the custom. But to admit dogs is the custom, and, being the custom, I suppose nobody thinks anything of it.

After the Alhambra, the great Mosque of Cordova is the most beautiful thing in Spain. Built by the Moors in 796, it still stands a monument of their glorious architecture. Charles V., in 1526, allowed a portion of it to be destroyed to make room for an ugly cathedral in the centre of it. When he saw the act of vandalism that the priests had persuaded him to permit he was deeply grieved, and exclaimed, 'You have built here what you or anyone might have built anywhere, but you have destroyed what was unique in the world!' You can imagine how beautiful it must be for the man who knocked down half the Alhambra to build himself a hideously ugly drab-stone palace to be grieved at its partial destruction. This mosque is the finest type in Europe of a temple of Islam. It is a forest of beautiful marble pillars, supporting the most exquisite Moorish arches. I spent a whole day in the mosque with an intelligent little Italian, who knew every nook and corner of it.

When you get to Cordova you are never sure that you will see the mosque. You may not find it. Cordova is built on the principle of the maze at Hampton Court, but there is no nice kind gentleman on a raised platform to extricate you from the labyrinth of lanes. Even the inhabitants occasionally get lost, and wander up this street and down that for hours until they accidentally get to their homes again. Many of the dogs in Cordova have their owners' names and addresses on their collars. This is a great help to the inhabitants. When a Cordovan gets lost he waits about and looks on all the dogs' collars who run past him. When he sees a dog who has his (the lost inhabitant's) street on its collar, he follows him, and is so guided home.

These things are not romances, but facts. Every street is exactly alike, and every street is crossed and recrossed by dozens of other streets, and they all wind in and out, and they are all about three feet wide—some of them are not two feet wide. Woe betide the stranger who ventures out alone, and does not know enough Spanish to ask to be guided home again! He may spend a week easily in trying to find his way back to the hotel.

The hotel in Cordova is one of the best in Spain, and is always crammed with foreigners. The best time to study the guests is at *table d'hôte*. I have always my ears and eyes open then. I am much amused by a young Frenchman who has been to London, and is entertaining the other French guests with an account of the marvels he has seen there. The English live entirely on mutton-chops and beefsteaks, and always have sauce out of bottles. They even put this sauce, which is black, over their pudding and into their tea. On Sundays the English have no dinner. They only have tea and cold meat. The French ladies hold up their hands and cry out that never will they venture into such a horrible country. The Frenchman then sends them into fits by describing the feet and boots of English young ladies. Their feet are enormous, and they wear big cloth boots with no heels to them. Many girls of only sixteen already have the gout. Englishmen drink beer out of pewter pots in the highest society. The Prince of Wales, even at his grand dinners at Marlborough House, always has beer in a pewter pot by his side.

Near the Frenchman who has been to London and gathered so much information sit an extraordinary family, who are the wonder of the hotel. There is an old gentleman who speaks nothing but English, and is married to a widow who speaks nothing but French, with two daughters by a former husband who speak nothing but German. It is the oddest family arrangement that I ever came across in my life.

Then there is a Russian gentleman who is three feet high and four feet across. His head is a big dumpling with two eyes and something that with the aid of a powerful magnifying glass you make out to be a nose. By way of compensation he has a mouth that goes right across his face and turns round each corner. His body is a larger dumpling, and for legs he has two boiled jam rolls.

We sit down 150 at *table d'hôte*, and 149 people leave off eating and sit in blank amazement when this little Russian commences operations upon an orange. With a series of snorts and a couple of wriggles he gets the peel off. He then puts the orange between his teeth and forces it into his mouth by hitting it hard with both his fists. During this operation the people opposite and on either side are continually ducking their heads to avoid squirts of orange-juice in the eye.

As soon as the little Russian succeeds in closing his mouth he goes black in the face, and remains so for about two minutes. At the end of this time there is a loud gurgle; then the great mouth slowly opens, and calmly and passively the owner allows the pulp from which the juice has been extracted to fall upon his plate in portions. Horrible as this description may sound, it falls far short of the actual truth.

The commencement of the last act of the Russian gentleman's orange tragedy is the signal for everybody to jump up from the table and rush from the room.

There is another gentleman at *table d'hôte*—a Spaniard—who wouldn't be a bad fellow if, after he had eaten a couple of olives between each course, he would put the stones anywhere except on the tablecloth. This gentleman is short-sighted, and has a pair of eye-glasses two sizes too large for the bridge of his nose. They drop into his soup, they come off into his wine, and they sometimes fall into the gravy of the dish the waiter is handing round. While the gentleman is fishing out his eye-glasses he drops his napkin. When the waiter picks up the napkin and presents it to him he drops his fork. By the time his fork has been restored to him his eye-glasses are in the dish again.

As the process is repeated with every course that comes to him, the gentlemen and ladies below him have several long waits during *table d'hôte*.

Many people will remember the case of the English doctor who shot a gipsy at Cordova. The gipsy was a well-known guide, who used to take foreigners to see the great mosque, from the tower of which an excellent view of Cordova can be obtained. Several tourists who had ascended the tower with him on previous occasions had either been seized with giddiness and fallen off, or committed suicide by throwing themselves over the parapet. The suicide theory was the one most generally adopted in the case of Englishmen, because the Spaniards still believe that all Englishmen suffer from a malady called El Spleen, and that El Spleen compels the sufferer to end his days and his sufferings in a violent manner. There are no coroners' inquests in Spain, and so no one ever troubled much to inquire into the deaths, which, as far as public opinion was concerned, were easily accounted for by El Spleen.

It was while turning to descend from the tower that Dr. Middleton found himself suddenly grasped round the throat by the gipsy guide, Heredia, and in such a manner that nothing but a shot from a pistol, which luckily enough he carried in a back pocket, could free him from his assailant. The doctor was acquitted, and the verdict was received with applause by a crowded court. There can be no doubt of the impartiality of Spanish judges, and of the friendly feeling which exists among Spaniards for Englishmen. That this feeling should have been expressed in loud applause in an open court in Cordova is all the more remarkable when we bear in mind that the gipsies who swarm in the city were actually thirsting for the blood of the Englishman who had taken the life of one of their race, and were threatening revenge on all those who ventured to express sympathy for Dr. Middleton. The gipsies of the south of Spain have always been a power in the country, and there are instances on record which prove that the Government has on more than one occasion been compelled to conciliate them by granting them small privileges. In the days following the revolution which led to the flight of Queen Isabella the gipsies became for a time a terror to all law-abiding and inoffensive citizens, and it was only by executing summary justice upon gipsy culprits that their power was broken.

The gipsies both of Cordova and Granada still, however, maintain the privilege of acting as guides to those who are foolish enough to take them. Outside the Hotel Suizo in Cordova there are always dozens of them hanging about. The reason of this is that it is utterly impossible for a stranger to find his way about Cordova alone. The narrow streets cross and recross each other in a perfect maze, and they are all exactly alike, so that there is no landmark for the pedestrian to steer by, and, as the streets are too narrow to admit carriages, a guide is a sheer necessity.

CHAPTER VII.

COSAS DE ESPAÑA.

FROM Cordova I came on to San Sebastian, the Brighton of Spain. How people can go to Biarritz while there is a San Sebastian, I cannot imagine. I have never seen such a beautiful watering-place, or one surrounded by such magnificent scenery. And all around is hallowed English ground, for here and at Pasajes are hundreds of graves of English officers and soldiers who fell in the siege. The graves on the hill at San Sebastian are terribly neglected. Many of the stones are overgrown with weeds, and the inscriptions are effaced. A few pounds judiciously spent would put them in order again. Wild and picturesque is the rough mountain cemetery of British heroes who fell in a far-off land; but, unless something is done, a few more years will see many of the headstones down, and the graves overgrown with weed and briar, and then no man will know where our dead braves lie.

Pasajes, the quaintest place in the world, is within easy reach of San Sebastian. It is a land-locked harbour, and looks for all the world like a lake surrounded on all sides by hills, until you come upon a gully between high, overhanging cliffs, when, after a few minutes' sail, you catch a glimpse of the open sea. One of the rocks is surmounted by a castle tower, and is called Castillo de Santa Isabel. Pasajes is a thriving town, and it is from this port that the Basques and Spanish emigrants sail for South America; but it is doubtful whether it has not missed its vocation. With a harbour the existence of which cannot be guessed from the sea, it is an ideal pirate's nest.

After a Spanish tour is over, the traveller divides Spain into two portions—the portion that was conquered by the Moor, and the portion that was not. Of the first portion he brings away a wondrous remembrance of glorious architecture and graceful decoration; of the second portion, the things which linger longest in his memory are the dances and the bull-fights.

To me the worst part of a bull-fight was the barbarous cruelty to the horses. They had *no chance*. They were simply brought into the arena to be gored, and, when they fell, they were beaten most brutally with sticks to get them to rise again. When they staggered to their feet, and tottered in the death agony, the Spaniards shouted with laughter. Even when the poor beasts lay in the last quiver of death, they were barbarously ill-used by the assistants, who tore the harness from them to put it on other victims. A more dastardly exhibition of brutality I never witnessed in my life. One feels sorry for the bull; but at least he has *some* sport. His treatment is cruel enough in all conscience; but he has four or five years of luxurious living in order to prepare him for his death. The poor horses only come to the arena to be tortured after wearing out their lives in the service of their master. Many of them are poor half-starved cab horses, and can hardly totter when they are spurred and beaten into the ring. If you say to a Spaniard that it is cruel to beat a horse like this, he stares at you and says, 'Ah, but he is not a good horse, no vale na; he is worth nothing.' There are some points in a bull-fight which command admiration for skill and dexterity. The espadas (the real heroes of the proceedings, the leading actors and stars) perform brilliant feats alone with the bull, and often incur great risks. But these would be far more worthy of admiration if they were performed before the bull had been tired out by baiting and weakened by loss of blood, instead of after. But it is useless protesting to a Spaniard. Bull-fights are their national pastime—the love of them is born with them, and you might as well try to mop up the sea as to put them down or abate their cruelty.

The horses and the horsemanship in Madrid are unequalled in any other town of Europe. The men ride as if they were born in the saddle. They ride horses that would cause every head to turn in Rotten Row over the stone-paved streets and in and out of the heaviest traffic. The Andalusian horse is a beautiful creature, and here is groomed to perfection. Everybody in Madrid keeps a horse and a carriage. Everything is sacrificed for show and outward appearance. There are families who go without meat for dinner that they may turn out in the drive in good style.

In Madrid I learnt the national cure for a cold on the chest. You squeeze the juice of an orange into a cup; you put in a heap of sugar, and you fill up with a hot decoction of marshmallow, which they call Flor de Malva. Then you go to bed and perspire. The next morning your chest is easy. I tried the remedy and found it efficacious. The drink is soothing and comforting. Try it. You need not wait till you have a cold.

Bad money is very common in all parts of Spain. Sometimes the coins have merely undergone the process of 'sweating,' more often than not they are altogether spurious.

Some years ago the newspapers announced that, on a certain day, new five-peseta pieces, bearing as impress the head of the little King, would be issued. No one had yet seen a coin with the effigy of the Rey chico, and so the issue of the new coins was awaited with eagerness. A gang of coiners immediately set to work, and early on the morning of the day announced they set forth to circulate them. One of them would enter a tramcar or omnibus and offer the conductor, when the latter came for his fare, one of the 'new coins.' The conductor naturally remarked upon it as the first he had seen, and examined it with interest. The curiosity of the passengers was roused; everybody was eager to see the new coins and the first portrait of the little King; and so when the owner of it explained that he had just come from the Bank, where he had received a number of them, and said that he was willing to exchange a few of the new pieces for old ones, his offer was gratefully accepted. Thus it happened that before a single genuine coin had left the Mint, Madrid was in possession of an immense number of false ones.

In a previous chapter I referred to the Spanish theatre, and I mentioned the peculiarities of the modern drama as it is understood in Spain. The favourite dramatist of the day, the Most Excellent Señor Don José Echegaray, had just produced a new drama at the Teatro Español, in Madrid, which only took him thirty days to write, according to rumour. The title of the drama is 'La Realidad y el Delirio' (Reality and Delirium), and there is a good deal of both in the production. The plot is a fair specimen of Echegaray's method and the kind of drama which the Spaniards accept as an evening's entertainment, and so it may interest the reader to hear all about it, more especially as since the Ibsen boom set in our English critics have taken Echegaray under their wing.

Gonzalo and Angela are newly married, and, like most newly-married folks, they love each other. Enrico is Gonzalo's friend; he is also a bad young man who has conceived an unholy passion for his friend's wife. One day he tells Angela that Gonzalo, who has just left home, pretending that he was to make a long journey on business, is really about to pay a visit to a young lady who lives in a certain house in a street close by. Angela is much upset by the communication, and becomes a prey to various conflicting emotions. Enrico, at last, while she is in a state of great excitement, induces her to accompany him to a lonely house, from the windows of which she sees Gonzalo entering the house of Julia, the young lady previously referred to. Angela faints and falls into Enrico's arms.

When she recovers from her swoon she despises herself in strong language and goes home. Gonzalo returns. He tells his wife all she knows already, but explains that he went to see Miss Julia in order to break off all relations with her. This noble confession fills Angela with remorse, and she bitterly repents her jealousy and wickedness. She spreads herself out in forcible and poetic language, and at considerable length, over the height of her husband's love and the depth of her own impropriety.

Enrico has promised Angela never to see her again, and, desiring to keep his word, he calls upon Gonzalo to bid him good-bye, previous to setting out on a long sea voyage. Gonzalo, who loves his friend, refuses to hear of such a scheme, and proposes instead that they should all go to Paris together. Enrico hesitates and is lost. He consents to go to Paris.

On the way to 'la Ville Lumière' an accident on the line causes Gonzalo to alight from the reserved compartment in which they are all travelling together. Gonzalo smokes a cigarette and strolls on the line and inspects the country; but he goes a little too far, and sees the train starting on its journey again without him. He runs after and catches it up (an easy matter in Spain, where five miles an hour is the express speed), but in the hurry he jumps into the wrong compartment, which is not the 'reservado,' but the one next to it. The night is dark, and the light from the illuminated 'reservado' throws a shadowy picture on the walls of a black cutting through which the train is speeding. Gonzalo, looking out of the window, sees the 'shadow on the wall.' He recognises the silhouettes of his wife and his friend. Suddenly he sees the shadows approach each other. One shadow puts its arm round the other shadow's neck and kisses it. Presently both shadows' arms are flung around both shadows' necks. Gonzalo waits to see no more. Hideous thoughts flash across his frenzied brain. He opens the door of the compartment, gets out upon the footboard, and is making his way along it to the 'reservado' to demand an explanation of the occupants, when his foot slips and he falls heavily upon the line.

Gonzalo escapes death, but he loses his reason. He is picked up and attended to, and in time he recovers from his wounds, only to be haunted by the memory of what he saw that fatal night. He raves wildly, madly. He does not know whether what he saw was real or a hideous nightmare: whether it was reality or delirium. In this scene the actor takes the middle of the stage and gives off some of the finest dramatic soliloquies that Señor Echegaray has ever written.

There is one person beside the guilty parties who knows the truth. This is the father of Gonzalo. He puts matters to rights by having a duel with Enrico and killing him. Enrico, repenting his villainy, makes but a poor defence of his life. The father of Gonzalo then forgives Angela, and Gonzalo recovers his senses and embraces his wife, and the curtain falls with Angela standing between father and son and representing, according to the author, 'the innocent victim of a villain's lawless love, purified by the suffering she has endured and the sorrow she has known.'

CHAPTER VIII.

OFF TO AFRICA.

'AFRICA' has not a very taking sound about it. When I told my friends and acquaintances that I was going to Africa, they had visions of lions and snakes, and jungles and swamps, and they insisted on my taking with me an armoury of guns and rifles, and a pharmacy of drugs and antidotes. I am going, however, to keep as much out of the track of the lions as possible; at least, I shall avoid the lions that have to be attacked with firearms, but the lions that you attack with a visiting-card I certainly hope I shall encounter. I have a beautiful letter of introduction to the reigning sovereign of Morocco, which I hope to present to him in his imperial palace (Dar Dabiba) when I go to Fez-al-jadeed and Fez-al-baleed, and I am assured that he will give me a royal reception, and trot out his dancing dervishes and his snake charmers for my edification. I have also a letter of introduction to a great Moorish General, a direct descendant of Othello, who will provide me with an escort of soldiers when I go to Wazan, which is a long way up country, and where I am bound to go, as I have a little business with the Grand Shereef, who resides there. I shall be obliged to have an escort, because the people of that district are so fanatical that there is no knowing what they might do to me. Mogador, Tetuan, and Tangiers are also on my visiting list, so that you may expect a great deal of Oriental imagery and barbaric splendour in these pages. In Algeria I shall sojourn awhile also, and I may pay a flying visit to Carthage, where I am desirous of making a few inquiries with regard to the career of a young lady named Salammbo. This is my programme as it is at present shaped in my mind's eye, Horatio. Whether I shall be enabled to carry it out, of course, depends on circumstances; but I shall get over a good deal of the ground mentioned, and I have no doubt I shall see some very wonderful things, and meet with many exciting adventures.

At present the Fates have brought me no further than Marseilles; but even the short distance from the capital of France to the Mediterranean seaport was not accomplished without a struggle. We were unable in Paris to secure seats in the 'train of luxury' one January night, but I was told there was another train at 7.15

which would do the journey to Marseilles in fifteen hours twenty-seven minutes by the time-table. The platform was crowded with dukes and duchesses with their footmen, and ladies' maids and lap-dogs, who, like myself, had not been able to get seats in the 'train de luxe,' and who were going by the 7.15, which was a first-class express with sleeping-cars, and all that we should miss would be the restaurant and the smoking-saloon. I brightened up at this information, and we called several porters to take our luggage and secure us a berth in the sleeping-car. The porters looked at us as though we had asked for a bit of the sun to put in our pockets to keep our hands warm. 'A berth in the sleeping-car, monsieur!' exclaimed the first porter who recovered his breath. 'Ha, ha! monsieur is joking; why, they are all booked a week in advance to Marseilles at this season of the year.' 'Well, then,' I said savagely, 'at least find us two corner seats in a smoking-carriage.' 'I will try, monsieur,' replied the porter, and away he sped. In a few minutes he returned, shrugged his shoulders apologetically, and delivered himself of the following elegant sentence: 'It touches me to the heart, and causes me profound sorrow, to have to inform monsieur that every corner seat is taken.'

It was true. I had heard a good deal about the fight for seats in the Marseilles express, but I realized it for the first time then. We were dragged up the train and down the train; we got on this step and on that, and peered into compartment after compartment. It was the same tale everywhere. Every coach was jammed as full as a cattle truck. At last there was a crowd of about fifty passengers for Marseilles all clamouring for seats, and there was not a single vacant place. Then the Chef de Gare most condescendingly informed me that he would put on another carriage. We felt deeply grateful. Having paid £4 4s. for a seat, we felt that the company was placing us under a life-long obligation by giving us one for our money. So we bowed to the ground to the station-master, and begged him to accept the assurance of our most distinguished consideration. He accepted it. Then we offered handfuls of francs to the railway porters, and these were also accepted. In return for our largesse, we told them we required them, when the extra carriage was joined on, to hold the crowd back until we had jumped in and secured the corners. When that extra carriage came, it was Waterloo all over again. But the arms of England (mine and Albert Edward's) were finally victorious, and we beat back four Frenchmen, a Russian, a German, two Poles, a couple of Arabs, and a Greek, and captured two corners. Directly we were seated the crowd poured in upon us, and at 7.15 we steamed out of the station—eight in the compartment, and about fourteen portmanteaux, nine hat-boxes, eight bundles of rugs, and ten parcels piled up to the ceiling on the top of us. It was an hour before we had sorted ourselves, and got the hand luggage packed away in the nets above and under the seats. By this time we were stifling. Both the windows were shut, the foot-warmers were burning hot, and the place was the Black Hole of Calcutta multiplied by eight. Albert Edward requested the permission of our fellow travellers to have the window a little way down, as we were nearly asphyxiated. Albert Edward asked the French passengers in French, the Germans in German, the Arabs in Arabic, and the Russians in Russian; and they all admired his linguistic attainments, but absolutely declined to allow the windows to be opened one inch, or for one second. They inquired in their various languages if he desired their immediate death. He replied that he did not; but that was the catastrophe he wished to avoid for me. I joined in gently but firmly, and brilliantly distinguished myself in all the languages except the Russian. But the enemy remained immovable.

Suddenly Albert Edward had an idea. His German-Arab features relaxed into an expression of sardonic glee. When everybody was dropping off to sleep he put it into execution. He struck a whole box of Vesuvians, one after the other. There was a simultaneous sneeze, six sleepers leapt to their feet coughing and gesticulating and swearing, and in an instant both windows were pulled down with a bang, and the fresh, pure air of heaven rushed into the black hole.

Over the agonies of that long night of intermittent suffocation I draw a partial veil. Now and again by some violent expedient, such as fancying we heard an accident, or pretending that we had run over a man, or that Mount Vesuvius in a state of eruption was distinctly visible on our left, we succeeded in getting a window down for a minute or two; but from 7.15 p.m. until 10.42 a.m. we were mercilessly smashed and stifled in a compartment which was not a first-class carriage, but a tin of compressed humanity.

At a little after eight o'clock in the morning we reached Avignon, and here we had five minutes for refreshment. I should like to have been an artist, to have made a sketch of the station as it appeared when the passengers alighted and dashed wildly at a little table set out with basins of hot coffee and rolls of bread a yard long. The ladies looked lovely, as they always do, but the circumstances were trying. Complexions are not at their best, nor is the coiffure at its apogee of excellence, when you have been sitting all night long in your clothes in a hermetically sealed railway-carriage. And the dirt and grime of travel will stain the most delicate cheek, and the flying grit of the engine will lodge occasionally on the most aristocratic nose, and get into the most lustrous and beautiful eyes. I say it without disrespect, but we were a seedy, pallid, untidy and unkempt lot that turned out on the platform of Avignon in the morning sunlight, and scalded our throats with coffee out of pudding-basins, and fought our way through the crowd at the buffet with the three feet rolls that were at once weapons of attack and defence. I was much interested in the duchesses *en deshabille*, also in the footmen in chimney-pot hats, and in the ladies' maids with smashed bonnets, who flew up and down the platform, vainly trying to arrange their mistresses' hair, and put them a little to rights, with a bowl of hot coffee in one hand, and a roll in the other. One clever maid put her coffee on the platform, and held her roll between her teeth, while with her two hands she dexterously arranged her lady's back hair in an ornamental and chaste design, and stabbed it with hairpins at the rate of ten a second.

But the most charming feature of that five minutes' wait was to me the way in which the dukes and earls and millionaires from the coupés and the sleeping-cars were deprived of their coffee and roll by their obedience to the will of their wives. A duchess said to her husband: 'John, I think Fido wants a walk.' And with her own fair hands she dragged a big black poodle from under the seat, and gave him to the duke. The duke accepted Fido without a murmur, and led him up and down the platform by his chain for the whole five minutes. Another lady handed her husband a little black-and-tan terrier to be exercised in a similar manner. Before the bell rang I counted seven husbands all walking their wives' pet dogs up and down the platform, and some even went outside the station with the dogs in order that the little dears might not fancy themselves debarred by surrounding circumstances from any of the privileges of the usual morning run at home.

All things come to an end in this world, and so did our journey to Marseilles, which I have related to show that the troubles of African explorers often begin much nearer home; but it is a wonder we didn't come to an end first. When, however, at noon I lounged on the harbour quays, amid such a wild, dark, picturesque crowd as few other European towns could produce, I was amply compensated for all my trials on the road. I never saw such a collection of flashing eyes and coal-black hair and sunburnt faces in my life. There were Italians and Spaniards and Greeks, and all the fierce and dusky sons of the Levant; there were Turks and Arabs and Egyptians and Syrians and African blacks, and the natives added to the picturesqueness of the crowd with their swarthy faces, fierce eyes, and splendid hair; and I stood with the motley crowd and lolled with my back against the wall, sunning myself as they did, and feeling beautifully Bohemian and lamentably lazy. It was such a treat, after the harsh travelling of the North, to find one's self wooed by the warm breeze and kissed by the burning sun, that I couldn't have taken my hands out of my pockets and left off lolling against that south wall if the Archbishop of Canterbury, or any other of my most intimate friends, had come by. For a whole two hours did I and Albert Edward loll about and frizzle and shut one eye, like dogs going to sleep, but I kept my other eye open wide enough to take a few observations, and make a note of them.

The Eastern custom of standing in a circle largely prevailed with the crowd of idlers. Here was a group of Greeks in full costume in a circle; there a group of Italians in a circle. The Marseilles sailors and labourers, and the Marseilles old ladies and the Marseilles young ladies, 'circled' also; they all stood and screamed at each other, and shouted at the top of their voices (this is conversation in Marseilles), but no one ever broke the circle.

The groups and the crowds of swarthy sons and daughters of the South were not exactly the sort of groups and crowds one would like to be alone in, with the Bank of England in one's pockets. I should say one might have manned a dozen pirate ships at any one quay in five minutes. Knives were worn handy, and there was a flash of steel more than once when argument became high. But for all that the men and women themselves wore a good deal of common jewellery; watch-chains by the score I counted across the woollen waistcoats of the sailors, and most of the men had heavy earrings in their ears. The scarlet sashes worn round the waists, the blue and green plush trousers, and the bright orange and red handkerchiefs twisted over the heads of some of the women, turban fashion, imparted to portions of the crowd an operatic look, and I expected every minute to hear them commence a chorus.

I had my boots blacked on the Quay du Port, and a marvellous boy in rags performed the office. Murillo might have been tempted to come out of his grave to paint him. When everything else fails, and I am quite tired of respectable life, I shall come to Marseilles, and spend the rest of my days in lolling on the quay and basking in the sun.

Yet perhaps I had better wait before I finally make up my mind on the subject of Marseilles, for down the harbour on my right there lies at anchor the ship which is to carry me across the blue Mediterranean to the African shore. And who knows?—I might like Algiers better.

CHAPTER IX.

ALGIERS.

'HIGH STREET, Africa,' is a very nice address to give to your creditors or to people who worry you with letters about nothing at all, and require an immediate and categorical answer; but it is not an address which facilitates the reception of the latest news from England. I have been able to leave nothing more definite at home for the guidance of the officials of the International Postal Service. For this reason I am in a state of the most blissful ignorance as to what is happening at home. I am sitting in the sun, I pluck oranges, gather bananas and prickly pears, and go into the garden after breakfast and pick green peas and dig up new potatoes. When you are where you can do this in the first week of January, it would be the concentrated essence of idiotism to bother yourself as to who is the responsible person for clearing away the snow and the slush that have stopped the traffic of Downing Street, and converted legislative pedestrianism into a process of slipping and sliding, and coming down bang on your back.

I like High Street, Africa, very much indeed. I have got so far along it as the Djur-Djura Hills, among the Atlas Mountains. I am on friendly terms with the great mountain tribes of Kabylia, and the lion and the panther are my next-door neighbours. But I did not get so far all at once, and as the process of getting there has been to me both novel and instructive, I fancy it may be the same to some of my readers—say eighteen out of the twenty millions. The other two millions can skip this chapter if they don't care about it, and read the advertisements at the end of this volume.

We left Marseilles, not by the Messageries, but by a much more 'up to date' line—the Compagnie Transatlantique. A more magnificent vessel than the *Ville de Tunis* it would be hard to find in the Mediterranean service, and she rushes through the water at the rate of nineteen-and-a-half knots an hour. But oh, that 'awful night at sea!' Tell me no more of your blue Mediterranean. I had it black—black and furious. It blew a gale nearly the whole voyage, and the ship rolled to such an extent that it was impossible to lie in one's berth. All night long it was a hideous crash of crockery and furniture, piteous groans of men, and the terrified cries of women, and the day brought no relief. For twenty-eight long hours did we roll from side to side in the trough of a raging sea, expecting every moment that the ship would roll an inch too far and go right over. If you don't know what it is to feel for a night and day that you are going to be drowned in a minute, you won't appreciate the feelings of the poor bruised and battered and bilious and broken-hearted passengers who sailed with me over that five hundred miles of misery that separates France from Africa, Marseilles from Algiers.

We made Algiers shortly before midnight on Sunday. But our troubles were not over. Beautiful in the moonlight lay Algiers, the houses and mosques of the Arabs glistening in pearly whiteness above the long line of lights of the European quarter, and the whole shut in by a background of far-off hills of snow. But we had to get there, and the ships don't go up to the quays. To the terror of the timorous it was explained that as soon as the ship's doctor had gone ashore, and certified that we had no cholera or infectious disease on board, we should be fetched off in small boats by Arab boatmen. And so we were.

There came about fifty boats manned by wild-looking Arabs. They crushed round the steamer shouting and swearing at each other, and gesticulating to attract the attention of the passengers. When at last the signal was given they swarmed up the sides of the ship, and at once laid hold of all the luggage that was unguarded. Two or three men would lay hands on a bag and fight over it. Presently all the hand-bags and the rugs were in the boats; but some of the passengers found themselves in one boat, while their rugs and bags were being carried ashore in another. We managed to keep our things together, but for a quarter of an hour we had a bad time of it, and I had begun to doubt that the French had ever conquered Algiers, because these boatmen were so much like pirates.

When we landed, we were taken in tow by a handsome, barefooted Arab lad of about seventeen, who insisted upon shouldering all our bags and rugs, and putting a heavy portmanteau on his head, and conducting us to the Custom House. Here, to my utter astonishment, the Custom House officer, instead of asking if we had tobacco, cigars, eau-de-Cologne, or spirits, demanded sternly if we had any 'verdure.' I hesitated before replying. I have a considerable amount of verdure. I am as green in some things as a country bumpkin, but I hesitated to confess it in public. I might have parried the question with a joke, by asking the grave official if he saw any verdure in my eye, but his solemnity of manner overawed me. I ventured to ask what he meant by verdure. A French officer attached to the Bureau Arabe, who had crossed with us and become friendly, hastened to the rescue, and explained that 'verdure' means 'green stuff' at the Custom House. The officials were merely anxious to know if I had any fruit, flowers, or vegetables in my baggage.

The key to the enigma was soon supplied. Algeria is in a state of morbid terror lest the dreaded phylloxera should be imported from France and destroy her vines. Not a green leaf, not an orange, not a flower is allowed to pass the Custom House. I assured the official that I had nothing of the sort, when, with a sudden yell, he sprang at me and seized me by the coat. Two soldiers ran to his assistance, a crowd gathered around me, and, amid the indignant cries of the multitude, a poor little faded rosebud was torn from my buttonhole. I had taken it from the dinner-table on board ship, put it in my buttonhole, and had forgotten it was there. I believe that the rosebud was put into a boat at once, rowed out ten miles to sea, and sunk in the Mediterranean by means of a big stone tied to its stalk. My own fate was less terrible. I was severely lectured and allowed to pass, but for many days afterwards, when I walked abroad in the town, the inhabitants turned and gazed after me with scowling faces, and muttered imprecations on the head of the 'Sale Anglais,' who had basely endeavoured to introduce the phylloxera into Algeria.

Once free of the Custom House, Achmet, our young Arab, conducted us to hotel after hotel. All were full. At last we succeeded in getting two rooms on a top landing. Achmet carried our luggage up, and then asked us for the ticket of the heavier portmanteaux, which were in the ship's hold, and could not be got out till the morning. I hesitated, but Albert Edward instantly handed it to him. 'Trust him,' he said; 'an Arab never betrays a trust.' And so Achmet walked off with the ticket of our portmanteaux.

At nine the next morning ragged, barefooted Achmet knocked at our door. He wanted the keys of our baggage to pass it at the Custom House. We gave them to him, and in an hour the lad came to the hotel and brought the baggage, and returned the keys. And not so much as a handkerchief or a pair of socks had disappeared. To me this is one of the most wonderful features of my journey. Here was a lad—almost a beggar lad—utterly unknown to us, we could not even recognise him in the crowd of Arabs that haunt the quays, and we had trusted him blindly and implicitly with the sole custody and control of valuable property. I shouldn't like to try the same experiment in London or anywhere else. And it wouldn't do to try it in Algiers with a European boy of the same position. This is one great feature of the Arab character. Trust them, and they would die rather than betray the trust; suspect them and guard against their dishonesty, and they will glory in robbing and tricking you at the first opportunity.

For his trouble and his civility I gave Achmet a five-franc piece. He grinned and smiled and chuckled, and tied it up in a piece of rag, and put it in his bosom. I asked him what he was going to do with it. 'Ah! monsieur, it will help to buy me a wife,' replied Achmet, and then he told us how he was saving up to get £5 that he might buy a wife. An old woman had told him of a very pretty girl, and the father only wanted 125 francs for her. I engaged Achmet there and then to do all my little commissions for me, and to accompany me to the Arab quarter, and show me everything; and I promised him that if he was good, before I left Algeria I would give him the balance he needed, and leave him a happy married man.

The Arab marriage system is curious but simple. There can be no love and no courtship about it. That must come after marriage, because the Arab husband never sees his wife's face, or speaks to her until the marriage ceremony has been performed. Old women are the match-makers. They see the Arab girls at home, and describe their beauty in glowing Eastern language to the eligible Arab men. A young fellow is kind to an old woman, runs errands for her (I am speaking of Achmet's class now), and in return she gives him 'the straight tip' as to whose daughter to buy for a wife. Achmet had saved his old lady friend from being insulted by a drunken Zouave, and she had rewarded him by telling him of the beautiful Saidah Bint Mohammed, the fifteen-year-old daughter of Mohammed Ben Omar, the old Arab donkey-driver of the Upper Town. Papa wanted 150 francs, but he would take 125. Achmet was in great terror lest some other young fellow should hear of the bargain first.

These young Arab women are rarely seen in the streets. The old women and the divorced women (women sent back to their fathers) go about, but closely veiled, so that only the eyes are visible. The Arab divorce is curious, and, like the marriage system, singularly easy. An Arab with too many wives who wants to get rid of one, or the poor Arab with one who wants a change in his domestic circle, says to the wife, 'I divorce thee.' This he must say three times at a week's interval. The girl then goes back to her father, and takes all her jewellery, and any property she brought with her. Divorce, however, is not very frequently resorted to. Husband and wife jog along together. Jealousy does not exist on the female side, and the wife has very little opportunity of causing her lord uneasiness. There is nothing in the domestic arrangements to cause words. The Arab husband does not dine with his wife, and it never enters into her head to object to his latchkey and late hours at the café.

The system of polygamy prevents the poor Arab from feeling the pressure of a large family, and the labour market is not affected by female competition. These people escape the difficulties of our London poor. A man's sons work for him at a very early age, and the daughters are all marketable. When they are very pretty they are really valuable property. Besides this, the Koran *commands* charity, and there is no such thing as an Arab who has been true to his faith dying of hunger. Arabs, again, are forbidden by their religion to drink intoxicants. An Arab can cross Africa from Morocco to the Soudan with nothing in his pocket. Shelter and food are offered him gratis by every tribe he meets. The rich help the poor, not as an act of charity, but as an act of religion. Islamism does not at present enjoy the benefit of the teaching of the Charity Organization Society.

With Achmet to accompany me, and Albert Edward to exchange Arabic pleasantries with the natives, I have been able to sit among them at their own cafés, to chat with them in their bazaars, and to visit some of them in their homes. To me this has been more instructive than wandering about the famous old town of the pirates and its picturesque environs. No one can look without emotion for the first time on this once blood-bespattered spot, on the wild African coast from which the scourges of Christendom sailed forth to sweep the seas and then desolate the neighbouring lands; to bring back thousands of slaves—the men to toil their lives away in cruel bondage, and the women to be sold in the great market to the wealthy lords of vast harems—no one, I say, can look upon this spot without feeling stirred and interested. But, after all, the proper study of mankind is man. The condition of a race existing is a more useful study than the story of a race which has passed away. Algiers has had its Dey, and now it has its Governor-General; but I doubt much whether the Arabs of Algeria are really fonder of the French soldiers than the Christians of old were of the Moorish corsairs.

The best way to get an idea of Algiers as a whole is to row out into the bright blue bay. Then you see as pretty a picture as ever was sent to a Royal Academy. The town seems to rise from the sea in a series of shining white marble terraces. Above the European quarter lies the old Arab town—white and weird and wonderful. But it is the background that makes the picture. The glorious green heights that frame the landscape are dotted with French villas and Moorish palaces, amid the rich colouring of tropical fruit and flower, and, high over all, stretching far away into the dim distance, are the snowclad summits of the Atlas Mountains.

But the greatest beauty of all lies in the sky and the sea and the sun, and the ever-glowing, smiling landscape. You can't describe this sort of thing—at least, I can't. My stock of adjectives is small, and I should exhaust it in a paragraph if I tried to depict the loveliness of this favoured spot.

The best of scenery soon palls on me, but the ever-changing, ever-moving crowd never does. I should like to have the great gathering-place of Algiers, the Place du Gouvernement, packed and exported to London for my especial benefit. Always at my dark hour, when I begin to wonder whether razors or poisons or water-butts are the best solutions of the enigma of life, I would go and sit down on the Place du Gouvernement, and my dark hour would give way to the dawn—nay, to the full glory of the noonday sun. What a marvellous crowd it is that saunters up and down! The stately Arab, spurning the ground as he paces it in white burnous; the gaudy Moor, in his bright blue, gold-embroidered jacket, short white trousers, and red fez; the Jew, with his yellow turban, his black jacket, and his many-coloured sash; the black Bedouins of the desert; the Greek; the Turk; the Maltese; the swarthy, fierce-eyed Spaniard; the French Zouaves and Turcos; the raven-haired, lustrous-eyed daughters of Spain and Southern Italy; the Arab woman, veiled upwards to the nose and downwards to the eyes—how you wonder what they look like behind that tantalizing gauze!—the Jewess, with her straight silk robe and slippered feet—all these races mix and commingle with the dandy Frenchman and the commonplace Englishman, and make a 'bit of colour' which it would be hard to find equalled anywhere.

How one despises broadcloth and chimney-pot and all the sober hues of cockneydom as one gazes on this scene! I feel that even I might begin to find a few minutes' pleasure in life if I could only dress myself up in one of these romantic garbs and wear a bright-coloured sash instead of braces, and shining buff boots or scarlet slippers. If I could wear these things and have a fierce black moustache and a turban or a fez, I am quite sure the world would also wear a different aspect. Of course I may be wrong. It is quite possible that these picturesque people who eye me as I pass are envying me my prosaic billycock hat and my tallow-coloured complexion and my commonplace black coat.

How these people ever get about Algiers without spoiling their finery is a great mystery to me. I have not been out five minutes before I am mud-colour from top to toe—not black mud; that does not exist here—but a brown-coloured mud, which dries *café-au-lait*, or fawn colour, and shows up splendidly on your dark garments. The roads of Algiers are awful. They are sometimes a foot thick in light, liquid mud. If you take an open carriage, you might as well put the mud on with a whitewash-brush at starting to save trouble. The administration of Algiers does not worry itself about such a thing as road-making or road-sweeping. The mayor is a learned professor, and the council probably join with him in learned discussions on abstruse questions. They never do anything for Algiers.

To take a good drive in the neighbourhood you want nerves of iron. One Sunday I drove a roundabout way to our Lady of Africa, the church that stands on the summit of the high hill of Bou Zarea. Two little Arab horses drew me, and the driver left the path to them. He only attended to the pace, which was the maximum all the way. Go up the side of a house and down the side of a house in an open carriage at full speed, then dash round the house on the extreme verge of the gutter, then, without getting out of the carriage, make your steeds jump from the roof of one detached house to the next, then drive straight across a row of roofs, taking the centre and never turning to the right or the left merely because a stack of chimneys is in the way—do all this, and you will then be able to understand the sort of drives my coachman takes me in Algeria. I am told the precipices and the ravines we pass over and the mountains we scale are grand and glorious. I can't say; I always, when I come to them, shut my eyes, and wonder whether they will think to join my pieces together before they pack me for transportation to England, just to see if I am 'all there.'

Our Lady of Africa stands upon a precipice overlooking the sea. Here I saw a ceremony which is, I believe, unique. The priests and the acolytes, and the whole religious procession, filed out after prayers and stood on the brow of the precipice. Then began a grand and beautiful service. The priest 'blessed the sea,' and then performed a solemn funeral service for all those who have died therein. It was a very impressive service, and it was a very lovely idea. Some of us were so touched by the solemn ceremony at the edge of that vast grave that we broke down a little. Amid the sad-faced women who stood around there were evidently some to whom the prayers for the dead who lay beneath the sad sea-waves brought back the loved face lost, the vanished hand, and the sound of the voice for ever still. The ceremony is one no visitor to Algiers should miss, but it leaves a sadness on the mind which does not soon pass away.

The interior walls of Our Lady of Africa are covered with votive offerings from the faithful, chiefly pictures of wrecks and narrow escapes by land and sea, from fire and water, which are intended to commemorate the miraculous intercession of the Holy Virgin; and there is also to be seen a very quaint statue of the Archangel Michael, usually hidden behind drapery, and which is said to be worth a hundred thousand francs, being made of solid silver. It is the property of a confraternity of Neapolitan fishermen. The church of Our Lady of Africa is the place of worship of Mediterranean seafarers, irrespective of nationality; and Spanish smugglers, Italian fishermen and French sailors forget their differences when they kneel down in prayer before her shrine.

The village of Bou Zarea, which is built on a slope of the mountain, lies 1,300 feet above the sea, and from it you can get some idea of what this coast must have looked like in the days of the Deys and the pirates. Every prominent point is studded with the ruins of a fort, or the tomb of a saint. These tombs, properly called koubbas, but usually styled marabouts by the French, are often exceedingly picturesque. Just behind us, half a mile up the mountain, there is the koubba of Sidi Naaman, a venerated patriarch who worked miracles while in the flesh, and whose fame is still green among the Arabs. But this is but one in a hundred, or a thousand, and there are few pretty spots on the seashore or in the mountain without a koubba.

One day, while wandering in the hills, I came upon one of these koubbas, the tomb of a very celebrated marabout, whose life had been one of holiness. I was quite alone, there was not a living soul to be seen, so I opened the door of the mausoleum and walked in. To my surprise, I found inside the tomb a beautiful bed hung with gorgeous draperies, and by the side of the bed was a little table, on which stood a plate of oranges, a plate of bananas, and a plate of dates. I fancied I had mistaken somebody's one-roomed house for a tomb, so I crept out cautiously and walked away. The same evening, while talking with a French officer, I related my adventure, and he explained the mystery.

The beautiful bed was for the marabout to sleep on, the food was for his refreshment. After sunset all holy men are believed to rise from the earth and lie upon the more comfortable bed, and take a little light refreshment. Some Arabs go so far as to put a pipe and some tobacco and a box of lights on the table, in case the dead saint should like a smoke. What a delightful idea of death! Why, the grave would lose all its terrors to some men if they could be sure of a pipe after dinner!

CHAPTER X.

SAINTS AND SINNERS.

I BRING a message from across the seas. I am requested by the venerable Father Antoine, of the monastery of La Trappe, at Staouëli, near Algiers, to make it known that the Trappists of Africa are very anxious to have an English brother among them. The monastery is delightfully situated. Its advantages are that you take a vow of perpetual silence; you only have one meal a day, which never includes meat; you labour healthfully in the fields, and, by way of recreation, you dig your own grave. The English brother will occasionally be relieved of the vow of perpetual silence, because his duties will be to receive the English visitors and conduct them over the monastery. I am absolutely in earnest. The request is a *bonâ-fide* one; and an English Roman Catholic willing to enter the order will be most heartily and cordially received.

I was much inclined to stay myself. I didn't mind the work and the grave-digging and the vegetarian diet. I am sure many of my ailments would have disappeared under the treatment. My stumbling-block was the vow of silence. In the interior of the monastery silence is rigorously enforced. Even visitors, after they pass the inner portals, are requested to hold their tongues. I couldn't do that even for ten minutes. I tried hard, but every now and then I found myself whispering a remark to my companions. The good Père Antoine smilingly rebuked me with a warning finger, and the silent Trappists gazed at me in mild remonstrance. No ladies are under any circumstances admitted. The utter impossibility of a woman remaining silent anywhere or under any circumstances is probably the reason for this rigorous exclusion.

On the day that I drove to Staouëli and visited the famous monastery, the African sun was pouring down its fierce rays from a sky of the deepest and intensest blue. The vast fields of scented geranium, from which the Trappists distil a famous perfume, were bathed in a great white heat. There hundreds of cattle lay about and lolled in the sun, and the great palm-trees in the glorious gardens of the monastery cast their long shadows over such a wealth of fruit and flower as I have never seen before. 'If it is sad to live at La Trappe, how sweet it is to die there,' says an inscription on the walls. I don't want to die there, but I am sure I should not have found it sad to live and labour amid such calm and beautiful surroundings, 'the world forgetting, by the world forgot.' It must be a very comfortable existence. All the brothers I saw looked very happy. No posts, no telegraphs disturbed the calm serenity of their labours, and they all sat down to their one daily meal with an appetite and a digestion that filled me with a great envy.

I breakfasted at La Trappe. Brother Dominic spread the feast, and Father Antoine himself uncorked the wines—made on the premises—with which the dainty fare was washed down. I was the only visitor, so I breakfasted in solemn state alone. I had first an excellent omelette, then some cold sweet potatoes, then some cheese and salad, then some bread and honey, then some raisins, some oranges, and some bananas, and after I had drunk a bottle of red wine, the good father produced a bottle of exquisite white sweet dessert wine; and after that I had coffee and a glass of the famous Trappistine liqueur. Father Antoine and Brother Dominic waited upon me hand and foot. They piled my plate and filled my glass until I was obliged to cry, 'Hold! enough!' only I expressed myself more politely. And then I was shown to the shaded seat in the garden, and told that if I liked to enjoy a cigar under the palm-trees, the brother would look the other way.

I have a few pleasant memories to look back upon—green oases in the arid desert of my life; but there are none so fraught with calm and holy peace as that hot January day I spent with the good kind brothers of La Trappe in their African home. They showed me everything—their cells, their beds, their library, their kitchen, their farm, their winepresses, their *laboratoire*, their stables, their cattle, their thousands of cocks and hens and pigeons and rabbits, and then they loaded me with ripe oranges and bananas plucked from their own trees, and choicest roses gathered from their own gardens; and all they asked me in return was to mention in my book that they wanted an English brother to come and live among them. Go, English brother, go; and I promise you you will be happy—far happier than staying in the turmoil of the world, to endure its thousand worries and heartaches and disappointments. Go and tell Father Antoine that the Englishman who smoked a pipe, and who *would* keep talking in spite of the rules, kept his promise, and sent you out to dig your own grave, and to make the English visitors who don't speak French welcome to the African home of the world-famed monks of La Trappe.

On the evening of the day that I visited La Trappe, I assisted at a very different scene. I received an invitation to be present at the Feast of the Assaouaï, a kind of religious fête, held in a Moorish house in the Rue Ben Ali, a narrow street in the top of the Arab quarter. The Arab quarter is a sight in itself. It is a labyrinth of narrow streets of steps and jumbled houses. You can only pass along two abreast, and the roofs of the houses hang over and almost join. To get to any given house, you must have a guide; for there are scores of streets crossing and recrossing one another, and they are all alike. Achmet conducted me at night to the Rue Ben Ali, and I witnessed a scene the like of which is to be seen nowhere else in the civilized world. I found myself in the courtyard of a Moorish house, open to the sky. Above me glittered the bright stars in a vault of blue. The courtyard was crammed with Arabs, and French and English 'strangers.' Next to me, standing on a chair, was Miss Jones of Clapham, with her mamma. I wondered how they got there, and what they thought of the Moorish ladies, who, dressed like the chorus in the Eastern extravaganza at the Gaiety Theatre, sat outside many of the houses in the narrow streets, and addressed endearing blandishments to the male passers-by. I blushed a little at much that I passed on my journey up the Arab quarter; but Miss Jones of Clapham and her mamma were possibly protected by their innocence from knowing what it meant. Before the Feast of the Assaouaï was over, they must have had their innocence severely put to the test; but I am bound to say they never blushed once.

The performance commenced with a dance of Moorish girls. The girls were lovely, and they were gorgeously dressed. They danced the Oriental dance, which is, perhaps, as absolutely and indelicately suggestive as any dance known to ancient or modern times. The French ladies present muttered 'Mon Dieu!' under their breath. Miss Jones of Clapham struggled for a closer view. Mamma pursed her lips a little, and once I thought I heard her groan, but she stood on tiptoe until a Moor's fez got in her line of sight. After the dance, the girls sang a love-song. Achmet explained the burthen of it to me, when I heard Miss Jones say to her mamma that it was very 'sweet.' I felt convinced that Arabic didn't form part of a young lady's education at Clapham seminaries. What the natives who understood the song and appreciated the dances must have thought of the English young woman who almost jumped on the Arabs' backs to get a good view of the proceedings, I have been wondering ever since.

After the songs and dances, the dervishes commenced their performances. A young dervish jumped into the ring, and swayed himself backwards and forwards for ten minutes, shouting, 'Allah! Allah!' while his motions became so rapid that I felt giddy. Then, having reached the required pitch of fanatical fervour, he began to cram live scorpions into his mouth, and bite off their heads and tails. I confess that if I could have got out of the crowd, I should gladly have been sick. Miss Jones of Clapham only murmured that it was very wonderful. Another fanatic, after swinging round till he fell down foaming at the mouth, ran skewers through his nose and under his eyelids, and left them hanging there while he bit pieces out of a glass bottle and chewed them to powder. Then he had an epileptic fit, or a paralytic stroke, and, as soon as he had recovered, sat down to rest on a pan of live charcoal. He then ran a knife through his tongue, turned his eyes out on to his cheeks, twisted his ears upside down, and stuck his nose full of red-hot needles. After this he bowed and retired, amid much applause, Miss Jones of Clapham almost splitting her dainty little kid gloves in her demonstrations of approval. Mamma, I am bound to say, whispered to her dear and enthusiastic child that she was not quite sure that she could stand very much more.

I didn't think there could be much more to stand; but a very old Arab gentleman stepped into the ring with a huge sharp-pointed sword in his hand. The sword was passed round, and we all felt the edge and the point. Miss Jones wouldn't let it go for at least two minutes. The sword was then held on the ground, point upwards, by two strong men, who lay down to do it. The old Arab gentleman then coolly proceeded to roll up his shirt round his neck, so as to leave his entire stomach bare. He then turned to the audience to show them that it was bare. At last Miss Jones of Clapham was disconcerted. Truth compels me to admit that she ejaculated, 'Oh, mamma!' and for one short moment she looked as though she would like to retire. But she recovered herself in a moment, and nearly knocked an elderly French gentleman's hat over his eyes in her endeavour to get a nearer view. The Arab 'undressed,' after trying the sword to see that it was firmly fixed, stepped back a foot or two; then, with a little run, sprang in the air, and, throwing himself out, fell with his bare stomach flat on to the point of the upright sword. He was absolutely impaled, and in this position he spun round and round. I turned away, and fancied I was on board ship again. If only there had been a steward handy, I should have called him to my assistance with the accompanying crockery; but Miss Jones of Clapham gave a little giggle, and cried out in maiden wonderment, 'Lor, ma! however can he do it?'

I stopped to see no more. Calling on Achmet to accompany me, I quitted the dancing girls and the juggling Arabs and the self-mutilating dervishes, and went out into the Rue Ben Ali. As I left the courtyard of the Moorish house, I looked up, and high above me in the starlight, upon the galleries of the house, I saw veiled Arab women looking down upon the scene. I wondered what they thought of the unveiled, bare-faced English girls who assisted, without a blush or a shudder, at such disgusting and depraved exhibitions. When I told Achmet that many of these young English girls would not be allowed to go to a stage-play in England, except at the Crystal Palace, for fear their modesty should be shocked, he opened his large Eastern eyes to such an extent that they looked like a couple of full moons. He says the Arabs can't understand the Giaour women at all, and I don't wonder at it. The French people in the town are themselves shocked at the idea of unmarried girls assisting at these exhibitions; but they are the first things that the English girls ask to be taken to see. If I had a son, I should be very sorry for him to accompany me to one. But English mothers take their daughters, and so I am driven to the conclusion that either I am extra squeamish, or that they are extra innocent. But the innocence that can detect nothing improper in the dance of the Moorish girls ought to be wrapped in cotton-wool, and taken back to the Garden of Eden in the days before Eve ate of the Tree of the Knowledge of Good and Evil. That is the only place, and the only period, in which anyone would accept it as genuine.

In bygone times the Assaouaï were a powerful religious fraternity. The founder of the order was an Arab, one Sidi Mohammed Ben Aïssa, and the members, whose mission it was to fan the fanaticism of the people in times of war, were all Arabs. But the Assaouaï of to-day are a mixed lot of Arabs, Berbers, and Negroes. Nevertheless, they still exercise considerable power over the imagination of their fellow-countrymen in the more remote districts of Morocco and Tripoli, where they are often the secret agents of rebellion. But in Algeria, owing to the revolts fomented by them, ending all in slaughter and defeat, they have lost their prestige; they are no longer 'invincibles,' only showmen living upon the profits of their performances.

The climate of Algeria is fearfully trying to the temper. If the Archbishop of York and the Archbishop of Canterbury came to stay here together, they would have words in a week. I won't say they would come to blows in a month, because they are Archbishops; but I think that two bishops would probably fight. Everybody in Algeria who is not a native becomes irritable and hasty and snappy very soon after landing. I, of course, retain my usual placidity of manner; but Albert Edward is awful. He bullies the landlords of our hotels; he challenges the post-office officials to come outside and fight; he even presumes at times to lecture me smartly upon my unreasonableness; and when he scolds the waiters, I blush for very shame. I generally go afterwards to these poor people and apologize for his violence. But I have to do it in secret, for I am myself afraid of him. The other day he fell over a piece of broken pavement in the Rue Bab el Zoued at Algiers, and his new hat went flying into the mud. This accident he declared was due to the culpable negligence of the authorities, and before I could stop him he had rushed off to the Hotel de Ville, rung up the concierge, and was flourishing his stick about, and giving most insulting messages to the mayor. His language to the clerk at the Poste-Restante was really shocking. Here I must say he had an excuse.

The method of doing business at the Poste Restante is not calculated to put an Englishman in a good temper. If he comes and gives in his card, he is handed all the English letters, and told to help himself. From Mustapha (the English colony, and at once the Clapham and South Kensington of Algiers) there comes a porter from the hotels. He generally takes all the English newspapers as a matter of course. The idea that anybody not residing on the Mustapha (a height above the town) should have anything from England is scouted as absurd. My English papers I only recovered after employing mounted Arabs to scour the hills in every direction, inquiring at every villa and every hotel and every farm where an English person resided.

I received a batch of letters nine days after their leaving London. They were due in four. I believe that they had been given to a sailor who came from an English yacht in the bay for letters, and mine evidently went for a short cruise before they were brought back. One thing I would impress on English people coming to Algiers—don't have your letters sent to the Poste Restante. If you do your time will be wasted, your correspondence delayed, and your temper will become as uncontrollable as my companion's.

The Post-office clerks cannot read English names. To show the hash that is made of them, I will quote from the list of fashionable arrivals at an hotel given in a local paper. The arrivals are all classified under the heads of French, Spanish, Italian, English, etc. Here is the English list *literatim et verbatim*:

'The Mistress Macandraw, Mr. Boom, Mr. Fegin, Mr. Fosdick, Mr. Dosgoity, Mr. Billies, Mr. Plumb, Mr. Sliebel, the O'Rori, the Mistress Lady Jon.' If the names are right, it is about the queerest collection of surnames I ever came across.

Achmet has just come in to tell me that a lion has appeared at a village some miles from where I am now encamped, and that his roaring has kept the inhabitants awake all night. I am off. To see a real live lion looking about for his breakfast, free and unfettered, is an unfulfilled ambition of my life. Hastily we grasp our firearms, leap upon our Arab steeds, and dash across the desert towards the hill where the lion is seeking whom he may devour. Whether I shall be able to let you know the result of our day's sport will depend very much upon which gets the better of the encounter—we or the lion.

Achmet, who brought me my letters and newspapers, also told me there had been an execution in Algiers of an Arab who had been found guilty of a very cruel murder. The guillotine is a fearful punishment for a Moslem, because the guillotine cuts the head off, and Mahomet takes the faithful when they are dead by the hair of the head in order to lift them up into Paradise. The poor fellows who are cut in two at the neck are in a fearful state, because when Mahomet takes hold of them by the hair of the head the body will naturally remain behind on earth. In the Mahomedan Paradise a gentleman with only a head would not be able to thoroughly enjoy himself.

A public decapitation strikes terror into the hearts of the Arab populace. The guillotine at Algiers is erected on a large open space in front of the Arab quarter, and the ceremony is made as imposing as possible, *pour encourager les autres*. Achmet told me that once when a friend of his had been guillotined, the relatives had gone to the Governor and begged the body and head back again. As a great favour they had been given up to them on condition that they said nothing about it to the other Arabs. When these people got the two pieces of their departed friend home, they sewed his head on again with a thick string, and then they practised holding him up by the hair to see if the stitches would stand when Mahomet came to lift him into Paradise.

The Arabs are none too well treated by *their* master. They have had to suffer for France's colonial policy. I don't fancy that France makes Algeria pay. It is a trinket on her watch-chain, and not the watch at the end of it. Algeria is in debt. She costs France far more to keep than she gives in return. The expenses of military occupation of the Government are great, and the produce is small. The Arabs complain bitterly of the excessive taxation; but they have suffered even more at the hands of the Jews than of the French.

Nearly all the Arab farmers and landed proprietors are in debt to the Jews. Their crops are mortgaged before they are gathered. One after the other their houses and lands have fallen into the hands of the Israelites. Money is dear. The legal rate of interest is from twelve to thirteen per cent., but the Arab pays forty, and sometimes more. I have been on some magnificent properties which only a few years ago belonged to Arab Caïds and Sheiks; to-day the gaudy villa of the Jewish owner has replaced the Arab house. They have passed from race to race at about one-third of their value. The extortionate interest has accumulated, and the property has gone to pay it.

Between the French Government and the Jew money-lender, the Arab proprietors of land in Algeria have come to the ground, or, to speak more correctly, have gone from it. How deeply the Arabs of Algeria feel their position was expressed in 1871. Gambetta appointed Crémieux, a Jew, Governor-General of Algeria. The great Arab chiefs flung down their French decorations, resigned their official positions, and called on their kinsmen to throw off the yoke of France. The rebellion was crushed, the Arabs were slaughtered and fined and impoverished, and to-day they sit and brood in a state of sullen resignation. The French have good reason for keeping a strong military force in Algeria.

But I am wandering into a political discussion. Good gracious me! and all my own personal adventures are going to the wall. I have spent so many nights in the Arab cafés with Achmet, and heard so much of these things from the natives, that they have saturated my mind. I hasten to unsaturate it. Bother the Arabs and their grievances! let us go and see the sights.

I told you I was just off to kill a lion. You will gather from the fact that these lines appear in print that the lion did not kill me. We found him, after a long search, in a lonely part of the Atlas Mountains. I never shot anything in my life, so when Albert Edward handed me his rifle I said, 'No. Perhaps the poor beast is the father of a family who are entirely dependent on him for support.' 'Oh, nonsense!' was the reply; 'pray don't let any idea of that sort interfere with legitimate sport. Besides, fancy the triumph of bringing home a lion that you have shot yourself. If you don't shoot him I will.' He levelled the gun. The lion saw it. A piteous look came into the animal's face. He gave one roar of terror, turned round, and bolted off with his tail between his legs. But he was not quick enough. Bang went the rifle, and the lion rolled over on his side a corpse!

Then I felt that I ought to share in the honours of the day. I assisted to pick the poor beast up, and we made a litter, and put him on it, and carried him in triumph to the next village. We expected a grand reception. To our intense surprise, when the inhabitants beheld the dead lion, they burst out into savage cries, and shook their fists at us, and cursed us in Arabic. We were arrested and dragged before the Caïd, and then we learnt for the first time what our offence was.

We had killed the 'show' lion of the district—a lion that had been imported at vast expense from the Zoological Gardens, London, and tamed and taught to run about the mountains for the amusement of tourists. The Caïd fined us £50 for destroying the property of the inhabitants, and discharged us with a caution. We asked for the skin, and were refused. That skin is to be stuffed and put up on the mountains in a natural position. African travellers who visit this district can shoot the first lion they meet now in perfect safety. They will injure nothing but the stuffing.

One cherished illusion I shall, alas! leave behind me in the Sahara. You know those beautiful lines the Arab addressed to his steed in the poetry-book of our youth—

> *'My beautiful, my beautiful, that stands so meekly by,*
> *With thy proudly arched and glossy neck, thy dark and fiery eye;*
> *Fret not to roam the desert now, with all thy wingèd speed,*
> *I may not mount on thee again—thou'rt sold, my Arab steed.'*

The poem is long. But it shows that the Arab is devoted to his horse. Well, I have seen the Arab's devotion to his horse, and I'm very sorry for the animal. The cruelty of the Arab to his steed is something beyond expression. The Arab starves his steed and beats it mercilessly. He works it to death. The steed is covered with raw and bleeding wounds, and when the Arab wants to make his steed go faster he runs a sharp stick into one of the open wounds. 'My beautiful, my beautiful!' O, Poetry, what sins you have to answer for! I shall never read those beautiful verses again without saying 'Bosh!' The Arab who loved his horse, and the horse that was so beautiful, have gone over for ever, so far as I am concerned, to the great majority—the majority of lost illusions.

While in Algiers I was indebted to my coachman for much of my information. My coachman was a Gascon, and he Gasconaded to his heart's content. He drove us about day by day, and told us stories which would have made Baron Munchausen look to his laurels. I let him have his fling, and then, in the language of the ring, I 'took him on.' I began to tell him stories of England. He listened at first in calm and childlike faith, but at last he saw that I was playing him at his own game. Then the old African hills resounded with his Homeric laughter, and he became my sworn friend. He slapped me on the back and said I was a fine fellow, and he liked the English because they were not proud like the French, but cracked jokes with a coachman.

My coachman's friendship became gradually a little too obtrusive. One day, having to rest his horses in order to take us a sixty-mile drive into the interior the next day, and having drawn twenty francs on account of his fare, he spent his spare time in drinking my health. Unfortunately, he strolled about the town as well, and was continually meeting me. Every time we met he insisted on shaking hands and slapping me on the back. I didn't mind it at quiet corners, but when I was talking to the Governor-General and his charming daughters on the Place du Gouvernement, I must confess that I was taken aback to find myself suddenly embraced by my affectionate Jehu, who, in accents slightly thick and alcoholised, called me his brother, and implored Heaven to witness that I was his best friend. The Governor smiled, the lovely daughters tittered, and I felt that my dignity as a distinguished stranger had suffered a slight concussion.

But my coachman was quite sober on the morning of our departure. He drove us to the quay, and refused any fare. He wept on both our shoulders, and as the Arab boatman rowed us out to the ship, the brave Gascon fell upon his knees upon the African soil and prayed that we might soon come back and gladden his eyes and shake his hand and tell him stories again.

Achmet, too, came to see us off. Achmet was married the day before we left. I made up his five pounds, and he bought his little wife and took her home. 'Well, Achmet,' I said, 'did the old woman tell you the truth?' 'Ah, Sidi,' replied the young man, 'I am the happiest young Arab in all Algiers. Give me your name, that I may call the first son that Allah shall bless me with after my benefactor.' I didn't give him my real name, but I gave him my *nom de plume*, and so I dare say before I visit Algiers again the followers of the Prophet will number among them for the first time in the history of the faith a Mohammedan named Dagonet.

CHAPTER XI.

MONTE CARLO.

'THE Beauty Spot of the Riviera' is the flattering title which a resident English physician has given to his book upon Monte Carlo. It is getting difficult nowadays to give a new name to a place which has been raved about, reviled, flattered, slandered, discussed, and described *ad nauseam.* That it is a paradise is a fact as widely advertised as that somebody's soap is matchless for the complexion, and that somebody else's mustard is the best. It is a paradise—a fool's paradise. All that Nature could do to make Monte Carlo beautiful she has done. She has painted the lily and adorned the rose in her endeavour to make the famous mount queen of the Riviera. Monte Carlo is a beautiful poem set to music; but the poem is the one in which the singer tells us that 'all save the spirit of man is divine.' When I arrived in Monte Carlo, my first impression was that I had made a mistake, and taken a ticket for Kempton Park; but the scenery was slightly against such a theory. I looked at the sea, and then I thought that in a fit of absence of mind I might have got mixed on the railway and in my dates, and that I had been landed at Brighton during the Sussex fortnight. The sun was hot, the sea was blue, and the bookmakers and the backers that one is accustomed to meet at a race meeting were airing themselves in light costumes and yellow boots along the principal promenades. But palm-trees, and marble staircases, and cacti and eucalypti, and prickly pear-trees, and sunny mountain slopes dotted with white villas are not the characteristic features of London-super-Mare. I gradually awoke to the fact that I was on the Mediterranean, and at Monte Carlo in January; but you can understand my being a little bit mixed at first when I tell you that the only people I met during the first half-hour of my sojourn in the principality were either English bookmakers, English backers, or English racehorse owners.

Let me briefly trace the interesting history of a place which is now world-famous, and is becoming every year more and more a place of English resort. In the old days, when the railway came no further than Nice, someone had permission from the Prince of Monaco to keep a roulette-table in the old town. There were so few customers that the game did not pay, and it was on the point of being given up when Blanc, knowing that the doom of the German gaming-tables was imminent, began to look about for a spot in which he could carry on his business when his German premises were closed. He came to Monaco, and saw the situation. He made an offer for the concession, took it over, and when the German tables were closed he transported his business to the shores of the Mediterranean.

All the world knows how the affair prospered, how Blanc died, how his daughter married Prince Roland Bonaparte, and how the affair was turned into a company. But what all the world does not know is that since Blanc's death the management has steadily degenerated, until it has become absolutely objectionable.

A special Providence seems to watch over this delightful, romantic, wicked, enchanting little spot. Monte Carlo escaped damage from the earthquake which shattered the neighbouring places, and she is always spared the snow and ice which occasionally remind one of winter in Nice. She seems, indeed, to bear a charmed life, for nothing affects her prosperity, and nothing damages her beauty. I fell an instant victim to her wiles. I had not been in the place half an hour before I wanted to come and live there for ever. Every turn reveals some new beauty, every hour brings some fresh pleasure, and you begin to wonder how it is possible that there can be so many melancholy looking people in such a heavenly spot, unless you remember that the little ball rolls from morning till night, and that the majority of people who come to Monte Carlo come to gamble, and, as a natural consequence, to lose their money.

From noon until eleven o'clock at night, despising the glorious scenery, the tropical vegetation, the balmy air, and the glorious sunshine, the great bulk of the people who come to Monte Carlo crowd round the roulette and trente-et-quarante tables in a series of close, stuffy, and gloomy rooms. The air and the sunshine are rigidly excluded. A dim, religious, artificial light falls upon the tables and the faces of the players. All is forgotten in the greed for gold. Faces are flushed, hands tremble, bosoms heave, and the gold passes slowly and surely into the coffers of the bank. Those who have lost fall out and go their way, with heavy hearts, out into the mocking sunshine and the beauteous Eden in which the 'establishment' has concealed its serpent. The winners stay on, and plunge and plunge again, only to come to the inevitable end; it is only a question of time. The unlucky lose at once, the lucky win at first, only to make their ultimate loss the more bitter.

I have the whole place to myself—always excepting the gambling rooms and the post-office. You can mostly find plenty of people losing all their money at the former, and wiring home for more at the latter. I came with the firm intention of climbing the mountain, basking in the sunshine, taking long walks by the blue Mediterranean, and generally enjoying the beauties of the poisoned paradise without paying toll to the Strangers' Club and Sea Baths Company (Limited). For a whole day I resisted the temptation to play. I drank in the warm air, I feasted my eyes on orange groves and avenues of palms, and gardens gay with the flowers that come to us only in summer. I climbed the mountain, and looked out over the hills dotted with white villas, and I looked down upon the sea that lay like a lake of still blue paint far below. I picked oranges and lemons from the boughs that hung down over the white mountain roadways, and in the lightness of my heart I whistled 'The Man who broke the Bank at Monte Carlo,' and shook my fist defiantly at the palatial building which has drawn all men unto the rocky home of the Grimaldis—with the accent on the rocky. I gambolled on the green turf like a lamb, instead of gambling on the green cloth like a donkey—and twenty-four hours afterwards a man with a stern set face and flashing eyes stood opposite that palatial establishment and cursed it in five different languages, specially studied up for that occasion. In spite of all his resolutions, he had gone in 'just to look on,' and he had put down five francs 'just for the fun of the thing,' and it had ended—ah, you can guess how it had ended—that man had won 5,000 francs, and that man was the man who didn't mean to play.

Then, like all winners, I went back again and again to the rolling ball that gathers all our moss. I didn't mind losing—in fact, I only lost the money I had won—but I hated myself for passing sunny mornings and moonlight nights in a heated atmosphere, amid exciting and unhealthy surroundings. It was so lovely out of doors, but Nature, decked in her fairest garb, wooed me in vain. It is so with almost everyone who comes to Monte Carlo. There is no one anywhere else, but the rooms are crowded. The grounds are deserted; there is never a soul upon the beach. Nobody ever goes out in a boat. Even the ocean at Monte Carlo is for ornament, and not for use. And it is an ocean which, anywhere on the English coast, would be a fortune to the proprietors of rowing boats and sailing vessels and bathing-machines.

Still, in spite of my annoyance at my own weakness in yielding to the evil influence of the place, I have managed to amuse myself and take a few notes, other than those handed to me by a croupier on the end of a rake.

One day there was an amusing incident in the rooms. An Englishman arrived early, and, sitting down, crossed his legs, and stuck one foot out in an attitude of ease. Suddenly there was a wild rush of everybody to the tables, and Italian barons, Spanish countesses, and Russian princesses fought with each other to get their gold and silver pieces on to 17. The croupiers stared, the inspectors looked nervous, and when 17 came up the entire staff seemed petrified. What had happened? Had the wheel been got at? Had some clever trick been played? Why had everybody rushed to back 17? The croupiers looked about and saw every eye directed at the Englishman, who, finding himself the object of so much attention, blushed violently, and burst into a profuse perspiration.

Then a roar of laughter went round the room, and the croupiers and the inspectors, and even the solemn attendants in livery, joined in it. The mystery was explained. On the sole of the Englishman's boot was the number 17 in chalk. He had just come from his hotel, and that was the number of his room, and the number chalked on the soles of his shoes that the boots might recognise them and place them outside the right door. We have heard of a man putting his own shirt on a horse, but it isn't every day that an entire company of gamblers put somebody else's boots on a number at roulette.

There have been the usual number of suicide stories flying about Monte Carlo. Last night two young Germans were discovered in the gardens about midnight; one had a pistol in his mouth, and the other had a clasp-knife open, with the point pressed against his heart. When they were seized they declared they were about to commit suicide because they had lost everything at the tables.

But a German gentleman came forward who had heard the lads say to each other a quarter of an hour before they were arrested, 'Let us do it. Someone will be sure to come along and see us, and we shall get a bit to go away.' This kind of trick is of the common or

Monte Carlo garden order, and has long since ceased to impose on the Casino officials.

In the good old days of M. Blanc, it was the custom (so the story goes), directly a suicide was found, to stuff his pockets full of bank notes. This was done to prove that his losses at play were not the cause of his hurried departure from the shores of time. The last person who received this generous treatment was, I believe, an American. He was found lying in one of the quiet alleys of the beautiful grounds, with an empty bottle, labelled 'Poison,' by his side. The secret agents of the bold Blanc instantly stuffed his pockets full of gold and notes, preparatory to giving information to the police. No sooner had they filled him as full of lucre as he could hold, than the suicide leapt to his feet, raised his hat, exclaimed, 'Thank you very much!' and went off to enjoy himself with his newly-acquired wealth.

A morning in the little post-office that stands above the sea on the terrace at Monte Carlo, and looks like the Paris Morgue's understudy, may be passed with profit by the student of men and manners. One day, when the mistral (probably having found out that I had come to Monte Carlo for the benefit of my health) was blowing its worst, I went into the post-office and sat down in a chair and wrote telegrams to the sovereigns of Europe, couched in brotherly language. I am in the habit of doing this sort of thing occasionally when I feel sad. I never send the telegrams, but leave them lying on the desk, saying to myself aloud in the language of the country, 'Ah, no; after all, I will write.' It is wonderful the respect with which you are treated in a Continental health resort when it gets about that you have telegraphed to the Czar of Russia, 'Sorry can't dine with you Wednesday, old fellow; gout keeps me here;' or to a Prince of the House of Hohenzollern, 'Come and take potluck with me Sunday week, if you are passing.'

Once in the old days before the war, when one could put one's gulden on the board of green cloth at Ems, at Wiesbaden, at Baden-Baden, and at Homburg, I was caught in a storm in the woods above Ems, and, spying a stranger standing under a dripping tree, I offered him half my umbrella. When the storm was over, he thanked me and went his way. That night at the tables we met again; he recognised me, and stopped and spoke to me, and asked me if I had had good luck. It is astonishing how polite they were to me at the tables after that. Although I only played in modest silver the croupiers would do their best to get me a seat, and treated me with the greatest distinction. I had entertained a Czarewitch under my umbrella unawares. The gentleman who had publicly asked me if I was having good luck was the heir to the throne of all the Russias. I have never since had a chance of chatting publicly with royalty, and have had to fall back upon sending it telegraphic messages, or, rather, leaving telegraphic messages addressed to it lying about unfinished on the desks of Continental post-office bureaux.

But in writing about the sovereign I am wandering from the subject. I went into the post-office one day and sat down at a table littered with spoilt telegraph-forms. I picked up some of them and read them. They were most of them little life-dramas in themselves. One ran: 'Dear Aunt and Cousins,—I have finished my life's journey. This is the bourne from which one traveller will never return. Farewell.' Here was a hint at a Monte Carlo tragedy. The next spoilt telegram I picked up was more definite. The tragedy was complete: 'Alphonse died at seven this morning. Break gently to his mother.' There was a little comic relief in another one: 'Send me fifty. Hôtel de Paris, return post. Am dead broke, and living on my watch. I only brought a silver one.' While I was turning over these telegrams, the writers of which had evidently on second thoughts couched their messages in other words, I heard a female voice exclaim, with a pronounced London accent, 'Does anybody here speak English?' I looked up, and beheld a young lady in a black hat and large ostrich feathers, and a silver chain and locket. I at once proffered my services. 'I want to know if I can send £500 through the post to London.' I explained that one can send a million if one wishes in a registered letter. 'Oh, that's all right, then,' said the young lady. 'I've won it, and got it changed into English notes, and I want to send it to my mother. I'm not going to let 'em have it back again at the table—not me.' The young lady then went to the counter, and, with my assistance, registered a letter containing £500 to Mrs. Hopkins, somewhere in the Caledonian Road, and, honouring me with a smile of thanks, went out gaily on a pair of those trodden-down high heels which are peculiar to the feminine toilette of Great Britain.

Her place at the *guichet* was immediately taken by an English clergyman in a brown straw hat and alpaca umbrella. He didn't speak a word of French, and he wanted a post-office order for four-and-threepence, payable in the Walworth Road. He asked about three hundred questions of the clerk, who did his best to understand him, and finally tendered for the order two French francs, two Italian lire, and wanted to make up the rest in English penny postage-stamps. When the clerk objected, the clergyman argued, and was especially indignant at the rejection of the Italian coins, maintaining that he had received them in the Principality of Monaco. Finally, after taking up nearly an hour of the clerk's time, and keeping twelve people waiting, he departed without the order, and with the loudly-expressed intention of writing to the *Times* on the subject.

There were applicants of every nationality applying for letters at the Poste Restante. Many a one that morning did I see turn away with a white, dazed face when the clerk shook his head and said, 'Il n'y a rien, monsieur.' The anxiously expected remittance had not come, and Monte Carlo is a bad place to be in when you have exhausted your funds and forgotten to make your retreat safe by taking a return ticket. Many of those who received registered letters opened them eagerly, and with feverish hands drew forth the bank-notes, thrust them into their pockets, and went off almost at a run along the broad pathway that leads to the gates of—well, 'the rooms.' A crowd of anxious faces does he gaze on day after day, this clerk who sits behind the *guichet* of the Poste Restante at Monte Carlo; and some sad, wild messages must the other clerk read who takes in the telegrams of the gamblers far from home. It isn't every day that a Miss Hopkins steps jauntily in to send a 'monkey' to her mother in the Caledonian Road.

One beautiful sunny afternoon I went over to Mentone. Sitting on the parade in the sunshine, it was difficult to imagine that it was the end of January. It was a day that an Englishman would have been proud of in August. I asked the landlord of the hotel where I lunched if the growing popularity of Monte Carlo had not injured Mentone. 'Oh no, not at all,' he replied. 'On the contrary, we have a great number of English people who come here because it is so close to Monte Carlo. They live here, and go to the rooms every day. No one suspects you of gambling when you are having your letters addressed to Mentone.' There is no doubt that Monte Carlo is not an address which everybody would care to give who leaves London for the benefit of his or her health.

I missed the train back from Mentone to Monte Carlo, and, not caring to hang about for two hours after the sun had gone down, I took a victoria from the public stand and drove back over the mountains. It was a nice drive in the twilight, but weird and lonely withal. Once in a gloomy gorge, when we came suddenly on an encampment of fierce-looking gipsies, I felt a little uncomfortable, and had visions of being carried off by brigands to a cave; but when we began, after a steep ascent, to go down a precipice at full gallop, I thought of nothing but my neck. The driver cracked his whip, and the horse flew like the wind. We swayed from side to side, and every moment I thought I should go over, and be found mixed up with trunks of trees and bits of rock on the beach below; but the horse was a surefooted little beast, and when I remonstrated with the driver he only laughed, and said he had driven that road for ten years and had never gone over the side of a precipice yet.

The last part of the journey was done by moonlight. I have no doubt it was very beautiful and romantic, but I don't care about it. There is a bit of roadway near Roquebrune which would try the nerves of a Blondin, and I never walk along it in broad daylight without turning giddy. When we got to that I insisted upon getting out and walking, and I was glad that I did. To avoid a piece of rock which had fallen, my charioteer took the extreme outside edge, and, walking behind, I saw one hind-wheel go actually off the ground and hang in the air. Had the horse stumbled or stopped, I should have had no fare to pay that night. Luckily he made a bound forward as he felt the carriage tilt, and the situation was saved. That steep bank was *not* the bank that broke the man at Monte Carlo.

I made up my mind that I would never take another moonlight drive over the mountains as long as I lived. For three nights afterwards I dreamt that I was rolling down a precipice, and woke up in such a state of abject terror that I had to get up and draw the curtains, and look out at Monte Carlo bathed in moonlight, lying silent and peaceful as a City of Dreams.

One morning, unable to go to sleep again, I sat at the window and saw the sun rise. I never wished so much for the power of word-painting as then. I would give a good deal to be able to describe that scene. As I looked out upon it, it seemed to me a sin that such a glorious spot should be the hell of Europe—the hotbed of all that is evil in human nature. The flaunting Casino, with its gaudy roof of blue and red and yellow, seemed like a painted harlot leering with a bold and brazen face as the fair earth woke and smiled at the kiss of her bridegroom the sun. But when I looked at it in this way, the last louis I had to lose had been gathered in by the remorseless rake of the croupier. Probably 'the Successful Gambler' would have seen that sunrise in a different light.

Everything is done to *force* the visitor into the bad atmosphere of the hot, unventilated gambling-rooms. No outside attractions are provided or allowed. Everything that may give pleasure to the visitor who does not wish to gamble is taboo. Even the railway is in the official clutches, and the means of escape from the place are made as difficult as possible. The Paris, Lyons, and Mediterranean Railway is, in the hands of the Casino people, made to injure the surrounding towns. You can get from Nice to Monte Carlo, for example, easily enough, but you find it very difficult to get back again. The hotel-keepers of Nice complain bitterly of what are called 'Les trains Blanc,' which are so arranged that the Nice visitor who goes to Monte Carlo cannot get back to Nice for dinner. There is an afternoon train, but it is '*facultatif*,' which means that it only runs when the administration chooses.

I met a young fellow the other day at the tables who at one time was betting in thousands, and losing his £5,000 a night at baccarat, and was the most notorious plunger in England. He told me he had been cleared out at trente-et-quarante. 'That's what I've got to get through the week with now,' he exclaimed playfully, as he showed me two francs and a bunch of keys. The next day he borrowed a louis and turned it into £50. The day after that he was 'broke' again, and the story goes that he went to bed without any dinner. I saw him yet again, and he had borrowed another five francs, and played it up into a thousand francs in the morning, only to be cleared out again before night.

It was this same young fellow who came to me and told me confidentially that he believed everybody was stony-broke. 'You wouldn't believe it, my boy,' he said, 'I've asked about forty fellows to change me a cheque for £50, and there isn't one of them that has enough to do it.' I smiled. Poor lad! If he had had more experience of the world he would have understood why all his former friends and associates, and even the wealthy men who had shared the bulk of his once vast fortune among them, had become so suddenly short of cash. Cheques are not changed with impunity at 'Charley's Mount.'

There has been a real suicide at Monte Carlo. There is nothing more difficult than to arrive at the facts connected with Monte Carlo scandals. Everything that is unpleasant, or that is likely to increase the prejudice against the pastime of the Principality, is hushed up with the skill which comes of long practice in the art of concealment.

The place at which the suicide was committed was a small house situated in the Condamine at Monaco. In front of it an Italian labourer was at work in the street. With this man I engaged in conversation, and asked him if he had heard of a young couple committing suicide. The reply was, 'I know nothing.' Then I told him what I knew, and rattled some loose silver in my pockets. 'Ah, as the Signor knows so much it cannot matter what I tell him,' said the man, and then he pointed out to me the window of the room in which the young couple had come to their end. 'Ah, I saw them often,' he said, 'this last few days, while I was at work on the road here. They used to come out arm-in-arm. They were very loving, and I said to myself, "It is a newly-married couple." '

Having fixed the position of the room well in my eye, I entered the hotel, and found it practically empty. The proprietress came out to receive me. I explained that I was looking for rooms for some friends of mine. Could I see which apartments were vacant? 'Yes, certainly.' I was taken into most of the rooms, but none suited until I found myself in the apartment of the romantic suicide. I said nothing to the lady, nor she to me. The room was a small but comfortable one. Two wooden beds stood side by side. These were the beds on which two days previously the lovers had stretched themselves to die. The sun shone in at the open window; the blue Mediterranean glinted below, and as far as the eye could see all was peace and beauty and the joyousness of life. It was from these windows that the young couple had taken their last look upon earth. They had looked out upon the sunny land and the deep blue sea with a fixed purpose of self-destruction in their hearts—with the letter already written which was to tell their friends the story of their last days. It was to this pleasant little room in which I stood that they returned on their last night together, with their last hope gone, with the knowledge in their hearts that when the sun rose again over the palm groves and orange-trees and the white cliffs and smiling seas they would have passed from this world to eternity. What a last walk in the moonlight that must have been!—the man of twenty-nine, the woman of nineteen—lovers, fugitives from their homes—she a married woman, he a married man, and—— But let me tell it you, beginning, middle, and end—this perfect French tragedy, this curious study of morals and manners and Monte Carlo, this romance of the passions, this little life-drama taken 'palpitating' from the pages of the modern Boulevard novelist.

A young married man of Lyons fell in love with a young married woman. They met secretly, adored each other, and agreed to fly together—to put the seas between themselves and their families. But there was a slight difficulty in the way. They had very little money for a long journey, and they wanted to be far, far away—in America for choice. Then the idea came to the man that they would take their small capital of a few hundred francs and go to Monte Carlo, and make it into a fortune—a fortune which would enable them to live in peace and plenty on a far-off shore. So it came that one day, with a small box and a portmanteau, the fugitives arrived at Monte Carlo, and put up in this little hotel, where for eight francs a day you can have bed and board.

They had only a few hundred francs with them. In the letter which they have left behind they explained that from the first their arrangements were complete. They foresaw the possibilities of the situation. They would play until they had won enough to go to America, or they would lose all. And if they lost all they would die together, and give their friends no further trouble about them.

They were a few days only in Monte Carlo. They risked their louis only a few at a time, and they spent the remainder of the days and evenings in strolling about the romantic glades and quiet pathways of the beautiful gardens, whispering together of love, and looking into each other's eyes.

The end came quickly. One evening they went up in the soft moonlight to the fairy land of Monte Carlo. They entered the Casino. They had come to their last few golden coins. One by one the croupier's remorseless rake swept them away, and then the lovers went out of the hot, crowded rooms, out from the glare of the chandeliers and the swinging lamps, into the tender moonlight again. Down 'The Staircase of Fortune' arm-in-arm they went, along the glorious marble terraces that look upon the sea, on to where at the foot of the great rock on which Monaco stands there lies the Condamine. It was their last walk together. The lovers were going home to die.

That night, in some way which I was unable to ascertain, the guilty and ruined man and woman obtained some charcoal and got it into their bedroom. They then closed the windows and doors, and prepared for death. They wrote a letter—a letter which an official assured me was so touching that, as he read it in the room where they lay dead, the tears ran down his cheeks. Then the girl—she was but a girl—dressed herself in snowy white, and placed in her breast a sweet bouquet of violets. Then the charcoal was lighted, and the lovers laid themselves out for death, side by side, and passed dreamily into sleep, from sleep to death—and from death to judgment.

These are the facts of 'The Romantic Suicide at Monte Carlo.' It is not a moral story; it is not a new story. I have told it simply as it happened.

One morning I went over to breakfast with a friend of mine at Roquebrune, a picturesque point near Monte Carlo. The proprietor showed me over his villa and his grounds. While we were in the back garden a Frenchman, who rented a villa in the neighbourhood, came in, in a towering rage, to complain of my friend's cat trespassing on his grounds. After a heated discussion, the Frenchman exclaimed angrily, 'Very well, sir, I shall lodge my complaint with the mayor. Where is the mayor?' My friend's gardener, who was busy digging up new potatoes, suddenly looked up, and, raising his battered hat, exclaimed with dignity, 'M'sieu, je suis le Maire de Roquebrune.' Tableau and curtain.

CHAPTER XII.

GENOA.

FROM Monte Carlo to Genoa by rail in a hurricane doesn't sound anything very tremendous, unless you happen to know that the rail runs for almost the entire distance at the extreme foot of the

Maritime Alps, on the uttermost verge of the coast; so close, in fact, to the sea, that in many places if you dropped your hat out of the window it would fall into the ocean. To walk along the line would turn many people unaccustomed to exercise upon the tightrope giddy, for, as well as running along the beach, it occasionally takes the outside edge of precipices, against which the deep waters of the Mediterranean are dashing themselves in their mad fury at not being able to get at the train and swallow it up.

Under ordinary circumstances the journey, which takes ten hours by the 'omnibus' train, is romantic. Taken as we took it, with a hurricane spending its full force on the coast, it was absolutely thrilling. Over and over again our trim little engine, as it toiled up cliffs and crept cautiously over massive rocks, was nearly blown to a full stop, and the way in which the whole train rocked from side to side made several of the passengers sea-sick. Our guard told us that he had never made such a journey in all his experience; and, after we had left the Italian frontier at Ventimiglia, and had passed San Remo, it began to look as though we should have to let discretion be the better part of valour, and pull up until the storm, which came rushing down the mountains and lashing the sea to fury, had abated. Over and over again the seas dashed up, and flung a great volume of water and small pebbles against the carriage windows. It was a question whether further on the sea would not have made the line unsafe, or perhaps washed it away altogether. But at every station we got the signal that it was all right at present, and that we could come on; and so on we went, recompensed for all our doubts and delays by the grand sight which the storm-swept coast and seething sea presented to our anxious and yet delighted gaze.

It was nearly eleven o'clock at night when we reached Genoa. We had taken eleven hours to perform a journey of about 112 miles, and all that time we had had nothing to eat. There was no buffet all along the line after Ventimiglia until we reached Savona, and then it was past nine o'clock. We grew so desperately hungry about six o'clock that when the train stopped for a few minutes we rushed out into the rain and the hurricane and requisitioned supplies of a small wine-shed by the roadside. All we could get was some dry bread, and some mysterious slices of something, which we were assured was 'carne,' or meat. The word isn't appetizing, and, hungry as we were, we couldn't tackle the food. It was so strongly impregnated with garlic that after we had given it to a dog our carriage retained the odour, and for days afterwards our clothes reeked of the pungent esculent. In despair we fell back upon the dry bread, and when we had eaten that we tried to remember what people did on rafts, and we unpacked our portmanteaus and looked out our boots, and wondered whether patent leather or ordinary walking boots would be the easier of digestion. So ravenous did we become that we sent on a telegram from one of the stations to the hotel at Genoa ordering beefsteaks to be ready for us the instant we arrived, and when at midnight the omnibus deposited us at the Grand Hotel we didn't stop to wash or take off our overcoats or look at our rooms, but rushed into the *salle-à-manger* and fell on our knees to the head waiter and begged that, ready or not, our beefsteaks ordered by telegram might be brought to us; and when they came we fell upon them with savage glee and short, sharp cries of joy, and the manager and the waiters and the porters came crowding in to watch the extraordinary spectacle. I think they fancied we were mad or cannibals, or that we had escaped from a penal settlement and had not tasted food for months.

Genova la Superba, Genoa the Proud, has indeed something to be proud of. She is proud of her port, of her people, of her palaces, and of her prosperity. Her people, high and low, rich and poor, are brave, independent, and public spirited, and her nobility stands at the head of the nobility of the world for deeds of good citizenship and benevolence. From the days of Christopher Columbus, who, when Genoa was stricken with the plague, wrote to his bankers to give half his fortune to the poor, to the present year of grace, when the Duchess Ferrari-Galliera spends hundreds of thousands of pounds on colleges and hospitals and model dwellings for the poor, the rich and the titled of Genoa have been world-famous for their deeds of noble charity.

Genoa itself is a stately city; seen from the sea, with its villa and palace-crowned amphitheatre of hills, it is superb. It has whole streets of marble palaces, full of wonders for the eye of the connoisseur to feast upon; and beyond its ancient grandeurs and its modern magnificences, its heart pulses with the vigorous, healthy blood of modern progress and prosperity.

Genoa delighted me from the moment I set my foot in it and began to take its measure. I liked its busy port, with thousands of bronzed, red-bonneted porters hard at work upon the huge quays, crowded with merchandise. I liked its blue houses and its pink houses, its yellow and green houses, and its houses painted all over with pictures of lovely ladies. I liked the Municipal Palace, in which I was shown Paganini's very own fiddle, and several letters written by Christopher Columbus with his very own hand, and I liked its Campo Santo, or cemetery, which is one of the wonders of Italy.

Imagine a glorious garden rising in terraces—a garden all aglow with red and white roses and fragrant with blossom—imagine this garden surrounded with noble open galleries lined with magnificent white marble monuments, and all shut in by great sunny green hills, which stand around it like sentinels guarding the silent and sacred camp of the dead. Imagine all this, then put above the roses and the blossoms and the fragrant trees, and the yellow immortelles and the green wreaths and the glorious marble statuary, a blue sky and a bright sun, and you have a faint idea of 'Genoa's Holy Field.'

But you cannot imagine the monuments and the memorial statuary. You must see them to understand them, because they are so utterly unlike anything we have in our cold, prosaic land. In long marble galleries, open to the air and the sun, the monuments at first give the cemetery the appearance of an art exhibition. You fancy you have wandered into a sculpture gallery by mistake; but the wreaths of flowers with broad silk sashes attached, the swinging lamps, and the memorial tablets undeceive you. Each monument has, as it were, an arch of the gallery to itself, and is placed against the back wall. The figures are rarely allegorical. A man in his habit as he lived stands life-size in white marble above his own tomb. A little girl in a short frock, with her lap full of flowers, seems dancing on the column that records her death. Over another beautiful tomb is a family group, life-size. The father is dying. He lies on his deathbed, and the sculptor has realized every detail of drapery. The wife kneels by the bedside, some of her daughters supporting her. The old mother sits in an easy-chair, her eyes raised to heaven, her lips seeming almost to move in prayer. On the other side of the bed the eldest son stands up and supports one of the daughters, who has utterly broken down. It is a marvellous piece of work. It is the 'Last Adieu' realized in marble. It is naturalism and it is art. It is realistic, and so perfect in detail that you would recognise any of that group of mourners if you met them in the street.

One turns from the group, and near it is a dear old lady standing alone above her own tomb. She is wrinkled, and wears a big cap and a woollen shawl over her shoulders. No kindred are near her, but she is sincerely mourned, for she was the friend of the poor. In her hand she holds the bread she was in the habit of distributing to them. She is a dear old-fashioned old soul—a typical English 'granny' of the Christmas number—and her puckered, smiling face seems to make one at home in the cemetery directly.

Some of the groups are more imaginative. A magnificent vault is faced with a black-and-gold gate. On the steps leading to it a lad and his sister kneel and gaze heavenward. They are watching their mother being carried up into heaven by the angels. The whole scene is reproduced in sculpture, and so exquisitely is it done that the dead woman and the angels actually seem to be floating upward towards the skies.

Over another tomb, where a husband and wife lie buried together, this old couple sit in two armchairs, holding each the other's hand. On another a man lies dead on his bed, and the young wife reverently raises the sheet and gazes for the last time upon his face. Over another tomb is the statue of the man who lies within. On the steps of the tomb stands his wife, and she holds their little girl in her arms, and lifts her up as though to kiss the dead papa. The door of another vault is represented as half open. The husband lies dead inside. The wife knocks at the door and listens for her dear one's voice to call her in.

There are hundreds and hundreds of these beautiful groups in the Campo Santo. What makes them the more extraordinary to the English traveller is that the living and the dead are all habited in modern everyday costume, and no detail is spared to make the groups and the single figures triumphs of realism. One remarkable piece of sculpture I have omitted to mention. It is over the tomb of a beautiful Italian lady who died a short time ago. Her bed is represented with a perfection of detail. The lace on the pillows is perfect. The lady is dead, but the angel has come to fetch her. The angel takes the dead lady's hand, and the lady gets out of bed to go with the angel to heaven. This is the moment depicted by the sculptor. The lady sits on the edge of the bed, and the angel points upwards in the direction they are to travel together.

All this is very beautiful, but its intense realism may jar on some. It did on me after a time. I felt that something of the sublimity of death was taken away in the process, and I turned with a little sigh of relief to some of the humbler graves which dotted the sunny garden of fragrant roses that lay so bright and beautiful under the blue Italian sky.

Walking in the streets of Genoa one afternoon I met a nice-looking, stout, middle-aged lady in the most wonderful bonnet I ever saw in my life. I was so attracted by the bonnet, which was of the Leviathan order, that I did not notice anything else at first, but presently I saw that she was bowing in answer to many salutes. Then I knew she was a public celebrity, and I inquired who she was. 'That,' said my companion, a Genoese, 'is the daughter of Garibaldi!'

The daughter of Garibaldi is a great favourite in Genoa. She has married a gentleman in the army, but people don't trouble to remember his name. He is always spoken of as the gentleman who is the husband of the daughter of Garibaldi.

The daughter of Garibaldi is the proud and happy mother of twelve sons. If they are as good as their grandfather, the lady deserves well of her country.

On the same afternoon that I met the daughter of Garibaldi I also met an old gray-haired gentleman and lady trotting quietly along the Via Roma. My Genoese friend pointed them out to me, and told me their story. Twenty years ago a rich Englishman and his wife came to Italy with a foreign courier. In Genoa the gentleman was taken ill and died. He was buried in the town, and his wife stayed on at the hotel. After a time she married the courier, and from that day to this they have lived in Genoa—going in the summer to a villa on the Lake of Como which they purchased. Neither has ever set foot in England for twenty years.

I saw many things in Genoa which most people see, and which are doubtless fully described in the guide-books; but I saw something also of which the guide-books make no mention. I have mentioned the great public spirit of the Genoese nobility. There is in Genoa a beautiful building on the heights overlooking the sea, which is called the Hotel of the Poor. This was founded and endowed by a Genoese marquis. Here respectable workmen, when they are past work, can come and end their days in perfect peace.

Another nobleman, when it was proposed to move the University to Padua for lack of room, instantly gave up his magnificent palace to the town, saying, 'This is henceforward your University.' But all deeds of this sort are put into the shade by the princely charities of the Duke and Duchess of Ferrari-Galliera. The Duke, shortly before his death, gave one million pounds sterling towards the building of the new port. The Duchess, continuing his good work, has founded noble charities which are almost unique of their kind. One of them has such direct bearing on the great question of the day—the housing of the poor—that I cannot resist the temptation to give the reader a few particulars.

First let me say that the Ferrari-Galliera fortune is estimated at ten million pounds, and then you will understand how the Opera Pia, or pious works of this noble family, are carried out on such a gigantic scale. I had been told a great deal in Genoa about the Duchess's scheme for housing the working classes in model lodging-houses, and so, obtaining proper credentials, I called upon the Duchess's agent, and he most courteously had me personally conducted over the new working class dwellings. Built in blocks, somewhat on the Peabody system, these dwellings are perfect in every detail. The tenant must be a genuine working man, of good character. In the Duchess's model lodging-house, for the accommodation of himself and family, he has five rooms—five lofty, big rooms: a sitting-room, three bedrooms, and a kitchen, fitted up with a capital range and every requisite. Besides these there are cupboard room and a larder. These rooms have all tiled floors, and the walls are painted or whitewashed. The rent is *eight francs a month*, and this includes all necessary repairs, which are done by a staff of workmen attached to the central office. Every month every room is inspected, and the slightest damage instantly repaired.

My visit to the dwellings was quite unexpected. I drove straight from the office to one of the blocks, and took the inhabitants unawares, so that what I saw must be taken as a fair specimen of the general condition of the tenements. I knocked at a door, was admitted, and made my inspection, much to the astonishment of the children, who wondered why the 'strange man' should come prying into their kitchen and walking into their bedrooms. I inspected four blocks, and took a suite on each floor, and everywhere I found the most perfect cleanliness and the greatest comfort. The women were mostly the wives of working men earning from twenty to twenty-five francs a week, but their homes were perfect pictures of neatness and order. The floors were swept and garnished, and the kitchens were little models of tidiness. One good soul was horrified when I asked to see the bedroom. The bed wasn't made, she explained, and she was afraid I should think she was a careless housewife. As I went over these homes of the Genoese working classes, I could not help thinking of some that I knew at home. What would some hard-working Englishmen and their wives give to get such 'model lodgings' as these, and how gladly would they pay double and treble the rent that the lucky Genoese pay for such accommodation!

As I came out of the block I had a look round the big courtyard in the centre. At one end I found a large public washhouse; at the other end baths fitted up for the inhabitants, and also on the premises I found for their accommodation a bakehouse, in which the frugal wives who make their own bread have it baked free of charge. And what could you wish for more?

The Duchess has founded also, for the education of the poor children of Genoa, a free college. To all who attend it breakfast is given, and also a mid-day meal. Each boy is for one year 'under observation.' If his conduct is good, he has a right to stay on and receive a liberal education. If his conduct is bad, he is struck off the school list. A poor boy who is industrious and shows any talent can even choose a profession, and be specially educated free for that profession until the age of seventeen. Young Genoa has certainly a chance to distinguish itself in the future.

But the Duchess's crowning work is the grandest of all her charities. She has already built and endowed two hospitals—one for children and one for incurables; the third, which was to be a general hospital, was not yet opened, but by the courtesy of the Duchess's agent I was conducted over the whole building and everything was explained to me. As the hospital is undoubtedly one of the finest and most complete in the world, I must tell you something about it.

But first let me tell you the sad story which is bound up for ever with it—a story which the Duchess herself has handed down to posterity by having it inscribed upon a marble tablet in the grand entrance-hall. This tablet states that the building of the hospital has been delayed for four years, 'owing to the treachery of my agent.

General So-and-So.' The Duchess names her treacherous agent, who was her own cousin, and so brands him for all time to come. His treachery was this: He decamped with £800,000, the money paid to his credit by the Duchess for the building of the hospital. Poor old gentleman! He is eighty years of age now, and he is said to have hidden himself from the world in a monastery, there to expiate his fault. They say that the money did him no good—that he is poor. That he took it to save from shame the son he idolized—the son who was leading a life of extravagance, and who had involved himself in such a way that the poor old General had to use the Duchess's money to save him. Whatever the truth may be, the General used the money, and his treachery is 'writ large' upon the walls of the magnificent hospital, the building of which his unhappy act delayed for four long years.

The hospital itself stands in a magnificent position above the sea, and is the perfection of every modern principle. It is so perfect and so full of marvellous appliances and inventions that one feels, in walking about it, that it is one of Jules Verne's ideas. The glorious halls and corridors, the massive marble pillars, the splendid marble staircases, indicate wealth, but the perfection of the sanitary and scientific arrangements tells of long years of anxious thought and study and research. So perfectly is this marvellous hospital built that, in the event of plague or cholera breaking out to such an extent as to infect the building, the whole of the inside of the hospital can be removed and another hospital will still be left standing as complete as the other. To accomplish this the hospital is being built double, with a space between the walls.

It would not interest the general reader for me to go into technical details of the wonderful arrangements for the patients, and the magnificent system of baths built on the premises, which includes every kind and variety; but the general reader will understand the value of a tramway system over the entire basement for the conveyance of stores, linen, provision stores, officials, patients, etc.; and the advantage of pure air conveyed straight from the adjacent mountains through underground tubes, and distributed all over the building. This palatial hospital looks on to the sea and on to the mountains, and, in order to isolate it and give the inmates gardens and terraces and glorious views, the Duchess has purchased a whole street of houses in the neighbourhood and demolished them, that nothing shall detract from the perfect sanitation of her glorious gift to the city of Genoa.

Genova la Superba! Genoa the Proud! Proud indeed, and with good reason, with such a city, such citizens, and such nobles! In what other town in Europe can you find, as here, a whole street of palaces given up by their owners to the people?

CHAPTER XIII.

FLORENCE.

SOME time before I left London, while indulging in the pernicious habit of reading in bed, I was much amused and instructed by the narrative of travel of a distinguished *confrère* who had set out in search of sunshine. The writer's name is a household word in England, and in Italy it is also a 'household word' in the most literal manner possible, for you find a 'Sala' in nearly every house. I don't remember whether the 'Prince of Specials' found all the sunshine he wanted, but if he did not he had better come out to Florence at once with the biggest bag he can get into the train.

I am writing at the present moment in a room looking on to the Lung' Arno, and the sunshine is overpowering. In order to write with a slight amount of cool-headedness I have to sit in a bath and to work with an umbrella over me, which is damped at short intervals. For the past week it has been the same—a fierce, blazing, beautiful sunshine, in which you could cook a mutton-chop by holding it out of the window on the end of your walking-stick for ten minutes.

Most of the Italian cities boast of special distinctions. Just as we say 'Genoa la Superba,' so Florence has been dubbed 'Firenze la Gentile,' 'Florence the Refined.'

Florence is beautiful to the tourist in search of art, but it is apt to grow monotonous to staid and sober citizens who do not care to risk rheumatics for life in order to see an altar-piece, or to take a certain chill as the price of gazing at the real original Venus de Medici in the icy passages known as the Uffizi. True, that the streets are full of grand and solemn old palaces that carry the mind back through the centuries; true, that every hole and corner is rich with art, but on the Philistine all this palls after a time. I can understand how classical and cultured minds can spend day after day lost in admiration before virgins and martyrs who bear the closest resemblance to each other, and I quite appreciate the rapture with which they gaze at statues which, when all is said and done, are but men and women imitated and undraped. I can worship with the best of them, say, six pictures and six statues per diem, but galleries I cannot endure, and I fear I never shall. As one jam-tart is pleasant to the tooth, and twenty produce nausea, so is one good picture pleasant to the eye, and two hundred are apt to give one headache.

Now, if you flee from galleries and churches, there is little left you in Florence town but the side of the Arno. This is the one place where all day long the sun shines out in splendour, and you can saunter and dream, and ask yourself with the Misses Leamar, 'Why is the world so gay to-day?' You turn away from the Arno at your peril. To enter any side street is, to an Englishman, dangerous in the extreme. The long, narrow streets shut out all sun and all light, and you pass into them from the Lung' Arno as from the kitchen fire to the ice well. I am tired of the Lung' Arno. I have worn the brim of my hat threadbare bowing to the thousand Florentine princes, dukes, marquises, and counts, who smile at me in the Cascine—the Hyde Park of Florence—and I am going to walk right away from the palaces, the churches, and the galleries, right away over the Arno to the high hills I can see shining in the sunlight far away. Of Art I am tired; a little Nature will do me good. I tell the people in my hotel I want a good ten-mile spin—where had I better go? The Porter crosses himself, and the Director murmurs the name of his patron saint. Ho! but here is a mad Englishman, who, having loose lire in his pocket, wants to walk ten miles. They point me out a way, however, begging me to provide myself with cognac, in case I fall by the road, and I go. I am sure the Director is debating whether he shall have a hot bath, a doctor, and some leeches ready for my return.

Once outside the hotel, the torture of my life in Florence begins. There is a carriage-stand opposite the door, and the moment I show my nose every man wildly whips his horse up, and drives full gallop at me. They are all sure that I want a *carrozza*. I endeavour to evade them, but they drive round and round me in a circle until I look like the ring-master at Astley's directing the performance of 'the flying charioteers.' At last I make a wild dash between two vehicles and rush up the street. But the enemy is not so easily defeated. The drivers dash after me up the Lung' Arno, and follow me over the bridge. The pride of the Florentine flymen is stung to the quick. An Inglese has escaped them. The watchword passes, and at every rank we come to the flymen there lash their horses and join in the pursuit. Before I have gone a quarter of a mile there are nearly one hundred flys pursuing me. Panting and breathless, I still urge on my wild career. The honour of England is at stake. In this unequal conflict I must conquer or die, for, as a patriot, the reputation of my countrymen for obstinacy is dear to me. Heedless of my course, I dash down narrow streets, through ancient gateways, and round old squares, and at last I reach the city walls. The Porta Romana is passed, and I am out in the suburbs. The flymen waver. It is all uphill now, and their horses—poor beasts!—are blown and leg-weary. One by one they turn round, and drive slowly back to the city. For one day, at least, I am safe from the flymen of Florence.

I walk my miles on ever-rising ground till all the fertile valley lies at my feet. I wind round and round till I reach the great height whereon stands Galileo's observatory and the villa in which, under the cruel eyes of the Inquisition, he spent his last years. From this spot the view is worth a pilgrimage that should have lasted a lifetime instead of two hours. All the city of Florence, the distant Apennines (their crests all crowned with snow), the blue waters of the Arno lie before me. I breathe the pure, bracing air, I feel the warm sunshine on my face, and the weight of my years is lifted from me. Give me a green hill, a blue sky, and a square mile of God's sunshine, and you may have all the pictures and all the statues in all the whole wide world.

I seem to have a speciality for coming upon horrors. In Florence the first night I go out, in a quiet, dark, back street, a gentleman walking ahead of me suddenly reels and falls dead from an apoplectic stroke. I should not allude to the circumstance but that it brought before me a quaint and solemn phase of Italian religious life. The poor man was carried into a confectioner's shop and a messenger despatched to the Misericordia—the establishment of the Brothers of the Misericordia, a curious order, which renders the last offices to the dead. Presently there arrived a man with a torch, and, following him, half a dozen of the brothers, clothed from head to foot in a black garb and a hood and mask. Nothing is visible of them but their eyes, their features being completely concealed by the masks and hoods which cover the head and face. Weird and solemn beyond description the brothers look in the moonlight in this strange garb, and when presently they came out, bearing the dead in an open bier, and formed in procession, headed by the torch, and slowly moved away into the shadows of the dark, narrow, winding streets, I shuddered, and fancied myself back in the Middle Ages.

The history of the order is curious and interesting. It was formed during the great plague, when people died faster than professional undertakers could bury them. A body of gentlemen then undertook the task, concealing their features while plying their solemn labour, in order that they might not be recognised and shunned by the Italians, who have a great horror of death and all that appertains to it. To this day the order remains a secret one, and the outside world does not know who the masked men are who tend the dying and the dead. The greatest and the smallest belong to it, and the prince and the artisan rub shoulders in it. It is often a refuge for wealthy men who have met with great disappointments, and of talented men whose careers have been blighted, and who want something to do to keep them from nursing their grief and their wrongs.

While in Florence I saw most of the minor theatres. 'Stenterello,' the Florentine Punch, has the big part in all the pieces at the people's theatre, and is a unique specimen of theatrical art. In order to appreciate him thoroughly, I have sat out several evenings' amusement under rather distressing circumstances. When you pay sixpence to go into a theatre, and sixpence more for a *posto distinto* or reserved seat, you must not grumble if your neighbours are not of the *haute noblesse*. But the *manteaux noirs* in which the Italian common people wrap themselves during the winter are, when worn with Florentine thrift for, say, thirty years, apt to get unpleasant, and the wearers have besides unpleasant little ways, and are curiously afflicted, and—— But I will not go into details. I have endured much by passing my evenings in the popular parts of popular theatres—I mean the theatres patronized by the masses—but I have gained an experience which ought to be valuable. I shrink at nothing where my favourite study—the people—is concerned.

How shocking—isn't it?—to waste one's time studying the people of to-day—living, breathing flesh and blood: tragedy, comedy, and farce all packed together under a ridiculous modern costume—while there lies all around one a whole population of stone and marble and painted ladies and gentlemen, all classically draped or equally classically undraped, and not one of them less than a thousand years old at least! I cannot help preferring the living flesh to the dead marble, the country to the canvas, and all that is wicked and philistine in me rises in rebellion as I peruse the guide-books and catalogues and find nothing but galleries and churches considered worthy of a tourist's observation. I am not blind to the beautiful in art, I hope. A modern picture gives me often the greatest of pleasure, and so, for the matter of that, does an old one if it has a story to tell, and tells it well; if out of the painted eyes there looks forth a human soul, if in the grouped figures there is some suggestion of human feeling. But the things which are as a red rag to a bull to me are the Virgins and Children, the Holy Families, the saints, the martyrs, the portraits of painters' mistresses, labelled now a heathen goddess and now a Catholic saint. For tourists to spend as they do day after day contemplating these things, worrying away at a note-book with a pencil, and then chevying off to spend more hours staring at churches and cathedrals and listening to the droned-out lies of the cicerone, while a people as interesting in their manners and customs as any in the wide world live and move around them, under their very eyes, despised, unstudied, and unnoticed, is to me incomprehensible.

At all the theatres, save those where grand opera is given, everything—tragedy, comedy, and farce—is 'con Stenterello.' Punch is dressed always the same, no matter what the period of the play may be. He is the low comedy man, and has all the funny lines, but at times he utters noble sentiments, and becomes pathetic over the sorrows of the heroine, who is habitually protected by him.

No matter how tragic or pathetic the situation, Stenterello, with his queer costume and painted face, has a share in it. The bereaved wife wails out to Punch her sorrow for the dear departed, the betrayed maiden reveals to him the name of the villain at whose hands she claims retribution. The Medicis of old cannot plot and plan without Stenterello, the masher of to-day has Stenterello as his companion when he goes a-wooing, and after a round of the Florentine playhouses I was considerably astonished to find that 'Othello' was played at the Teatro Tommaso Salvini without a Stenterello. I quite expected to see him turn up as the devoted friend of Desdemona, or as the virtuous foiler of the wicked schemes of Iago.

Stenterello is literally worshipped by the Florentines. In every play he talks in the Florentine dialect—that is to say, in the *patois* of the people.

The late King Victor Emmanuel used to come in the good old days to the little theatres, and roar as loudly as anyone at Punch's wheezes, and one evening expressed his delight at the performance by making a knight there and then of the Stenterello who had given him so much amusement. The history of these Punches would make a long magazine article. They are classical in Italy. Stenterello is indigenous to Tuscany. Other provinces have their Punch, who appears in nearly all the plays, but in a different garb. In Naples it is Pulcinella who is the omnipresent comic man. Pulcinella is dressed in a loose white costume, and wears a black domino, with a beak to it—a property which deprives the actor most effectually of the aid of facial expression. But Italian actors and pantomimists do not need their faces to tell a story. They use their hands most marvellously, and will tell a whole five-act drama with gesture alone. In one little theatre the other evening I saw a *mime* hold an audience spell-bound for fully ten minutes while she described a tragedy, and showed how it was to be revenged, without uttering a single word.

At the bulk of the Italian theatres you can enter by simply paying fifty centimes or a franc for the *ingresso*. This entitles you to stand in the large vacant space at the back of the stalls, which takes the place of our pit. If you want a numbered seat or a box, of course you pay extra for it. Once having paid your *ingresso*, you can go to all parts of the house where there is room to stand and see. If you have friends in a box, you walk in and sit with them, as each box is sold as a whole, and is never split up into seats. The Italian theatre consists entirely of stalls and private boxes and 'standing room.'

At many of the theatres smoking is allowed all over the house during the performance. Even the musicians smoke their cigars during the *entr'acte*, and lay the half-finished ends on their music-stands when the conductor waves his bâton.

To see the reckless manner in which matches are struck and flung about would strike terror to the panic-monger's heart were it not for the fact that the houses, being built mostly of stone and marble, are not very inflammable. The audience is always a wonderful study. The Italians fling their hearts into the scene. The drama or farce is to them no play, but a reality. They hoot the villain, they encourage the hero with reassuring words, they cap Stenterello's jokes with original ones of their own, and they keep up a running fire of comment on the story as it develops. They are as loud in their disapproval as they are in their commendation. They will hoot a bad actor or singer off the stage mercilessly, and if the moral of a play or its dénouement does not interest them they will howl with rage till the curtain falls.

One remarkable feature of the popular playhouses is the prompter. This gentleman sits in the centre of the stage, covered over with a green wooden hood. I had a box one night on the stage, and I heard the prompter deliberately read the whole play to the company a line in advance of each actor, who repeated it like a schoolboy. The turn of each actor to take up the text was indicated to him by the prompter's finger pointing at him. This continuous prompting is, of course, only necessary in minor theatres, where the bill is changed almost nightly, and the actors have little time for study.

I was seriously thinking of buying a title while I was in Florence. Without a coronet one is so insignificant in Italy. I counted one hundred and twenty houses in a straight line in Florence, and only eight gates were without a coronet. Go over to the 'Surrey side' of the Arno, and it is the same thing. Every 'slum' has a dozen palaces, and every palace has a coronet. Prying about, after the manner of my species, in out-of-the-way holes and corners, I became acquainted with the fact that the nobility nearly all sell their own oil and wine. Near the gateway of the palaces there is generally a little hole just large enough to pass a bottle through. Over this is written, in small letters, 'Cantina,' and just by the side is hung a board with a tariff of the price of 'our wine.'

Dukes, marquises, and earls, they all retain the produce of their vineyards and farms. You can buy a bottle of the ordinary for a franc, and my lord's servant will hand it you with a smile, and take your coin with a condescending 'Grazie.' It is very quaint to see a workman come along, stop at a palace about three times the size of Newgate, and suddenly bob his head in—apparently through the stone wall—and presently bob back again with a bottle in his hand.

I was determined to study this phase of noble life myself; so I knocked at the hole in the wall of one of the most magnificent palaces of Florence, and when the little slide was opened I bobbed in my head and asked for a bottle of gingerbeer. 'Gingebre?' said the man inside. 'I do not think that is a wine of our vineyard.' 'Oh yes, it is,' I said. 'I met an English Duke at the Palazzo Corsini yesterday, and he told me I should get a bottle of gingerbeer here.' 'Ah!' said the ancient servitor, 'then I will ask the Marquis, my master.' He was absent for a few minutes, and presently returned with the Marquis, an exquisitely polite old gentleman of the good old school. 'I fear, illustrious stranger, you have made a mistake. I know not the name of "gingerbeer" as a wine of the country. Certainly I grow it not myself.' I apologized profusely, and withdrew my head from the aperture just in time to allow an old lady who was waiting, to bob hers in, and ask for two soldis' worth of the Marquis's best olive-oil, which she would take in the coffee-cup she held in her hand. And she took it.

CHAPTER XIV.

ROME.

I CAME, I saw, and I—was conquered. For once I prefer the old to the new, and Rome has exorcised the evil spirit that has taken up its residence within me. I came into Rome from Florence on a day that would have passed without attracting attention in Camden Town, Nunhead, or even the Seven Dials. The rain was pouring in torrents, the streets were rivers, and in the filthy byways, much affected by coachmen as short-cuts, the stucco was peeling from tumble-down tenements, and all was dirt and darkness and desolation. I have come into a good many Continental cities, in the course of a long and virtuous life, depressed and dyspeptic and disappointed, but I have never been made so utterly miserable by anything as by my first introduction to Rome. I jumped at once to the conclusion that travellers and guide-books had grossly deceived me, and that the famous capital of the Roman Catholic faith and United Italy had been made, like Somebody's pills and ointment, by persistent advertisement.

But with the morrow came the sun; the nightmare was over, and a pleasant dream had begun. Pagan Rome had made me—yea, even me, my brother—a little more respectful in my attitude towards antiquity. I came to scoff, and I remained to pray. I have been in the Forum, and when I sat on the great columns I tried to remember my Roman history, and muddled up the Cæsars, and wished that I had paid more attention to my books at school instead of making surreptitious catapults with the elastic I pulled out of my new spring-side boots. I have roamed—should I say Romed?—up the Appian Way, and lost myself in the mighty Baths of Caracalla; I have been down into the Catacombs and seen the bones of some Early Christians, and I have dreamed dreams, and wandered about in fancy in a toga, and given off Latin orations to the winds, and have only been aroused from my reverie by the voice of a fair creature inquiring, with the choicest American accent, if it was in the Forum that Julius Cæsar used to fight with wild beasts and play the fiddle while Rome was burning.

But all the ancient glories, so far as I am concerned, sink into insignificance beside the Colosseum. In this, the mighty ruin of the greatest arena the world has ever seen, the most ordinary mind—mine, for instance—loses itself. The present fades away; the guardian who follows you to see that you do not put stone and marble pillars in your pocket is lost sight of. You are back again in the year 72 A.D. You hear the cruel whips of their masters cracking merrily over the 12,000 Jewish captives who laid the first stones of the Colosseum, and in the year 80 it is complete, and Titus dedicates it, and the great arena is soaked with the blood of 5,000 wild beasts. The years go on, and human blood alone can satisfy the cruel thirst of the Romans. Over the seats and benches, now mouldering ruins, you see a mighty populace swarming. In the vast arena, where your modern foot, clad in a buttoned kid boot, now stands, thousands of gladiators, their huge muscles standing out like iron bars, fight, and dye the ground with their gore. The fiercest beasts stand at bay, with trembling captured slaves, and the nobles and the people—ay, even the women—shriek with delight as quivering flesh is torn, and the life-blood of man and brute spirts out in crimson jets. You can see it all, if you have a spark of imagination—the whole bloody, revolting scene becomes so real that at last you turn away and hide your eyes, and cry 'Faugh!'—come to your senses, and thank Heaven that such cruel days are over for ever.

And outside, even as you are expressing your gratitude, you will see a long line of weary, wretched animals dragging their heavy loads, while behind them walks a Roman of to-day lashing their quivering, bleeding sides with brutal fury, even goading their poor starved carcases to further effort by thrusting a sharp stick into their open wounds. I can imagine what the Roman horses and mules and oxen would say if they heard anyone rejoicing that cruelty died out with the Pagans and the decay of the Colosseum. I have seen such cruelty to animals under the shadow of St. Peter's that I doubt if the Colosseum ever saw worse. Beasts had at least a speedy death there. It is reserved for the modern citizen of Christian Rome to make a dumb brute's torture last its whole life long.

A Roman is very proud of being a Roman, and he does nothing menial. The fly-drivers are Romans, but they do not groom or attend to their horses. They have Neapolitans to do that. There is a good deal of the old dignity still surviving among the people. At a Roman pastrycook's a Roman waiter brings me an ice with the air of an emperor. An emperor would have done it more quickly, though, as his time would doubtless have been valuable. A Roman is always wrapping himself in an imaginary toga, and that dress is a much better one to pose in than to bustle about in and perform the vulgar task known as earning one's daily bread.

Anyone who travels must be struck with the extraordinary way in which the same waiters turn up all over the world. The man who spreads my humble repast of polenta and dried figs in the Hôtel Londra, in Rome, last waited upon me at the hotel at Seaford, in Sussex, a pleasant hamlet, which generally consists of six inhabitants, two visitors, and a pedestrian passing through from Newhaven. In Milan my waiter reminded me that he had often had the honour of waiting upon me at the St. Enoch's Hotel, at Glasgow, and in a restaurant in Florence I was recognised with a broad grin by the former oberkellner of a pleasant hostelry upon the Rhine, where I sojourned in '78. Most travellers can multiply instances of this sort of thing, but it is just a little wonderful to meet in Rome your old garçon of sleepy little Seaford, in Sussex.

More wonderful still! I have just been into a coiffeur's in the Via Condotti to be shaved, and the young gentleman officiating, after lathering me, said in the most unconcerned way possible: 'Let me see, I thinks that you like him a razor fine, if right I remembers?' I stared at the man in astonishment, and stammered: 'Do you know me, then?' 'Ah, sare,' was the reply, 'I shave you often last year, at the Toilet Club, Brighton. No you remember?' The world is decidedly small. I am looking about Rome now with some hope of coming upon the cabman to whom I gave a sovereign instead of a shilling in the Old Kent Road in the summer of '81. I really don't see why he shouldn't come round the corner accidentally.

Rome has just recovered from the incursion of the pilgrims to the tomb of Victor Emmanuel, and Society is returning to the capital. The 'pilgrimage' business scared many people from the city, for there was a good deal of wild talk about riots and I know not what. You see, this pilgrimage has been an organized Government affair, got up entirely for political purposes. The vast horde of folks who flocked from all parts of Italy came, not to show their attachment and devotion to monarchical institutions, but to see Rome and enjoy themselves. The railway companies brought 'pilgrims' at a reduction of 75 per cent. on the regular fares.

Although nothing has appeared in the papers, it is common talk in Rome that one train-load was stoned by the mob, and in several places this 'loyal' demonstration was hissed and hooted. Italy teems with dissension and discontent, and how fully the Government is aware of the fact is best proved by the enormous pains that have been taken to organize and carry out this solemn farce of a national pilgrimage to the tomb of the late King.

It is fair to say that this view of the pilgrimage is taken only in clerical and Republican circles. I am assured by many Italians that it has really been a great success, from a political point of view. There is no doubt that the 'merry jests of King Victor Emmanuel' endeared him to a large number of his subjects, and the stories that are being told of him now would fill a book.

The stories of his hobnobbing with peasants and boors, and finding his pleasure in bourgeois life, have caused the old canard to be revived about his identity. My waiter in Rome imparted it to me confidentially one morning while I was struggling to eat some *gnocchis à la Romaine* without injuring all that is left of my liver for life. I will give it as I received it:

'Wunst was a fire—big fire, while Vittor Emanuele he was baby in de palace. Real royal baby he was burn to death. To prevent being found out what happen, de nurse she put her baby in de place of other, and nobody not find out, so Victor Emanuele he really was one of de people, and dat was what make him so fond of sit in beerhouse and eat sausage and bread with a big knife.'

There is a big movement afoot in Rome to revive the Barberi races in the Corso. The Corso, as all my readers are aware, is a long, narrow street in the fashionable quarter of Rome, and the Barberi are poor horses who are let loose at the top with spiked balls fastened to their sides, which goad them almost to madness, and make them fly like the wind. Last year the cruel sport was abandoned, owing to its having caused a terrible accident just under the Queen's balcony the previous year. This time, however, there is a great outcry for a revival, and the chief sinners are not the cruel Romans, but the humane English and American visitors and residents.

As in these days of extended travel everyone goes to Rome, I should like to say a word about the nonsense that is talked about the unhealthiness of the climate and the danger of malaria. 'Roman fever' is a bogey which frightens hundreds of good folk from enjoying one of the greatest treats the world can give. There is very little danger to people who live carefully and don't rush. If people will go to Rome in the blazing heat of summer, and gallop about from place to place like madmen, now sweltering in the sun, and now burrowing into the icy depths of a ruined temple, or wandering in the cold galleries of a church, chills will follow, and fever may ensue; but in nine cases out of ten fear is the great cause of the illness of English travellers.

The Roman water, again, which some folks warn you not to drink, is the purest water in the whole wide world, and there is a supply, brought through the restoration of some of the classical aqueducts a distance of thirty-six miles, which is equal to 300 gallons per day for each inhabitant, and this is flowing day and night uninterruptedly. London Water Companies please note.

There is one thing which makes Rome unendurable to nervous, excitable people, and which, combined with the sirocco, has driven me away. To be harassed and tortured at every turn is death to a rheumatic, dyspeptic, quiet-seeking man whose nerves are champion jumpers. To show what I mean, I will exactly reproduce my last walk in Rome. I have read Mr. Hare's 'Walks in Rome,' but mine is the walk of a Hunted Hare.

A WALK IN ROME.

(*Enter a Rheumatic and Dyspeptic* ENGLISHMAN *from a Hotel on the Piazza di Spagna. Fifty single and double horse flys instantly rush at him.*)

ENGLISHMAN (*leaping wildly in the air*). No, no; I'm going for a walk!

(*Flys retire slowly, dropping off one by one as* ENGLISHMAN *continues to dodge under the horses' heads, to weep and wail, and beg to be allowed to go for a walk.*)

(*Enter a Man with Laces, a Man with Coral, and a Man with Views of Rome.*)

MEN (*surrounding Englishman*). Volete! Volete!

ENGLISHMAN. No, no; I don't want anything. Let me pass. I'm going for a quiet walk to calm my nerves.

(*After a quarter of an hour's race distances the three men, and stops and mops his brow.*)

ENGLISHMAN. At last! Now for a quiet stroll and a little calm meditation.

(*Enter an omnibus* R. *and a waggon* L.—*there are no raised pavements in Roman side streets*—*both coming full speed.*)

DRIVERS (*shouting*). He! Ho!

ENGLISHMAN. Oh dear! I shall be crushed. Where can I go? Oh dear!

(*Climbs up a waterspout on to the sill of a first-floor window, and escapes with the loss of his boots, which the waggon draws off.*)

ENGLISHMAN (*coming down*). Dear me! the stone is very cold to one's feet without one's boots. Never mind; now for a nice saunter.

(*Enter Flower-sellers—Mother, Father, and Four Children. They surround* ENGLISHMAN *and offer flowers.*)

ENGLISHMAN. No. Oh, do go away, please! I have left my purse at home.

(*Family stick flowers in* ENGLISHMAN'S *buttonhole. He flings them back. They throw them on his hat. He shakes them off. They put pansies in his pockets and roses down the back of his neck—fact! He shakes himself free and flies.*)

ENGLISHMAN. Phew! The sirocco is blowing, and I'm all in a perspiration. Let me enter this cool church a moment and rest in a pew.

(*Chorus of beggars at church door, holding out withered hands, half noses, wrapped up in paper, mangled legs, etc.*: 'Io muojo di fame! Date mi une soldo!')

ENGLISHMAN. Die of hunger, and be hanged to you!

(*Pushes through them and enters the church.*)

CUSTODIAN (*in church*). You vould like for to see pitchers an' statchers, eh, sare? Come vid me.

ENGLISHMAN. No; I'm going to rest a minute. Go away.

(*Enter Two* CICERONI.)

FIRST CICERONE (*in French*). Take you over the church, sir? Show you some funny things.

SECOND CICERONE (*in Italian*). Come with me, sir; I understand the antiquities.

ENGLISHMAN. No, no, no!

(*Kneels and prays to Heaven to be left alone one moment.* CICERONI *pursue him. He exits shrieking, rushes back to his hotel in a high fever, barricades himself in his room, and, drawing a revolver, threatens to shoot the first person who disturbs him.*)

(*Enter Two Sisters of Mercy to beg for the poor.*)

ENGLISHMAN. What! cannot I even have a minute to myself in my own room? (*Shoots himself.*) Now I'm dead perhaps I shall have five minutes!

(*Enter a Dozen Men masked, who seize* ENGLISHMAN.)

ENGLISHMAN. Here! leave me alone; I'm dead.

MASKED MEN. All right, but you must be removed at once. You've got to be underground by to-morrow in Rome, you know.

ENGLISHMAN. Oh, hang this! I'm off, then!

(*Rushes to railway-station, has a fight with fifty porters, who struggle to carry his umbrella and his overcoat for him, leaps into a train, and departs for England.*)

DOCTOR IN ENGLAND (*feeling Englishman's pulse*). Why, you're in a raging fever, and your nerves are overwrought, and you're quite delirious!

ENGLISHMAN. Yes, doctor. I unfortunately went out for a Quiet Walk in Rome!

One thing that has surprised me more than any other in a land of so much art as Italy is the striking mock modesty which has ruthlessly disfigured the statuary in the galleries and churches. The suggestion of putting the legs of a table into drawers is only paralleled by what one sees in the Uffizzi and Pitti galleries of Florence, and in St. Peter's at Rome. In the latter, a marble figure is actually adorned with a ridiculous zinc petticoat. The force of the ridiculous can only go a step farther, and put Achilles into trousers, and the Gladiator into a Highland kilt. A hundred years hence the Venus de Medici may have to be studied through a *robe de chambre*, and Hercules in an ulster and chimneypot hat may be the last contribution to the adaptation of ancient art to modern views.

What we shall do with the pictures I don't know. Many of them are quite as undraped as the statues, and several are absolutely indecent if we are to take the figures as modern ladies and gentlemen, living under the police regulations of the nineteenth century. One might just as well paint petticoats on to the females of Rubens as give zinc bathing-drawers to the *chefs d'œuvre* of Michael Angelo and Canova.

There is one picture which was very objectionable to an elderly English lady in the Uffizzi. It is a charmingly-executed figure of Venus performing a kindly office for Cupid with a smalltooth-comb. I suppose by-and-by the comb will be painted out, and Venus will be supplied with a piece of flannel and some soft soap.

I am sorry to say that I have had to leave Rome without the honour of an audience of the Pope. I have seen the King and the Queen and the Prince of Naples, for they all three drive about daily without the slightest escort, and we—that is, I and the Romans—just bow and smile and murmur 'How d'ye do?' and pass on. We mix so freely with the Royal Family—I and the Romans—that we get quite friendly, and find ourselves saying 'Fine day, isn't it?' to the King as we pass him in the Corso; and the King, taken off his guard, says, 'Very; but I don't think it will last.' But with the Pope it is different. He is the prisoner of the Vatican, and comes no more forth. Privileged persons, however, now and again he receives, and I had every reason to expect an invitation to attend at the Vatican, when I was compelled to leave Rome and go further north. I had, however, every opportunity afforded me of seeing all that the Vatican contains, and cannot let this opportunity pass of expressing my gratitude to his Holiness's Private Chamberlain, the Cavaliere Cassell, who procured me every privilege.

I know how interested ladies are in all that concerns housekeeping, for many are the charming letters which reach me on the troubles and torments of the modern domestic interior. For their private perusal, therefore, let me make a note of a custom which prevails largely in Italy, and which, I think, would do away with a great trouble and annoyance from which all unfortunate individuals who do not live in hotels or dine at clubs continuously suffer. In some parts of Italy, when you engage your cook or *chef*, you simply say to him: 'There are ten of us in family. For breakfast we like so and so; for dinner so and so. How much?' Thereupon the cook thinks it over, and he reckons it up, and presently he says: 'Sir' (or madam), 'I will keep your family for so many francs a month.'

The bargain is struck, and you have no further housekeeping worries at all. The *chef* buys everything; he has contracted to cook for you, and to supply all you require.

If his dinners are not good enough, or if you think his contract is too high for what he is giving you, you send for him, and you say: 'I cannot afford to pay so much; you must keep my family for less.' If you are overpaying, the cook will accept a reduction. If you are not, he will say: 'Very well, madam, then I must leave, as any reduction would leave me no margin of profit.' Then you know that your *nourriture* is being supplied at a reasonable rate, and you allow the contract to stand or not as you think fit.

Now, just think what a lot of trouble this will do away with. No more bother with butchers and bakers and grocers, no more journeyings to and fro to co-operative stores. The good housewife has nothing to do but play with her children and read the latest of Mr. Mudie's three-volume frivolities. All the cares of housekeeping are gone. I intend to try the plan directly I return. Only, as I am not rich enough to afford a *chef*, and shall have to rely upon a female, I shall watch her very closely when she goes out on Sunday. If, after she has contracted for me for three months, I find her going out with six ostrich feathers in her hat and a diamond ring outside her gloves, and hailing a hansom at the corner to drive her to the Café Royal where she is going to entertain a few Lifeguardsmen and some lady friends at dinner, I shall begin to think that the contract will bear reconsideration and a little reduction.

'Comfort' does not enter very largely into consideration, except at the great national theatres to which foreigners as well as natives flock. In Rome it is usual to give two representations, one at half-past five, and the second at half-past nine. I went one evening to the 'Metastasio.' At a quarter to ten I had the house to myself. I groped my way up a dark passage, and found a woman asleep on a bench. I showed her my ticket, and she shouted, 'Hercules! Hercules!' Presently a little lame dwarf answered to the name if not to the description, and unlocked the box. It was a dingy hole, with a bare brick floor, and contained two rush-bottomed chairs. 'Hercules' handed me a cushion to put on the chair, and for this I paid 'by the tariff' half a franc. Presently the house filled. In the box next me a Roman lady administered its natural sustenance to her baby. All around the men smoked the local cigar. The performance was fairly good. The costumes in one act were suggestively indecent, and the scenery ridiculously wretched. The stage footman walked about all through the acting, and cleared the stage frequently for the next scene while the hero and heroine were in possession of the boards. There was a real rain scene, which so delighted the audience that they had it all over again, and, as usual, the prompter steadily read the play aloud from end to end.

CHAPTER XV.

NAPLES.

NAPLES! What marvellous scenes that one word conjures up! Everybody knows Naples. Those who have not seen it have read about it, and its thousand marvels are familiar as household words. Vesuvius is known to every street arab who sells matches in the street. The story of Pompeii is as the story of Noah's Ark. And Naples itself! Are not Neapolitan ices sold from barrows at a halfpenny each wherever the English language is spoken—from

Hampstead Heath to Donnybrook Fair? The Neapolitan fisherman, in his red cap, who sings choruses from 'Masaniello'; the little Neapolitan girl who sings 'Santa Lucia'; the lazzaroni, the Bay, the Chiaja, the house of Emma Lady Hamilton, the grottoes, the blood of St. Gennarius, the storytellers on the Port, the puppets, the poor horses with open wounds—all these things are now as A B C to Englishmen; and there is not a boy or girl in the fourth standard who couldn't tell you that '*Vedi Napoli e poi mori*' means 'See Naples and then die.'

Shall I confess that, having been taught from my earliest infancy to believe in the Naples of romance, the Naples of the operatic stage, the Naples of the guide-book, and the Naples of the tourist, I was just a little disappointed when I first found myself in the famous city? My first disappointment was the complete absence of choruses of red-bonneted fishermen, singing, 'Behold, how brightly breaks the morning.' My second disappointment was the utter absence of colour and costume on the quay and in the city; and my greatest disappointment of all was that the bay was not blue, the sun was not warm, and the people were not gay. I arrived in Naples on a day which must have left London last November, and have remained hidden somewhere off the coast until it heard of my arrival. It was a dark, dull, lowering day—a day such as my good friend the oldest inhabitant could not remember the like of. Vesuvius in the background was shooting up a black volume of smoke that made him look like Sheffield in the distance more than the time-honoured mountain of the London matchbox, and the sky was as dirty and grimy as the lava pavement of the city. It wasn't the fault of Naples that it so belied its character. It was my fault. I had brought my own weather with me, and spoiled Naples as I had spoiled the Riviera.

But in the morning all was changed. The sky was a cloudless blue, and the sun shone brilliantly, and I sallied forth to lounge away the day, and to steep myself in Neapolitan life. Much of my first disappointment was atoned for, but still I searched in vain for picturesque costume. Naples is no longer the Naples of old. The curse of the billycock hat, which has spread over Europe, has not spared Southern Italy. The common people wear the castoff clothes of the well-to-do, and the well-to-do dress in the London fashion. As a natural consequence, the Neapolitan porters and fishermen and lazzaroni have little to distinguish them from the London labourer and the London costermonger. Naples has also in a great measure been ruined by the rich foreigner, who insists on carrying his own manners and customs with him. The old habits of the people yield to foreign influence, and one great city becomes as another great city. The English and the French and the Germans come to spend their money at Naples. They must be pleased. To please them everything that is English and French and German is introduced, and one by one the Neapolitan characteristics disappear.

Still, the industrious searcher who leaves the beaten track of the visitor and plunges into the side streets and the poorer quarters can find plenty of reward for his pains. He who would see Neapolitan life and study the people, their amusements and their customs, must shun the great hotels, and turn a deaf ear to the words of porters and hotel guides. As a rule the hotel people know nothing of the town. As an instance, take the hotel at which I stayed. The proprietor was a Swiss; the hall-porter was a German newly arrived from the Midland Hotel, St. Pancras; the head waiter was, during last season, sitting-room waiter at the Old Ship at Brighton. My sitting-room waiter came from the Queen's Hotel, Hastings, and my chambermaid's last place was the Schweizerhof at Lucerne. You can imagine for yourself what these people are likely to know of Naples. I had not been two days in Naples before I was able to tell the hall-porter of a dozen places which would be most interesting to English visitors, but of which he had never heard. Yet every day I heard English tourists inquiring of this man what they ought to see, and he gave them the stereotyped answer. He sent them to Pompeii, Vesuvius, and one or two well-known places, and for their evening's amusement invariably recommended them to try the opera at San Carlo. San Carlo is the largest theatre in Europe, and the opera is magnificently given there; but there are a score of things to see in Naples of an evening which are far more amusing and instructive and novel than a night at the opera.

One such place I found for myself, and I will tell you what I saw there presently, but first I must get over my ascent of Vesuvius. It is an awful journey from Naples to the edge of the crater, but the adventurous voyager is well repaid for all his trouble, especially if he is as fortunate as I was on the day of my visit. Vesuvius is a great fact in the history of Naples; but for Vesuvius there would be no Herculaneum and no Pompeii, and Vesuvius has had a tremendous influence on the Neapolitan character. People who live at the foot of a volcano, within sight of buried cities and islands and mountains which disappear in a single night and reappear again, sometimes after thirty years of submergence, are naturally superstitious, and equally naturally strongly pervaded with the sentiments of religion.

Nowhere are the people so devout as in these parts. Shrines are everywhere, and no house is without its cross. The priests flourish in the midst of the people, and are beloved and revered by them. New ideas come slowly to minds filled with simple and childlike faith, and free thought makes but slow progress among a populace who are ever in the presence of Nature's most sudden and most awful catastrophes. Grant that the Neapolitan is bigoted, superstitious, incapable of great mental or physical effort. Who can wonder at it? Climate, race, and surrounding circumstances account for it all! Live in Naples and be energetic under that clear blue sky, in that hot sun, in that dreamy atmosphere, if you can. Live under the shadow of that ever-seething volcano, knowing not at what moment it may pour forth its fiery deluge and bury the villages for miles around under a molten mass, and scoff if you dare!

All my life long I had wanted to see Vesuvius. My youthful imagination was fired by the picture on the fusee boxes. It was not until the month of January, 1888, that I found myself at last within measurable distance of the grand old volcano.

I was in Naples for some days before I made the excursion. Every morning I used to gaze at the great mountain celebrity, and from the respectful distance of my bedroom window at the Grand Hotel watch him 'smoking his morning pipe'; but Vesuvius, as seen from Naples, is a very different affair from Vesuvius as seen from the mouth of its crater. I was a long time making up my mind to 'do' Vesuvius, because Naples is a place where one does not go to bed particularly early. Every evening found me at one of the theatres, generally the magnificent San Carlo, and as the opera in Naples is frequently not over until past midnight, and there is life to be seen at the Café de l'Europe, in the Via Nazionale, 'after the opera is over,' it was often two o'clock in the morning ere I walked back along the lonely Chiaja to the Grand Hotel. Now, to see Vesuvius properly, and get back to Naples before nightfall, it is necessary that you should make a start at eight o'clock in the morning. Naples is the last place in the world in which a man wants to get up early in the morning—Naples is the home of the *dolce far niente*. Mendelssohn declared that in Naples he felt the greatest disinclination to do anything at all. 'I lounged about the streets all day,' he says, 'with a morose face, and would have preferred lying on the ground without the trouble of thinking, or writing, or doing anything. The atmosphere of Naples is suitable to grandees who rise late, never require to go out on foot, never think (for this is heating), sleep away a couple of hours on a sofa in the afternoon, then eat ice and drive to the theatre at night, where again they do not find anything to think about, but simply make and receive visits.' This peculiarity of 'Neapolitans at the play' I may refer to on another occasion, when I write my long-contemplated article on the theatres of Europe; for the present I only wish to draw attention to the intense laziness which the climate engenders. You will now understand why I remained in Naples a whole week before I summoned up sufficient courage to get up at eight o'clock in the morning to go to Vesuvius.

However, I managed it at last. This is how I got up at eight o'clock in the morning: I returned from the theatre at one in the morning, sat up in my room with my companion, the now famous Albert Edward, native of Finland and citizen of the world, smoking and talking till three. Then we settled ourselves down in easy-chairs and went to sleep without undressing. At seven we were aroused by the waiter, who, according to overnight instructions, entered with considerable noise and some hot coffee, and after giving us half an hour's grace took us by the shoulders and forced us downstairs.

Even when we stood outside the hotel, and found it cold, we said we would go back and go to bed; but the landlord, who had promised us faithfully to prevent any weakness on our part at the last moment, was a man of his word, and, assisted by the waiter and the porter, thrust us into the carriage, banged the door, and bade the coachman drive off with us at once to Vesuvius.

Finding that further subterfuge was impossible, we turned up our coat-collars, wrapped ourselves in our rugs, and presently we fell fast asleep, the rhythmic snoring of my companion alone breaking the silence of the lonely roads along which, at a cruel crawl, our wretched animals proceeded.

Oh, the poor horses of Naples! They have haunted me ever since I saw them. There is not, I should think, any place in the civilized world where dumb beasts are treated with such wanton brutality as in this glorious Naples. Some of the horses are mere skeletons—bags of bones—and their starved bodies all one mass of gaping wounds and hideous sores. The Neapolitan flyman always keeps a wound or a sore place open on his horse's body. It is into this wound that he thrusts a sharp-pointed stick when he wants to urge the poor beast to further effort or increased speed. I have seen a poor little pony, one mass of sores and dead lame, dragging a *calesso* containing fourteen people, and being goaded into a gallop the whole length of a journey of ten miles.

I have referred to the subject of the Naples horses elsewhere, but it cannot be referred to too often. I am, in common with many other writers who have seen the awful cruelty of Naples, hopeful that some day public opinion will grow so strong on the subject that even the Neapolitans will be shamed into something like ordinary humanity to their dumb slaves.

Let me briefly, while our own wretched animals drag us wearily along the road to Vesuvius (it takes four hours to get to the base of the cone from Naples), tell you something of the Naples beasts of burthen.

The *calesso* which I mentioned above is a long, narrow cart with three benches or seats in it, and two poles sticking out behind, on which a board is placed which seats more people. These *calessi* belong mostly to the villagers and the costermongers. The sides are painted sometimes with pictures of the Virgin, sometimes with ballet ladies, and sometimes with apocryphal figures. But however much they differ on the outside they are always the same inside—that is, they are always full. The proprietor of a *calesso* drives half the village to town and back again for nothing if they are his friends; for a small fee if they are not. All the morning you see these loaded *calessi* coming into Naples, and all the afternoon you meet them going out again. Sometimes, instead of the usual lame, raw, starved pony, a donkey draws the terrible load; occasionally a horse in the last stage of break up and break down is harnessed to the shafts. The heavier waggons are drawn by teams. Sometimes four horses, sometimes a horse and a donkey, are harnessed together. Sometimes a horse, a donkey, and a cow limp along side by side. Upon one occasion near Pozzuoli I met a horse, a cow, a mule, and a donkey drawing a load, but the most frequent 'pair' is a horse and a cow.

Up in a secluded corner near the tomb of Virgil, just at the entrance to the old grotto of Posilipo, I came one day on a dirty, broken-down looking stable. On the door I saw written up 'Society for the Protection of Animals.' After seeing the animals, I was not surprised that the society took such a back seat. After all, what can it do in a country where everybody tells you it is wicked to think of animals—animals have no souls! Well, it may be so. I am far from sure about it, but animals have hearts, and in this respect they have the advantage of the people who torture them so cruelly in return for their willing, life-long drudgery.

We arrived at the foot of the cone at last. The last part of the journey had been a zigzag climb over miles of lava and black mud and shapeless rocks, the cooled down 'vomit of Vesuvius.'

At the foot of the cone is a funicular railway which has been rendered familiar by the advertisements on most of the Continental railway-stations.

The price of a seat in one of the cars is £1. We step in, and are hauled up to the top.

It is something like going up the side of a house on a switchback, and the process is so alarming that many people still prefer the old-fashioned method of ascension, and either climb up laboriously or are carried up in chairs by the guides and porters.

I had an uncomfortable feeling that the rope might break as I made the ascent, and I was intensely relieved when we reached the mountain station and stood once more on *terra firma*.

But there is still a further ascent to make on foot to reach the actual mouth of the crater and look down into the yawning hell that night and day, for ever and ever, is belching forth flame and smoke, and hurling large stones and masses of rock into the air with a report that can only be compared to the discharge of artillery.

As we alight from the funicular, we find ourselves in an awful atmosphere. We are nearly choked with the noxious fumes of the volcano, and our eyes are stung and blinded with the sulphurous smoke that envelops us. The earth trembles beneath our feet, the huge mountain throbs and gasps from beneath, and thick as hail around falls the shower of stones that the volcano, with a thunderous roar, hurls unceasingly into the air.

Still we determine to go on. I have sworn to look into the fiery jaws of Vesuvius, and I will. Slowly we climb up that 'awful' summit—a summit seething and boiling and steaming at every pore. Only those who have made the ascent can realize the awful grandeur of the scene which awaits the intrepid excursionist.

I use the word 'awful' advisedly. The stoutest heart will quake at the spectacle which he beholds for the first time, and the surroundings are not calculated to diminish the feelings of terror.

During the week I made my ascent a rumour had been published to the effect that an Englishman who made the ascent of Vesuvius without a guide had been lost. It is quite possible to be lost on the summit of Vesuvius. Enveloped in smoke and steam, you may easily, if you are incautious, become asphyxiated and fall into the crater of the raging volcano, never to be heard of again.

The Englishman turns out to have been a German, and he has probably turned up again at his hotel safe and sound, but there was plenty of justification for the anxiety of his friends.

We take a guide. My companion was on the mountain during one eruption and had to fly for his life. While we are ascending he tells me the story, and that does not add to my sense of security.

It was the greatest eruption that had occurred during the present century, and took place on April 24, 1872. At 4 p.m. a new crater opened on the side of the mountain, and the lava from it made a circular sweep round the mountain, threatening to cut off the descent of all the people who were up above.

My companion, alarmed by the shouts of the guides, guessed something had happened, and made all haste to descend, and only got down just in time to find a narrow passage still open, through which he dashed.

By the time he reached the Hermitage the entire side of the mountain was a sheet of burning lava. He learned afterwards that forty people had perished on the volcano. The lava overwhelmed two villages—Massa and San Sebastiano—and at Resina, the village at the foot, nearly a hundred people were destroyed.

I had joked on the road about an eruption and what a fine thing it would be to write about; but standing within measurable distance of the seat of danger I am not only willing but decidedly anxious to postpone the experiment.

Our guide conducts us cautiously over the yellow masses of sulphurous rock and the yawning, steaming fissures, and the huge masses of coiled lava that look like twisted rope. Our feet are parboiled with the steam that rises from beneath them. The perspiration begins to burst from every pore. We are in a perfect Turkish bath, or, rather, imperfect one, in which the noxious fumes and vapours are allowed to escape and choke the patient.

We cough and sneeze, and I gasp out a prophecy that I shall be choked. My eyes smart as they have never smarted in the foulest London fog.

'Close your mouths!' yells our guide. We close our mouths and make frantic efforts not to inhale the awful fumes of Vesuvius through our nostrils, and still we stagger on with trembling limbs and anxious faces, and at last we stand on the edge of the crater and peer down into the abyss below.

The sight is terrible, and yet sublime in its grandeur.

Even as we look, blinded and choked, there is a loud report, and hundreds of large stones are hurled high in the air.

The ground rocks beneath us. There is another report, and another, and this time huge masses of rock are flung aloft from the infernal depths of the crater.

I am fascinated by the scene, though I am in a state of mortal terror. My companion urges me to come away. He has had enough of it, and is thinking of the day when he had to fly for his life. No one who has ever seen the burning lava pour down the sides of Vesuvius, and has been in its path, ever wants to behold the sight again.

I, too, am thinking, but my thoughts have flown farther back than my friend's. I am thinking of all the scenes of horror and death and desolation of which this stupendous volcano has been the cause. I think of the buried cities that lie around me, hidden for ever beneath the deadly vomit of the mouth into whose insatiable jaws I stand and gaze.

Herculaneum and Pompeii are below me, and hundreds of villages have been swallowed up in the bygone centuries, and have left no record on the pages of history.

I don't know how long I should have remained gazing down into the jaws of the volcano, terrified, yet too fascinated to move, had I not felt symptoms of dizziness coming over me.

Not wishing to share the fate of the gentleman named Empedocles, who in the year 400 B.C. toppled over into the crater of Mount Etna, I made a violent effort and stepped slowly backward from the mouth of the crater, and gradually staggered over the rough rocks and piles of lava until, steaming and caked with sulphur, I returned to the little restaurant which has been obligingly built by the authorities at the foot of the cone.

Here I sat down to rest my weary limbs and recover my dazed senses. We had a bottle of Vesuvio—a wine made from the grapes which grow on the southern slopes of the mountain—and then we made our way to the world-famous observatory on the side of the mountain, over which Professor Palmieri presides, and which contains a marvellous instrument called a seismograph.

Professor Palmieri has made Vesuvius the study of his life. By the aid of his instrument he is able now to know twenty-four hours in advance whether the intentions of the mountain are honourable or not.

By the kindness of the aged professor I was enabled to examine the seismograph at my leisure, and I will briefly explain what it is.

It is a marvellous piece of mechanism, so arranged that certain wires are agitated every time Vesuvius breathes. It is a long way from the crater—in fact, it is actually on a neighbouring spur, but so perfectly is it arranged that every movement of the volcano is recorded. While I watched it the wires trembled—Vesuvius had thrown up a few stones. So delicate is the mechanism that if you put your wrist within the glass case which contains it your pulsation causes the wires to be agitated.

In the night, when the 'observers' sleep, the seismograph still records the force of every breath the volcano draws. Attached to spiral wires are a red pencil and a blue pencil, and underneath the points of these a piece of tape—such as is used in telegraphing—winds itself round a reel. Any force or agitation in the centre of the crater brings the pencils down upon the tape, and causes them to mark it. A spasm of one kind causes the red pencil to mark the tape, a spasm of another kind sets the blue pencil off. In the morning the member of the staff on duty simply looks at the tape, and he can tell exactly what 'Old 'Suvy' has been up to in the night. This is only a rough outline of what this wonderful instrument of Professor Palmieri's can accomplish. To understand it thoroughly you must see it yourself.

After we had spent a pleasant hour in the observatory, chatting with one of the attendants, who, by-the-bye, was formerly in the chorus of the Royal Italian Opera in London, we went down the mountain to the inn at which our horses had been stabled, and as soon as our coachman was ready we drove back again to Naples.

I was tired out and fell asleep, only waking up once, just in time to listen to a pious *pifferari*, who was making music at midnight before the shrine of the Madonna.

I had a day's rest after doing Vesuvius, and then I set out for Pompeii. You can go by rail, so I didn't this time have to rise at an abnormally early hour. The train that left Naples for Pompeii might have been a special from the Tower of Babel. Certainly every European language was represented in it. When I arrived at Pompeii I was hungry, and I adjourned at once to a restaurant, where a *table d'hôte* breakfast was being served in every language under the European sun. At the little table at which I managed to find a seat we were English, French, German, Italian, Spanish, Roumanian, Russian, Pole, and Swede, and the other Continents were represented by a couple of Australians and three Americans. But it is an extraordinary thing that, when we conversed together in scraps of our various languages, we found we were all making the same joke about the food. The omelette was made with eggs discovered in Pompeii, which had been laid eighteen hundred years ago. The beef was from a cow which had been dug up petrified during the latest excavation; the apples had been found in the house of Diomed, where Diomed had left them when he fled from the rain of hot ashes that fell upon his doomed villa on November 24, 79. We all laughed at the joke, and the waiter—a polyglot personage, who talked fourteen languages all mixed up together at the same time—laughed too, and told us that it was on record that ever since there had been a restaurant in Pompeii every traveller who refreshed at it had perpetrated that very identical joke. And then he looked very hard at me, and said: 'But, pardon, sir; do I know you? Is it not that you are Mr. ——?' 'You have guessed it the first time,' I replied, putting the idiom into German as well as I could on the spur of the moment; 'but where have you known me?' 'Ah, you no remember John! I am John, as was your waiter in sitting-room at the London North-Western Hotel at Liverpool.' Oh, these jack-in-the-box sons of the Fatherland! They pursue me everywhere. Fancy meeting your Liverpool German waiter at Pompeii!

Of Pompeii itself what can I say in these pages? I want a whole book to write what I think about it, and then I shall only have said what hundreds have said before me. To wander about that old-world town, rescued from its ashes after centuries of oblivion, is to stand aghast with astonishment at the little progress which civilization has made with the centuries. The Pompeians had probably forgotten far more than we shall ever know. One stands absolutely open-mouthed and with starting eyeballs before the cases in the museum, which contain the Pompeian lady's rouge-pot, and the Pompeian doctor's surgical instruments, and the pass-out checks for the Pompeian theatre; and the hair of one's head stands erect as one comes to a wall in Pompeii, and reads what a rude little Pompeian boy had chalked upon it just seventy-nine years after the birth of our Saviour. They knew how to live and how to enjoy themselves, did those old Pompeians, and the art of making the house beautiful was far more theirs than ours. Beautiful and perfect as works of art as are the relics of that past civilization already recovered, it is almost certain that buried deep down in old Herculaneum are works of far greater beauty and of still higher art. But new towns have risen above the old ruins, and the treasure will now probably never be recovered.

The museum at Pompeii suffers from the best things found in the city having been sent to the Naples Museum. In the Pompeii collection, after the dead Pompeians in glass cases, there is very little to see, but they are wonderful enough to satisfy the greatest curiosity hunter. It gives one a little flutter of excitement to look at a man, perfect in form and feature, lying just as he died on that terrible November day in 79—to see his hands clenched and his teeth set, and the very look of horror on his face that came there as he fell, fleeing from the doomed city—fell to rise no more. And in another case lies a beautiful girl of Pompeii, who died with her arm across her eyes, shutting out the sight of the swift death that was overtaking her. And near her lies a poor little dog who died that day. He still wears the collar and chain that bound him to his kennel and prevented his escape. The poor little Pompeian bow-wow, who lived one thousand eight hundred years ago, lies upon his side, his limbs drawn together in agony, his lips parted just as they were when they gave the last dying whimper of terror and despair. Poor little dog! He will be handed down perhaps for thousands of years yet to come, for the wondering eyes of a new race of human beings to gaze upon. That little dog of A.D. 79 may—— But I mustn't lose myself in building up a Rider Haggard romance about that dog. He has achieved immortality, and, like a good many four-footed immortals, he paid a good price for the advertisement.

In the Naples Museum the rescued statuary and bronzes and ornaments are very wonderful; but what interested me much more was the bread taken out of the oven where it was recently found. It was put in on the day of the catastrophe, and taken out some years ago. It was new bread then; it is absolutely the stalest bread in existence now, for it is 1,800 years old. After the loaves of bread such minor curiosities as the dessert from a nobleman's table, a bottle of wine from the cellar of Pliny, and a patent latchkey found in a Pompeian gentleman's pocket, fail to attract more than passing attention. My only astonishment was that nowhere in the museum could I find any traces of the electric light of Pompeii, and that among the rescued literature exhibited there was not a single copy of the Pompeian daily sporting paper. But when I asked the custodian for these things he took a noble revenge by showing me a challenge from the Jem Smith of Pompeii to fight the Jake Kilrain of another town, and the score of a Pompeian tosspot which had been chalked up behind a tavern door. After this he would be a bold man to deny that people were quite as advanced in their civilization in 79 as they are to-day.

All around Naples there are wonderful ruins and natural curiosities, and, of course, I explored them all. I went to the great sulphur mine of Pozzuoli and sulphured myself, and I went all over the Temple of Serapis in the same place, and thoroughly explored the great amphitheatre in which the famous seafights or Naumachia were held by the Romans. The centre of the amphitheatre was filled with water, and then hundreds of slaves and prisoners rowed in and hacked each other to pieces. It was while exploring the dungeons underground in which the prisoners were kept that a terrible adventure befell us. Our guide was a local old gentleman of about ninety—the real genuine oldest inhabitant in the flesh. He carried a tow torch to light us through the damp, noisome, winding passages that led to the cells below the earth, and just as we got into the darkest dungeon the old gentleman fell down in a fit and his torch went out.

The situation was awful. We had not the slightest idea where we were, and we hadn't any matches with us. We shouted aloud, but only the mocking echo of our own voices answered us. Just as the old gentleman fell he had told us that we were now in dungeons from which no sound could escape. We groped about in the dark, and tried to find a passage, but only with the result that I found myself in one dark dungeon and Albert Edward got into another, and we could neither of us find our way back to the old gentleman. We gave ourselves up for lost. We had not even the hope which the ancient prisoners had of being dragged out into the arena to make a fight of it. We should perish by inches in the secret dungeons of the great Roman amphitheatre of Pozzuoli. Just as we had abandoned hope, and I was trying to scratch a last message to the world on the wall with the point of my scarf-pin, a distant murmur reached our ears. It grew nearer and nearer. We shouted; on it came. We heard English words spoken by English lips. A guide was bringing another party to the secret dungeons. They entered and found us, and between us we carried the epileptic old gentleman upstairs into the light of day, and got him some cold water and brought him round. But I registered a vow never again to visit dungeons with an elderly gentleman subject to fits, and with a tow torch of limited powers of endurance.

In Naples my principal amusement was buying lottery tickets and going to the theatre. I didn't get much out of the lottery, but I was vastly amused at the theatre, as I sought out the smaller houses where plays in the Neapolitan dialect, with Pulcinella as the principal comedian, were given. One evening's entertainment was unique in my experience, and will remain impressed upon my mind while memory maintains a sitting position. I had heard much of the marionettes and puppet-shows, and so one evening I found my way to the Teatro Mercadante, where marionettes were announced to appear in a grand play, entitled 'The Universal Deluge,' and in the great ballet of 'Excelsior.'

I fancied, of course, that I was going to a small puppet-show. Imagine my astonishment when I arrived at a real theatre with a real box office, and found that the prices of admission ranged from one lira (equal to a franc) to twenty lire. I paid ten lire for a private box, and on entering the theatre found a huge audience assembled—an audience not of children, but of grown men and women, of well-dressed ladies and gentlemen armed with fans and opera-glasses—just the same kind of audience, in fact, that assembles at the Lyceum, or the Criterion, or the Gaiety. There was an orchestra, too, of twenty performers, and programmes were sold, and when the curtain rose on 'The Universal Deluge,' the great grown-up audience settled itself down to enjoy the tragedy enacted by wooden dolls.

When I saw the scene, and Noah and his sons and daughters and the priests came on and conversed, and raised their arms to heaven, and generally conducted themselves in a manner worthy of Sir Henry Irving's company in 'Hamlet' or 'King Lear,' I was speechless with surprise. The talking is, of course, done at the wings, but the gestures of the puppets were perfect. There was a little lack of dignity occasionally in the walk off, because the feet sometimes did not quite touch the ground, but the figures being made to appear life-size by the dwarfing and arrangement of the scenery, the illusion was at times simply marvellous. Noah embraced his children; he fell on his knees and raised his hands to heaven; he denounced the wicked, and he gave off long and impressive speeches with such perfect dignity and appropriateness of gesture that he speedily established himself as a great actor in the eyes of the audience. He made his points amid rounds of applause, and at the end of a really magnificent piece of acting he got such a terrific recall that he came on and bowed his acknowledgments. Never did well-trained actor take a call so gracefully as this wooden puppet, and never did trained actor more thoroughly carry his audience away.

The second scene was the day of the Deluge. The skies were stormy and ominous; peals of thunder were heard. Noah made one final appeal to the wicked crowd of dolls, who only mocked him and went off to continue their evil ways. Then Noah knelt down, and, joining his hands, indulged in a short prayer, after which he opened the ark doors, and his sons and daughters, each embracing him, passed in. Then he had a grand exit speech, and walked up the plank into the ark, turning at the door with true stage instinct to give off his exit speech. Then, the human beings having taken their places, the animals commenced to arrive two by two. The animals were wonderful wooden imitations of the real thing, and they walked and pricked their ears and wagged their tails, each species stopping just at the ark door to roar, or to bark, or to neigh, or to crow, or hee-haw, as the case might be. The two donkeys displayed great courage on the eve of such a catastrophe, for they kicked up their heels and relieved the scene with considerable low comedy, retiring at last amid roars of laughter and rounds of applause. Then the serpents wriggled up, and then came the birds. Unfortunately a number of the birds were real ones, and some of them flew into the theatre instead of into the ark. Instantly the huge audience, with true Neapolitan cruelty, set up a yell, and stretched out their hands to capture the frightened little things, and the gallery boys hurled their caps at them, and the crowded house rose and hooted and shouted, and was only satisfied when the poor birds had been caught and killed. After all the animals were in the ark, the door was closed; then a terrible rain descended on the earth—the best rain I have ever seen on the stage. It was so real that I found myself picking up my umbrella in my private box. Now the waters rose rapidly, the ark began to pitch and toss, the wild lightnings flashed, and the audience was hushed to a silence that might be felt. In a moment the wicked were seen climbing to the mountain summits, only to be washed off and carried away. Mothers clung to their children, husbands clutched madly at their drowning wives, and the angry billows were thick with struggling human beings—I beg pardon, struggling with puppets. How all these figures were worked so naturally is a puzzle to me. The action was never jerky or mechanical; it was natural—so natural that the scene became painful. One poor doll mother held her doll baby in her arms and smothered it with kisses as the cruel wave swept them away, and a doll husband perished in agony locked in his young doll wife's embrace. But safely, amid all the horrors and the cries of the doomed, the brave old ark rode the angry waters, until the dove flew out, and presently returned with an olive-branch. Then the waves were still, day dawned over the scene, and Noah, with the limelight full upon his patriarchal head, knelt at the ark door and returned thanks to Heaven for its mercy to him and his, and then the band played soft, sweet music, and the curtain slowly fell upon 'The Universal Deluge.'

If this was wonderful, what can I say of the ballet of 'Excelsior' which followed? I have seen this famous ballet at San Carlo in Naples, at the Eden in Paris, and at Her Majesty's in London, but I have never seen it performed with such vigour as by the wooden troop of artists engaged at the Mercadante. The complete ballet was given, with the music, the scenery, the dances, and the various tableaux. The *corps de ballet* went through the complicated figures with a precision that would have gladdened the heart of Monsieur Jacobi at the Alhambra, and the leading lady, Miss Emma Wood, as she was playfully called in the playbill, won all hearts by the grace and finish of her dancing. She leapt a little higher perhaps than Palladino or Pitteri ever did, and now and then she didn't trouble to touch the boards with her twinkling little feet; but here, as in the tragedy, the action was excellent, and when, after a magnificent *pas seul*, Miss Wood was called, she came on and bowed right and left with the most exquisite grace. The dramatic scenes of the ballet were perfectly played, and from start to finish it was thoroughly appreciated by the audience, who remained in the theatre from eight until nearly midnight, applauding and enjoying the really artistic performance of these wooden actors and actresses. When the curtain had descended and we all filed out into the street, it seemed to me that I had at last discovered the secret of true happiness for a dramatic author. It was to live in a country where his plays could be interpreted by puppets. And oh, what a paradise such a land must be to the theatrical manager! No quarrels among the company, no trouble with the leading man, no indisposition of the leading lady, and no salaries to pay, except those of the voices at the wings and the men who work the strings of the puppets from the flies.

From that night I went only to puppet shows. Even a grand opera at San Carlo could not tempt me away from them. I saw dramas and comedies and farcical comedies played by dolls, and I saw everywhere packed audiences roaring with delight at their antics, or weeping in sympathy with their sorrows.

Funerals at Naples are among the curious spectacles of the town. Being of a cheerful disposition, I always run after a funeral. The body is carried on a bier by four masked men, and a procession of masked men follows. These masked men are the Brethren of the Misericordia. Rich funerals have a grand open hearse in which the coffin is placed, and two priests, with lighted candles, sit inside at the head of the coffin. The coffin is always smothered in flowers.

The practice of exposing the dead to the public view still obtains in Naples. Recently, in one of the small streets, a baker lost his only daughter, a very beautiful girl of sixteen. I saw her after she was dead, because the baker had cleared all the bread from his shop-window and put his pretty dead daughter there instead. And for a whole day she lay there, surrounded with beautiful white camellias and lovely flowers, until it was time for her to be placed on the bier and carried off to the Campo Santo.

The lottery playing in Naples is the curse of the town. Almost every second shop is a lottery shop, and all ranks gamble from week to week. The system is not to buy a ticket, but to back certain numbers to come out. The numbers run from one to ninety, and five are drawn every week. You can play the single number, the ambo, and the terno—that is, two numbers or three, and four and five if you like. If you play the ambo you name two numbers to come out, and if you are right you are paid by the Government three hundred times your stake. That stake can be what you like, from a penny to a pound. If you back a terno you get proportionately more; if you name all five you get sixty thousand times your stake.

With this game brought within the reach of all classes, you can readily imagine that the lottery shops are besieged all day long. Every peasant, every servant, every beggar plays at the lottery. The vice is national; it is in the blood; it is part of the Neapolitan character. There are a hundred superstitions among the people concerning the lottery. If you meet a white horse you play such and such a number: if you meet a funeral, if you hear a donkey bray, if you see a man with red whiskers—whatever happens, the Neapolitan takes it as an augury of a certain number, and he plays it accordingly.

Some of the priests have great success in foretelling successful numbers. One of the monks who walk about soliciting alms once had a great reputation. To anyone who gave him charity he whispered a number. He was so successful that at last he could not move out without being surrounded by crowds, who demanded a number to play. He lost his temper, and refused to tell anybody. The crowd thereupon seized him, and he was carried away and shut up in a cellar in a house, where he was beaten with a stick to make him tell the number. Still he refused, and they swore they would keep him prisoner until he consented; but the poor priest fell ill, and then, getting alarmed lest he should die, his assailants took him out and put him in the street, where he was picked up by the police. He was taken to the hospital, where he died, but before he breathed his last he gave 'numbers' to the sick in his ward. They told others, and the entire hospital—patients, doctors, and nurses—played the poor monk's numbers, an ambo, and those numbers came out of the wheel. The Naples lottery lost an enormous sum, but it gained again next week, when every living soul put every shilling they had got in the world on the poor monk's terno, which, fortunately for the Government, didn't come out as the ambo had done.

There is one remarkable feature about the Naples Museum, which is, that each of the old gentlemen who act as custodians of a room quietly whispers into your ear that he should like to do business with you. One dear old boy actually found out my hotel, and arrived in the evening and asked to see me, having with him a book about the museum which he was sure I should like to buy, as it was very rare and very curious. When I had bought it I discovered that it was the 1888 edition of a work published in Ludgate Hill, London.

The English are the special prey of the touts in the Museum—in fact, they seem to be special prey everywhere. Everybody in Naples knows enough English to waylay them with. Even the objectionable 'guides' who stand outside the Café de l'Europe at night, and in the expressive language of the country are called 'ruffiani,' ply their highly objectionable calling in the Anglo-Saxon tongue. And a little barefooted Neapolitan imp who sells matches outside the San Carlo Theatre shouts morning, noon, and night, in a shrill treble, 'Here yare, sare—vant some matches!' In addition to this a peripatetic trade in Holywell Street literature and art is openly plied by men in the streets, who expatiate upon the character of their wares in fluent English, and follow the British or American tourist for a quarter of a mile in their endeavour to persuade him to become a purchaser.

After all, England is not such a great place in everybody's eyes as it is in our own. I travelled with an Italian priest from Naples to Pompeii, and we told each other stories in French—not French stories, *bien entendu*. He had just come from Sicily, where he had been tutor in a great Duke's family, and when he wanted to teach the Duke's son some English history, the Duke said: 'Nonsense! let him learn the history of Sicily first; what is the use of his troubling about the small countries like England?' I met a Neapolitan, too, not long ago—a Neapolitan Count from Otranto—who asked me many questions concerning England. I told him it was a great country. 'Is it as great a country as Greece?' he said. 'Oh, much greater!' I replied; 'the two are not to be compared.' The Count shook his head. 'I can't believe it!' he exclaimed; 'I see many Greek ships at Otranto, but very seldom an English one.'

CHAPTER XVI.

VENICE.

IT was an awful journey from Naples to Venice. I had another half-hour in Rome *en route*. 'Half an hour in Rome'—doesn't it sound terrible? Fancy being in Rome and going no further than the refreshment-room in the railway-station! And at Bologna I was nearly frozen to death. The snow lay thick everywhere, and the mountain passes looked like seas of ice. When I arrived in Venice there was a dull November fog lying over the city, and my heart went down into my boots. But I recovered myself sufficiently to get into a gondola, which, however graceful it may be on a fine day, looked on this occasion more like a frowning hearse than ever. I asked if I couldn't have a carriage and drive to the hotel, as it was so foggy on the water. The gondolier stared at me in blank amazement. 'And where would monsieur get the horses?' he said; and then I learnt for the first time that there are no horses in Venice, and that the gondola is absolutely the only means of locomotion. Some of the Venetians, those who have never been to the mainland, have never seen a horse in all their lives. A showman once brought one to a fair, and called it a monster, and the factory girls and boys paid sixpence each to see the marvellous curiosity.

This utter absence of wheels and animals makes this city in the sea a city of silence and of perfect rest. A sense of perfect bliss steals over the tired traveller from the towns of noise, and he glides along past the marble palaces in his gondola as in a dream. And Venice is a dream. The wonderful stories of her Bridge of Sighs, the weird tales of the old romancers and poets, are all dreams. At any rate, they are not true. But Venice is beautiful, and, though much of the romance that enshrined her has been swept away by the ruthless hand of the modern literary inquisitor, 'A Day with the Doges' is a day to be remembered in one's life, and Venice remains a city unique in the world. My gondolier took me down short cuts—waterways all of them—which were overpowering in their odour. We glided swiftly over waters that were simply floating refuse heaps and dustbins. But out of the fishy water rose now and then a glorious palace that made amends for all. Cutting into the Grand Canal from one of these water-lanes, we grounded on the mud, and stuck there for four or five minutes; but the spirit of romance breathed o'er the scene, and I felt that I could have stuck in the mud for ever and not found the position monotonous.

I was lucky enough to see the beginning of the Carnival in Venice, and to make the acquaintance of a gentleman who has a palace on the Grand Canal, and who was kind enough to take me about in his gondola and show me everything. On the Rialto one afternoon, wanting to find out where Shylock lived, I approached a gentleman, who was smoking a cigarette and lounging about. I asked him my question in Italian. He replied in English, with a strong German accent: 'That's the house—that one yonder, Mr. ———,' giving me my correct name. I stared at him. 'Ah,' he said, 'I thought you didn't know me. I'm at Danielli's Hotel here, but I used to be coffee-room waiter at the Palace Hotel, Aberdeen. Don't you remember me now?'

One of the great show places of Venice is the museum of the Arsenal. Of course I stopped enraptured before the magnificent gold barge in which the old Doges went forth and married the Adriatic, flinging a gold ring into the sea; but what interested me most was the case which contained relics of Duke Francesco Carrara, commonly called 'the Tyrant of Padua.' I was in a very bad temper myself the day I saw his 'relics.' The bitter cold had upset my liver, and made me extra fiendish, and so I felt in perfect sympathy with the gentleman who wreaked his vengeance on his enemies in the most ingeniously diabolical manner possible.

The first 'specimen' which attracts your attention is a beautifully decorated jewel-box—all velvet and gold, and set with precious stones. Duke Francis was in love with a lady who one day snubbed him before company. Francis smiled a sweet smile and bit his lip, but never by word or deed allowed the fair charmer to see that she had trodden on his corns. But when her birthday came round he sent her anonymously this beautiful box, with an inscription upon it to say that it was from an unknown admirer to the Queen of Beauty. When the box was delivered the lady was out, so her maid took it in, and, with the natural curiosity of the female sex, she began to wonder what the beautiful box contained. It was delivered uncovered, and attached to it by a ribbon was a little golden key. The maid thought to herself, 'I'll just open this, and see what lovely thing is inside it for my mistress.' She put the golden key in the lock, she gave it a turn; up then flew the lid, and all that remained of the inquisitive maid was gathered up from the floor and scraped off the walls. The Duke's notion of a birthday present for a lady who had rejected his addresses was decidedly original, was it not? He must have been the ancestor of the gentleman who, when Sir William Harcourt was Home Secretary, used to send him such curious hampers and brown-paper parcels.

Another delightful relic of the life and times of the Tyrant of Padua is in the same case as the beautiful box. It is a simple key—about the size of an ordinary door-key. It was the key of the Duke's library in his private room. When he wanted to get rid of any of his suite or any person of his household, he used to ring his bell and ask for Mr. John to be sent to him (fancy name, of course). When John entered, the Duke would say: 'Oh, John, I wish you would go to the bookcase in my private room and bring me Lecky's "European Morals."' 'Certainly, your grace,' Mr. John would say; and away he would trot with the key in his hand. When he got to the library, he would put the key in the lock of the bookcase and turn it. But directly he turned it, out of the handle of the key shot a long poisoned needle, which stabbed the hand of the holder, and instantly shot back again. John would take his hand from the key, and say: 'What the deuce was that?' He would look at his hand and see only a small dark blue spot. He would think nothing of it, but all of a sudden he would begin to feel queer in his head. Presently someone would come in and find him in a fit on the floor, and the household would be alarmed. 'Mr. John has had a stroke or a fit,' the people would say. A doctor would be sent for, but his services would be of no avail. In twenty-four hours Mr. John would be dead, and everybody would think that he had died through a fit. There were no bothering coroners' inquests to upset the plans of clever fellows like Duke Francis in those days.

Everybody knows what a Venetian gondola is, but I doubt if everybody knows why they are all of one pattern, and all black and funereal. My Venetian friend gave me the information. What brought the subject up was this. As we passed along the Grand Canal, he pointed out to me Sir Henry Layard's palace. Sir Henry's gondola was waiting at his door. 'Why,' I said, 'it's exactly the same pattern as yours; everybody here seems to have the same pattern and colour. Wouldn't it be gayer if there were a little variety?'

'It would,' replied my friend, after he had pointed out to me the palace of the late Comte de Chambord and the palace which Taglioni, the famous danseuse, bought for her son, and which the naughty son lost in one night at cards. 'It would,' replied my friend: 'but the fashion is the result of a sumptuary law of olden times. In those days there was constant rivalry between the nobles and the wealthy merchants of Venice. The merchants went out in glorious gondolas that cost thousands of pounds. The nobles tried to outdo them. The liveries of the gondoliers cost small fortunes. At last the nobles, who were not so rich as the merchants, found that they were crippling themselves to have more magnificent gondolas than the merchants. So, like artful fellows, having influence in the council of the city, they got a law passed which compelled every gondola on the canal to be of one pattern and one colour, whether private or public.' The design was the gondola which to-day walks the Grand Canal like a thing of li—— like a thing of death, because it is a floating funeral-coach, and nothing else.

A funeral at Venice is very curious. A gondola in black and silver comes for the body at the house of mourning. The coffin is put into the open boat, and the family and the priests then get in and sit round it. The gondoliers are dressed in black and silver, and they row away towards the cemetery, which stands in the middle of a broad lagoon. The sight is a mournful and impressive one. It is far pleasanter to see the great canal and the glorious city bathed in moonlight, and to watch the gondolas filled with gaily-dressed masqueraders and masqueraderesses in all their Carnival finery as they float along to the sound of music and of song. I have never been so carried away by the dreamy beauty of a scene as I was when a boat-load of laughing damsels in dainty costumes stopped just under my sitting-room window one night and serenaded me. It was a delicate little attention, for which I found I was indebted to my Venetian friend.

CHAPTER XVII.

MILAN.

I AM going to see a gentleman cremated at the famous monumental cemetery of Milan. I am specially invited to be present at nine o'clock in the morning, and if my courage does not ooze out of my fingers' ends, I shall certainly go in the interest of my readers who may wish to be cremated, and who would like to know beforehand what they have to go through and what it is like.

To the 'crematorio' of Milan people are brought from all parts of the world. The room in which the furnace is situated is a very nice comfortable one, and there are black chairs set against the walls, in which the friends of the deceased sit and wait while his body is in the oven. The process is very simple. Suppose you want to be cremated. You are brought into the room dressed in a nice white shirt and drawers, and you are gently laid on an iron plate that looks like a large tea-tray turned up at the ends. As soon as the oven is sufficiently heated the door is opened, and you are pushed into a receptacle inside on the tray, much on the same principle as a baker puts bread into the oven. The door is then closed for two hours, and then the iron coffer is taken out. Inside it your friends see a nice white powder and a few fragments of white-coloured bone. That is you. You are then put into an urn, or glass box, or anything you like, and put away in a nice little locker in the great hall of the cemetery. Outside your locker is a lid with your name and the date of your cremation inscribed on it.

I was shown in this hall, in a glass case, the ashes of a lady, aged twenty-six, who was cremated a year or two since. She left her body in her will to be burned, and afterwards shown in the interests of the Cremation Society. Outside, in the grounds, there is a monument to her, and on it in a glass frame is her photograph. She was a very pretty lady, and it is difficult to imagine that she is the same person as the little heap of white ashes in the glass jar. But she is.

It is a general I am to see cremated. He has been brought a long distance in a coffin, and is temporarily deposited in the cemetery. The performance is public, and there are no reserved seats. From what I have seen it is absolutely devoid of offensiveness in any way, and all the officials are smiling, happy-looking folks. I took so much interest in the place that the chief official fancied I might one day be a customer. He pointed out to me that in the hall of the cemetery the places for 'urns' to be deposited were booking fast, and would soon be quite full. He had a capital stall—I mean locker—to let in the third row and one in the fifth. The offer was very tempting, but I didn't close with it.

I don't know whether many people, when they are exhilarated by Nature's champagne, cry out, 'I'm glad I'm alive.' I do sometimes, and just at present I have very good grounds for the exclamation. I have been cremated, and that is enough to make any man rejoice that he can see and hear and eat and smoke a cigar.

As I told you, I had an invitation to the 'crematorio' of Milan to see a general cremated, which I accepted. Wonderful things have happened since then, and that they may be understood let me proceed methodically. On the day preceding the proposed cremation I made up my mind to spend the evening at La Scala, with the exception of the San Carlo at Naples the largest theatre in the world. I sent to the office for a box, and was told there were none; they were all let. If I wanted one I must apply to a subscriber who did not intend to use his that night. Off I started in search of a subscriber. I inquired of the ladies and gentlemen I met in the street, all in my choicest Italian, 'Pray, have you a box at La Scala, and do you intend to use it?' At last in the Galleria Vittorio Emanuele I met an old lady, who told me her master, the Count Somebody, was out of town. I could have his key for fifty francs. I sent to the address she gave, and received the key, and in the evening marched into the theatre, unlocked my box, and was, for the time being, *chez moi*. It seems droll to an Englishman to buy a key instead of a ticket, but this is a common way of doing business in Italy, where, in some of the theatres, the boxes are bought right out by nobles and others for a lifetime. This perpetual proprietorship accounts for the fact that the boxes are many of them differently decorated and lined. Some are blue, some green, some red—all are furnished after the fancy of the owner, and the general effect to the foreign eye is *bizarre* in the extreme.

The performance was, of course, magnificent. They know how to sing and how to mount an opera at La Scala, and there were some processions and stage pictures in 'Don Carlos' that Sir Augustus might have studied, and Sir Henry made notes of. After the opera there was a ballet. It was a prologue and six acts, and I was very interested in it, so much so that I forgot for a long time to look at my watch, and when I did, in the middle of the fourth act, I found it was 1.30.

I went home and to bed at once. I had to be in the cemetery by nine in the morning to see the General cremated, and was terribly tired. I awoke in the morning at 8.30. Then began a struggle in my mind. Should I dress and rush up to the cemetery without my breakfast? I hesitated. A man wants a meal before he sees a sight like that. I hesitated, and I was lost, for I turned over and went to sleep again, and when I woke it was 10.30. The General was finished, and I had not been there to see.

I was sorry that, like my Lord Tomnoddy who went to the coffee-house opposite Newgate, I had slept too long, but after a ballet that lasts until 2 a.m. a man may be excused if he doesn't get up in time for a cremation at nine. I had made special arrangements with the officials and a famous scientific gentleman of Milan, who was most anxious for me to publish an account of the proceedings in England, and the thing worried me a little all day; but at night I stepped into a compartment in the sleeping-car for Lugano, and forgot all about the matter. Just, however, as the train was starting and my eyes were closing in sleep—I had dined well an hour previously—who should enter the car but the scientific gentleman. 'They told me where to find you at the hotel,' he said. 'Come out at once; there's a cremation to-night.' 'But my ticket,' I said; 'I must go on to Lugano.' 'Bother your ticket! Come with me, and see what I'll show you. You'll never regret it.' Before I could expostulate further he had me out of the station and into a cab, and we were soon driving along through the night in the direction of the cemetery.

As we entered the gates the moon was high, and the figures of angels and women in white marble, keeping guard over the graves, had a ghostly effect. It was with something like a shudder that I passed through the black doors of the chapel-like building where the crematory rites are performed. The furnace was roaring already, and the heat was intense. I glanced at the metal tray raised to the level of the oven, expecting to see the body ready, but, to my surprise, this was empty. I turned to my guide. 'Where is the person to be cremated?' I asked. 'Here,' was the reply, and he touched me on the shoulder. Instantly I was seized, and bound, and gagged, and hoisted on to the awful tray, where I lay dumb and helpless. 'You wished to have a thorough knowledge of cremation,' said the fiend who had lured me to this awful place. 'You shall have it.' I tried to scream; I tried to burst my bonds—all, all in vain. The great doors of the oven were flung open, and there came forth a great gust of heat that seemed to scorch my living flesh. Slowly the tray moved nearer and nearer to the mouth of the oven. I was going to my death—to be cremated alive! The heat grew more and more intense. I scorched and singed; my eyeballs started from their sockets; my body seemed to swell and crack. Suddenly with a violent jerk I was shot forward into the oven, the great doors closed on me with a clang—— and—and—the conductor of the sleeping-car came rushing into my berth to know what was the matter.

I woke with a start. The heat was intense, the fumes of the charcoal terrible, and I had been dreaming a dyspeptic dream in my berth. Moral: Never travel by an overheated sleeping-car after thinking about cremation all day.

CHAPTER XVIII.

A REVOLUTION IN TICINO.

ALL things come to those who wait. I have waited nearly a fortnight in Ticino for a revolution, and I have seen it at last. I have seen the soldiers charge the mob, and I have seen the mob stone the soldiers. I have seen the soldiers retire with cracked skulls, and I have seen the citizens flying to the chemists and the doctors to have their bayonet wounds dressed. I have seen a town suddenly seized with panic, the streets cleared, the shops shut, and the cafés barred and bolted. And it all happened in a minute, without the slightest warning. It all happened just when I had packed my portmanteau and was going to leave Ticino because the excitement was over and everything was getting insufferably dull, and the weather was giving the Ticinese a seasonable hint to keep indoors by their wood fires and to abandon politics as an outdoor amusement.

Last Sunday was the day of the general election all over Switzerland for members of the National Council, which sits at Berne. In Ticino the greatest interest attached to the election, because of recent unfortunate events and the terrible pitch which the enmity long existing between the Liberal Party and the Conservative Party had reached.

On Sunday in Ticino things went off pretty quietly. I was in Lugano, and spent the morning watching the voters as they went to the poll and the populace that stood about the public squares and discussed the situation. The Liberals made a big show in Lugano. The trees of liberty, surmounted by the hat of William Tell, were everywhere decorated with the red flag of Radicalism. To some of them were affixed wreaths of laurel 'offered by the Liberal ladies of Lugano'; others were ornamented with Liberal inscriptions couched in language that, to say the least of it, was thorough. The Italian—I beg pardon, the Ticinese—politician is given to discuss matters as much with his hands as with his tongue, and all day long an energetic crowd indulged in vehement finger-wagging and hand-elevating, which would have given a stranger not used to the wealth of Italian gesture an idea that St. Vitus's dance was a national disease.

The Liberals were easily distinguished from the Conservatives by red ties, by red feathers worn bravely in enormous brigand hats, and by red flowers in their buttonholes. Every Liberal sported a little red, and even the Liberal ladies had arrayed themselves in accordance with their political sympathies.

Apart from the idea that the election of October 26 might lead to a little revolution, I was interested in it for another reason. Was not my old friend Agostino Gatti, of the Adelaide Gallery and of the Adelphi Theatre, a Consigliere di Stato? and was not Agostino Gatti up for re-election as one of the six members for Ticino in the National Council of Switzerland?

It was a great day for all Ticino. Every man was expected to vote, and nearly every man did. Some of them travelled miles and miles to fulfil the duty of citizenship. I soon found out how seriously the Ticinese take politics. Very early on Sunday morning my waiter hurried me over my breakfast with a thousand apologies; he was going to vote, and his native place was in a valley across the lake ten miles away. The porter brought me a day's supply of wood to my room before I was up; a thousand pardons, but he had to catch an early train that he might go home to vote. There was not a flyman outside my hotel when I went out; they had all gone to vote. The boats upon the lake lay floating empty on the wave; the boatmen had all gone to vote. When I went into the *salle-à-manger* I quite expected to see a note to the effect that, 'In consequence of all the waiters having gone home to vote, there will be no *table d'hôte*.'

Giuseppe, my sitting-room waiter, is a Conservative; Napoléon, the *salle-à-manger* waiter, is a fierce Radical. Between them I endeavoured to arrive at the truth of the various incidents which they narrated for my benefit. Giuseppe hails from the village to which poor Rossi belonged—Rossi, the unfortunate victim of the brutal outrage of September 11. Rossi was a young man universally beloved and respected. He had only joined the Government a few months. He had never done any man harm; he was only recently married, and he was assassinated in cold blood in the name of civil and religious liberty. Giuseppe trembles so violently with rage when he tells me of Rossi, his fellow-townsman, that I expect him to drop the tray every moment; but Napoléon talks of it calmly, says it was a pity, but won't have it that the Radicals are to blame for it. But I am digressing. Of Giuseppe and Napoléon more anon.

I wait patiently opposite the Municipio all day expecting a demonstration, and none comes. So I fill up my time by noting one or two minor matters. A gentleman selling fowls wrings their necks one by one *coram populo*, and I watch the process till I feel sick. A Conservative dog creates a diversion by having a furious fight with a Radical dog. The dogs are arrayed in their masters' colours, and the red dog walks up to the blue dog in a most insulting manner. Then the row begins, and all the dogs of Lugano rush to the square and take sides. Heaven only knows if it would not have ended in a dog revolution had the Federal troops not interfered. Two soldiers separated the combatants, and once more, thanks to the Federal bayonets, peace is restored.

In the evening we get the news. The Conservatives have gained a majority all over Ticino. The Liberals are glum, and, after a night spent in the cafés, I walk home with Albert Edward, and we both prophesy trouble on the morrow. We have heard what we have heard, and we have seen what we have seen.

On Monday there was general Conservative jubilation. The church bells rang violently; from the mountain-tops guns were fired and bonfires were lighted. The little boys formed themselves into processions, and waved flags and shouted through the villages, and dogs, decked out in Conservative colours, followed proudly at the heels of their little Conservative masters. And here, on the eve of the lamentable outbreak which took place at Lugano on Monday evening, let me give you a few particulars of the first revolution which led up to all the recent trouble and excitement.

The revolution was a prearranged affair. In Lugano they managed it this way. Some men went into a field and made a bonfire, which caused a great smoke. Then some of their confederates suddenly rang the fire-alarm from the church belfry. Out rushed the officers from the Municipio to see what was the matter, and in rushed the revolutionists and took possession of the building. The Government officers were seized and dragged to prison. The mob rushed into the cafés and laid violent hands on prominent Conservatives, yelling, 'To prison! to prison!' It was Bedlam broken loose, for surely there was nothing but madness in what followed.

Every Conservative was threatened by the Liberals—the active Conservatives were actually seized and put in prison—an instance of the height of absurdity to which this so-called 'revolution' was carried. The man on duty at one of the little piers where the steamers embark passengers was known to be a Conservative. He was seized and threatened with imprisonment. 'What for?' he exclaimed. 'You are a Conservative!' yelled his Liberal aggressors. The same thing happened to shopkeepers, to boatmen, to fly-drivers; the one cry was, 'To prison with the Conservatives!'—and all this was done in the sacred name of Liberty, Equality, and Fraternity.

It is really worth pausing for a moment to reflect that these things were actually done in a Republic, and by a party whose watchword was 'Liberty.' It is difficult to treat the thing as anything but a huge burlesque. 'In the name of Liberty I put you in prison because your political views are not mine.' Read, mark, learn, and inwardly digest it—reflect on it! Here is a Republic which claims to be the government of the free by the free, and in this Republic there is a party which calls itself the party of freedom, and its first act, when by force or by stratagem it has snatched temporary power, is to seize and imprison every fellow-citizen whose views upon politics and religion are at variance with its own.

My own belief is that the Liberals of Ticino in their discontent allowed themselves to be the dupes and the tools of a party of disorder, a party which has its headquarters over the frontier. I have seen upon the walls of Bellinzona a proclamation issued by a society which has its headquarters in Italy, and, putting two and two together, I look a little below the surface of what is generally called politics for the origin of the Ticino revolt against law and order. These things might perhaps be left for the Ticinese to settle among themselves, but unfortunately they have been done in the name of 'the Liberal party,' and Liberalism generally all over the world is injured and discredited by such a display of intolerance and persecution on the part of a section of those who profess it and make it their watchword.

But, after all, but for the brutal murder of Rossi, and some subsequent bloodshed, the whole affair might perhaps have been charitably dismissed as a display of what the German calls 'Kinderei.' The remark of a Cockney tourist who was in Lugano with me, that it was 'like a lot of kids playing at revolution,' is a fair translation of the German expression. The utter childishness of some of the proceedings which are now agitating the Swiss Republic is beyond dispute. The Ticinese have given us a revolution *pour rire*, and the whole thing, the murder of Rossi apart, is a cyclone in a coffee-cup, a hurricane in a half-pint pot.

So much for the revolution of September 11; now for the revolution of October 27. I have told you that the Conservatives of Lugano rang the church bells in their joy. On Monday afternoon the Liberals, having had enough of the Conservative rejoicings, thought they would have a turn. So they brought a cannon on the public square and began to discharge it. Now, cannon-firing in a public square is not exactly a parlour pastime, and an officer who was in charge of a small body of soldiers ordered the gay Liberal youths to 'cease firing.' They argued the point; the officer insisted, and then—well, nobody knows how it began. The Conservatives say the mob threw stones at the officer; the Liberals say the soldiers attacked the crowd; at any rate, stones were thrown and the mob was charged, and presently the soldiers were prodding the people and blood was flowing and stones were flying, and Lugano had another little revolution in miniature all to itself. I was with Albert Edward, and in the middle of it, and I am not ashamed to confess that we executed a strategic movement to the rear and sought the friendly shelter of the Farmacia Internazionale.

Half an hour afterwards the streets were cleared. Every shop and every café was shut, and only groups of excited men gathered under the arcades and discussed the situation. It had been severe while it lasted. I saw plenty of blood—less would have satisfied me—and unfortunately a number of women and children in the crowd were seriously frightened, and I believe a few of them hurt, in the absurd proceedings. A number of wounds were dressed by the chemists of the town that evening, and several of the soldiers were taken to the hospital.

All the troops in Ticino are from the German cantons. Between the German Swiss and the Italian Swiss there is no love lost. The troops have been attacked, and some of the soldiers injured by the people. Relations are now naturally more strained than ever. Some unlucky day something may happen, and then—— Well, let us hope for the best.

The journals of the rival parties and the placards of the rival parties are not going the way to mend matters. *Il Credente Cattolico* comes out every day with a black band round it, and it prints on its title-page 'Il Sangue di Rossi invoca Giustizia'—the blood of Rossi calls for justice. It also pleasantly describes the Liberals as the 'congrega di Satana'—the congregation of Satan. *La Liberta*, after a terrific onslaught, calls attention 'alle infami manovre Radicali,' and I count the words 'infamy' and 'infamous' fourteen times on one page. *Il Dovere*, a Radical sheet, hurls every awful adjective in the Italian language at the Conservative party, and finishes up with a fit of violent hysterics. The *Gazette Ticinese* can find no heading to its fierce wrath at the result of Sunday's election, and so contents itself with an inarticulate '!?!' while another journal declares the vote to be valueless, and writes in huge letters that the Conservative majority is an iniquity, and cries aloud in mighty wrath that 12,066 Liberals return only 35 Deputies to the Grand Council, while 12,833 Ultramontanes return 77. Both sides call each other assassins, and both sides call each other thieves, and the Conservative journals always speak of the Liberals as 'the party of brigands,' and it is evident that in Ticino a Republican form of government has not been productive of liberty or equality, and most decidedly not of fraternity.

The placards on the walls are all couched in fiery language, with the exception of Colonel Kunzli's proclamation, which simply forbids any public meeting to be held in any place in Ticino. 'Proibisco ogni assemblia populare in tutto il Cantone Ticino.' (What do you think of that in a Republic, my Trafalgar Square friends?) The Liberal addresses al Popolo Ticinese denounce the Conservatives as ruffians, liars, slanderers, thieves, and oppressors; and a proclamation which is posted up all over the walls of Bellinzona itself, within a few feet of the Government House, and signed by 'The Liberal Committee *in Milan*,' calls upon the people to drive out a Government which for years has tyrannized over the country and been guilty of intolerance, assassination, the liberation of the guilty, the condemnation of the innocent, persecution, swindling, extortion, robbery, 'and all possible subdivisions of these and other iniquities.' I have never read as much strong language in my whole life as I have been compelled to peruse during the last fortnight in Ticino.

To-day (Wednesday) we have had another 'incident' in Lugano. This morning a great hulking fellow told a little boy of twelve to go and insult the sentries on duty at the Municipio. The lad, nothing loath, trotted off and called the sentries all the bad names he knew. One sentry ordered him off. The boy, encouraged by some roughs, refused to go, whereupon the sentry, like an idiot, prodded him playfully in the arm with his bayonet.

Soldiers and populace alike seem to have lost their heads, and now are thirsting for each other's gore. A man in a café told me that if it went on they would fire at the soldiers from the windows. Good business this. O Liberty! Liberty! what crimes, etc.

That the military fear a rising is certain. When the train came in from Milan on Tuesday a guard of soldiers with fixed bayonets was posted at every entrance. A number of agitators from Milan were expected to come to the aid of the Luganese. 'My God!' exclaimed the station-master, when I asked him what the armed force at the station meant, 'one would think we were all murderers here.'

The Lucerne and Berne soldiers will be heartily glad to get back home. They have been badly treated in Ticino, where, although Swiss, and the real Swiss, they are looked upon as foreigners. The arrangements made for their accommodation have not increased the pleasure of their stay. Some of them have had to sleep and live in a church, lying down at night on straw spread about on the floor. The accommodation provided for the others is even worse, being at a disused seminary, where they have absolutely had no water-supply at all, and have had to go down to the lake to wash.

Let us turn from the revolution to more pleasant matters. To-day is market-day in Lugano. The greatest crowd is round a man who is displaying on a pole an enormous and highly-coloured picture of a man dripping with blood, who is stabbing a very *décolletée* lady in blue silk. The banner is labelled in huge letters, 'Jack, l'Assassino di Londra! Lo Sventratore di Donne!' The man is doing a roaring trade in a penny book which is no less than the life and adventures of our old friend Jack the Ripper.

The country people who have come from the mountains and the valleys are positively trampling each other down in their eagerness to purchase copies, and presently the vendor raises his price from a penny to twopence. What a reputation has Jack made for himself! All over the world he is famous. Gladstone is not in the same street with him as a European celebrity. Such is fame!

The women of Ticino are surely the hardest worked women in the world. In the lower classes they are simply beasts of burden. The little girl of twelve and the old woman of eighty carry huge loads everywhere, while the boys and the men carry nothing. I meet old women toiling up the great mountains with huge baskets on their backs. In these baskets they carry not only goods, but animals. I have seen a woman toiling along with a big calf in the basket on her back and a great bundle of faggots under her arm. In the town it is the same. All the heavy porterage is done by the women. At one of the steamboat piers yesterday it was a woman who came for the luggage, and she positively reeled under the weight of a Saratoga trunk, while the men sat with their hands in their pockets and smoked cigars.

From this same steamer there landed a couple of men of the peasant class. Their wives, with baskets on their backs, were waiting for them. The men had a number of packages with them.

These they instantly loaded on to their wives, and then, lighting their cigars, strolled off up the mountain path that led to their village. And behind them at a long distance, heavily laden, toiled their beasts of burden—their wives.

CHAPTER XIX.

LOCARNO.

FROM Bellinzona a local train conveys the traveller to Locarno, which is a small town at the extreme head of Lake Maggiore. I had heard a wonderful account of Locarno, and had been assured that in its perfect peace and pure air the malady from which I was suffering would rapidly disappear. I arrived at Locarno full of hope. I also arrived in a heavy storm of rain. I looked around me, and I saw nothing but water and mist and mud. The mountains were wrapped in black cloaks of cloud. The walls of the houses were covered with moss and mushrooms and toadstools, and in the roadways the bulrushes grew several feet high.

On the way to the hotel we passed a few shops. Every shop seems to deal in the same article—umbrellas, green umbrellas and red umbrellas. They hung in rows along the walls of the town; they were piled high in the shop-windows; every man, woman, and child carried one, and still the rain came down upon the desolate scene.

There is no mistake about the dampness of Locarno when it is damp. It is owing to the enormous amount of moisture which Locarno gets in combination with the full glare of an Italian sun that it boasts unique phenomena in the way of vegetation. You find the southern and the Alpine plant in absolute juxtaposition. At one moment your eye is dazzled by the full glory of a tropical garden; at the next you are gazing at peat bogs and into moist green hollows crowded with the sedges of the moors. Let me be fair to Locarno, for it has been fair to me. A fairer place (when it doesn't rain) it would be almost impossible to find. From the sunny shores of the glorious lake the mighty mountains rise, with soft green skirts of vine and caps of snow. In a hundred gardens the red and white azalea, the camellia, and the wisteria make great clusters of colour. Gaily painted villas, fair white spires, and picturesque villages dot the heights, and over all there floats a balmy southern breeze that bears upon its gentle wings the perfume of a hundred flowers.

Before we left Locarno we explored the beauties of the neighbourhood, and we started with climbing a mountain. One glorious mountain walk we had which will linger in my memory until the last guard blows his whistle, and I start for a country to which as yet neither Murray nor Bradshaw nor Baedeker has published a guide. We started from Locarno for Mergoscia, ascending the mountains by the path that leads to the Madonna del Sasso (Our Lady of the Rock). One starlit night in 1480 a monk kneeling in prayer looked up the mountain. Suddenly a glorious sea of light bathed the rocky peak that rises above the town, and the Virgin was seen surrounded by adoring angels. The monk interpreted his vision as a wish of Heaven that on this rocky mount a chapel should be built. The money was raised, and to-day Our Lady of the Rock, far above the town of Locarno, is one of the famous sights of Switzerland.

It is a toilsome journey up the mountain-side and past the countless shrines to the church, but the traveller is rewarded with many a quaint sight by the way for his pains. The old-world peasant population was probably gratified by the realism of some of the groups which are placed here and there up the hill like small waxwork exhibitions. You come to a kind of stone grotto; you peer in through the iron bars, and you start back astonished. You are looking into a stable, with real straw and real stalls, and in a manger you see the infant Saviour lying, and the Holy Family grouped around him. A couple of donkeys are peering into the manger, and nothing is spared that contributes to the almost sensational realism of the scene. A little farther up you peep into another cave, and you see a number of figures sitting at a long table laid with plates and glasses. In front of each figure is a small roll, and a waiter is just coming into the room with a big fish on a plate. You gradually recognise the fact that you are assisting at the Lord's Supper, and you turn almost with a sigh to think that a beautiful faith ever needed such coarse theatrical adjuncts to impress it on the minds of the populace.

Our Lady of the Rock is much resorted to by people in pain and affliction, and the naves of the church are lined with curious *ex votos*. No chamber of horrors ever contained a more terrible series of accidents than these pictures represent. Here is a little boy under a carriage wheel, rescued just as the wheel is on his chest. Here is a man falling from a bridge into a river, and just caught by the leg as he is going head first into the water. Here is a woman hurled over a precipice, and caught by the branch of a tree. In one terrible picture a man's nose is being blown off by his own gun; in another, a gentleman is accidentally mowing his own legs off with a scythe. It is a great relief, after gazing at these pictorial horrors, in which the blood is always laid on thick by the artist, to get out into the open air again, and climb higher up the hill to the narrow path that leads to the Alpine village of Orselina.

Through Orselina we pass over the spur of the mountain to Contra, another village which is perched up higher still. These Alpine villages look beautifully picturesque from the valley below, but they are sad and grim enough when you are in them. All the poetry is gone when you wind in and out through the little tortuous street and see the squalor and the poverty in which the people live. The rough stone walls look so forbidding; the rooms seen through the battered doors look so black and cheerless as the smoke of the wood fire curls slowly out of them. All the poetry is going as you peer into them, and there is no poetry at all left when you have seen the inhabitants. Old men toil painfully along with trembling hands; women, bent almost double beneath the burthen they bear on their backs, pass you with sad faces and dull eyes. The women in these Alpine villages do the work of animals. They are really beasts of burden. They are loaded as in our country we load carts and barrows. I have seen an old woman toiling up a hill with a great wicker basket on her back in which were two calves and a pig. The basket the women have perpetually strapped to their back is called a *gerlo*, and is made to contain anything, from an elephant to a packet of pins.

Half the houses in these Alpine villages are deserted, as are many of the houses lower down in the valleys. Only the old men and the women and children seem to be left in the others. The reason of this is not far to seek. The Ticinese have been the great emigrating race of Switzerland. The men of the hills and valleys are scattered over the world, and most of them have climbed the hill of fortune. Some of them have reached the summit. From a village near Locarno, which is now full of houses barred and bolted and falling into decay, have gone forth some of the richest men in California. In that far-off land the owners of these houses made a fortune by their industry, and then their fellow-villagers, hearing of it, set out to try and do the same.

Everywhere as one wanders over this part of Switzerland one finds that the manhood is gone. The Ticinese are far away in Italy, in France, in England, in America, and everywhere their industry, their business talents, and their thrift have carried them triumphantly to affluence.

But though he is far away the man of Ticino does not forget his old home, or his poorer brethren left there. From over the seas every year comes the emigrant's gold for the village poor, and for the Church, and for every good object that can be thought of.

The finest peal of bells in Ticino is the gift of a man of the valley of Maggia, who is far away in California. On one of the bells is this inscription:

> *'Anche attraverso sterminati mari,*
> *Degli Svizzeri il cor vola a'suoi cari,'*

which, being translated, reads:

> *'Though doomed beyond the boundless seas to roam,*
> *The Switzer ne'er forgets his childhood's home.'*

The fortune of the Ticinese emigrants now settled in California alone is estimated at nearly two millions, and from one valley in Ticino, the Vallemaggia, there are forty men who went out from a little cottage such as I have described, and who could now any one of them buy up almost the entire district. Splendid emigrants are these brave, determined fellows—emigrants who benefit not only themselves, but the lands to which they go, and who never, as they climb the rungs of Fortune's ladder, and build up new homes and new associations in the land of their adoption, forget the dear old home, or those less fortunate companions who still remain there.

I have interrupted my walk to say something about Swiss emigration, but it is a subject that must force itself upon you in whichever way you turn in this portion of Switzerland. Emigration is writ large in every valley. It accounts for much that you see which otherwise would be inexplicable. The subject was forced upon me when I came to Contra and saw the empty village homes of the rich men far away.

I don't mind confessing to you that after leaving Contra I grew a little nervous. Blondin used to get £100 a time for walking on the tight-rope. I got nothing for walking from Contra to Mergoscia, but there were times when I should have preferred Mr. Blondin's job, even if in addition to performing gratis I had had to pay for the rope and the pole out of my own pocket. Just after leaving Contra the road crosses a most fearful abyss. Down thousands of feet below you dashes a mad, roaring torrent. You clutch the side of the frail mountain bridge, and you peer over into the yawning jaws of death below. I have seen some grand sights, but never before have I seen anything so sublime in its grandeur as that wild rocky scene, the far-stretching vale, the roaring torrent in the gorge below.

We crept over that bridge on tiptoe. We neither of us spoke a word. The scene was too grand for words. We were both awestruck, and both just a little nervous, for after crossing the bridge the road became more awful still.

It certainly was a terrible feat we were about to attempt, but I had set out to go to Mergoscia, and I didn't want to be beaten. We had been told that, owing to a portion of the path having been carried down into the abyss by a landslip, the road was not very good, but we had never imagined it was so awful as it now appeared to us. The road absolutely led across the face of a perpendicular rock! To look down below was to turn sick, and there wasn't even the pretence of a wall on the outside edge of the path! It was barely wide enough to creep over, walking one foot in front of the other, and the rock above jutted out at places so that you were forced nearer the edge.

It was at this point that the road had recently broken away. While we were standing and hesitating before we stepped upon the ledge, a lad came up behind whistling, and with his hands in his pockets stepped boldly upon the broken path, skipped over some bits of rock which had fallen upon it, and was presently safe round the terrible jut and on the broader and sounder pathway that led direct to Mergoscia.

That was enough for us. Steadying ourselves and clenching our teeth, we stepped forward. It was a very bad minute as we nervously crossed the jut. We dared not look down the face of the rock, or think what lay below us. But we arrived safely on the other side, and then we paused to take breath, and we confessed to each other that we wouldn't do it again for a thousand pounds.

The village of Mergoscia stands at a dizzy height on the side of a sheer precipice. Looking back at the road by which we had reached it, it seemed impossible that anyone but an acrobat could traverse it. It was afterwards explained to us that the road was about to be repaired, that half of it had recently fallen away, and that while it was in its present condition the general way of approaching Mergoscia was from the opposite side of the gorge. That night, after I fell asleep, that awful path to Mergoscia came back to me in my dreams, and I woke up just as I was falling into the abyss below. The walk is described in a guide-book as 'one of the most sublimely grand and romantic on the Alps.' Romantic it certainly was, but besides the romance there was just a little too much reality about it to make it an unmixed pleasure.

There is a town on Lake Maggiore where all the cooks come from. It is called Brisago. The first person Columbus met when he discovered America was a cook from Brisago, which brings me to another of Albert Edward's jokes. He was talking to Lord Mayor Monico and the Right Hon. S. Gatti at Dongio, and he said: 'Ah, if William Tell had been a Ticinese, do you know what he would have done with the apple after he had shot it?' 'No,' said Lord Mayor Monico, 'I don't.' 'He would have made it into an apple dumpling, and opened a restaurant with it,' replied A. E. And everybody laughed so heartily that several avalanches fell in the neighbourhood.

There is one thing which cannot fail to strike the close observer of Swiss contemporary history, and that is the extraordinary contempt which the rival political parties have for each other. The Radical and the Conservative members of the Council never associate in private or in public life. They won't even sit at the same café, they won't put up at the same hotel, they won't walk on the same side of the street.

And oh, the dreadful things they say of each other! The Conservatives assure me that the Radicals would not hesitate to set fire to Switzerland, or to blow it up with dynamite upon the slightest provocation. The Radicals tell me that the Conservatives are ruining the country; that they want to make the people slaves, and divide Switzerland among themselves. It is a sight to see a Radical and a

Conservative meet accidentally. The scowl is a thing to remember for a lifetime. You can almost see them arch their backs at each other like rival tomcats, and you are quite astonished when they don't spit. There is no place in the world where political antagonism becomes such real and personal antagonism as in the land of the gentleman who immortalized the apple trick.

One fine day we went over on a specially-conducted expedition to the Val Gatti—the beautiful and romantic valley, some four or five miles from Biasca, from which the celebrated brothers came forth many years ago to conquer London. Our expedition was almost a royal progress. In Bellinzona we were entertained by Mr. Stephen, M.P. for Switzerland, at a sumptuous breakfast, at the fifteenth course of which Albert Edward broke down, and shed tears because he couldn't eat any more; then we all adjourned to the Presidential Palace, where we had cigars with the Government; and then it came on to thunder and to lighten and to hail, and presently—note this, for it is a remarkable fact—it became so pitch dark that we had to light lamps in order to see each other—and this was between twelve and one o'clock in the day. When in glorious Switzerland in the middle of May I saw the gas and the lamps and the candles alight in all the shops and houses at noon, I felt that I owed some slight apology to London for the unkind things I have sometimes said about it.

By one o'clock, however, the storm was over and gone, and the sun shone out, and then we took train for Biasca. At Biasca we alighted, and found a carriage and four horses, and postilions in magnificent uniforms, waiting to take us over the marvellous four miles of mountain road that lead to Dongio, the beautiful spot in the Val de Blenio in which the Palazzo Gatti is situated.

It is impossible for me to describe that drive. My adjectives would not hold out, and my neck is still aching with the twisting I gave it while endeavouring to gaze up at the kaiser crags and monarch mountains that stand like solemn sentinels guarding the glorious Gatti valley. The drive was spirit-stirring and sublime, and the face of Stephen, M.P., positively beamed as he saw how much we were impressed with the glory of his mountain home. We only had one or two trifling accidents by the way. Once the postilions took a road that the M.P. didn't wish them to go 'for fear of our nerves,' and, in endeavouring to turn round on a wooden bridge across a torrent, they came so near landing us all upside down that the author of a hundred melodramas jumped out for his life. Unfortunately, he hopped out of the frying pan into the fire. Our carriage righted itself; but he jumped badly, and fell on his nose, and his hat went over into the roaring torrent, and the big waves banged it merrily against the rocks, and the last he saw of it it was going down the valley at the rate of fifty miles an hour.

Avalanches fall occasionally in the Val Gatti, and sides of mountains come down without being invited to do so by the inhabitants. I must confess that every now and then, as we dashed along a narrow road, with a yawning abyss below us and about a couple of billion tons of overhanging rock above us, and it began to look like thunderstorms on the weather quarter, I began to think that an Alpine life has its bad quarters of an hour. But we arrived safely at last at Dongio, and, when we reined our reeking steeds up in front of the Palazzo Gatti, and a deputation of Dongio maidens came and presented us with bouquets of mountain flowers, we felt that we had not risked our precious lives in vain.

In front of the Palazzo Gatti the Tree of Liberty is planted in honour of Mr. Stephen, M.P. for the Valley. From the tree float flags and emblems and ribbons. It is by this tree that you know you are on the domain of a patrician, a citizen of renown. There are plenty of beautiful houses scattered about the valley, and any amount near Dongio. 'English,' says the Dongio M.P., and you gather at once what he means. The owners are of the London-Swiss division. The names of most of the grandees of the valley sound familiar to a Londoner's ear. The mayor of Dongio, who gives us a right hearty welcome, is Signor Monico. I fancy I've heard that name in Piccadilly. Our host at Aqua Rossa, a health station higher up the valley, is Signor Gianella. I think that name is to be found in London day by day. Whenever I say to the M.P., 'Whose palazzo is that?' he mentions a name that is familiar to my cockney ears. One pretty villa, standing a little way out of the village, specially attracts my attention. 'Whose house is that?' I say. 'That,' replies the M.P., 'is the house of our manager at the Gallery.' I uncover my head and bow to the residence. Without knowing it, I have been leaning over the garden wall of the Palazzo Gallizia!

From Dongio we drove to Aqua Rossa. As we pass every hat in the village flies off, and all the old ladies drop curtsies. Mr. Stephen is a great man in these parts, and our progress is a triumphal one. While our host has gone into a house to pay a call we converse with our driver. We ask him, through Albert Edward, who speaks Italian as his mother tongue, many little questions, and he is filled with admiration and reverence for the great men of the valley who live far away in London. He assures us that the whole valley belongs to the Gattis, and that he thinks all the mountains do too. He isn't quite sure if they have any more valleys anywhere else, but they could have if they liked. We asked him if he has heard that the Gattis are going to buy up Switzerland, and turn it into a public company. He thinks a minute, and says, No; he has not heard that, but he thinks they have something to do with the big hotel at Aqua Rossa, where, right in the heart of the mountains, there are to be the electric light and the telephone, and your hair is to be brushed by machinery.

We go up the valley to the hotel at Aqua Rossa, which is being enlarged. The 'Red Water,' from which the Grande Stabilmento Balneario takes its name, is a marvellous cure for dyspepsia, skin diseases, bronchitis, etc. The situation of the hotel is magnificent. Five miles up the valley, far from the busy hum of men, you can look from your window over a glorious panorama of mountain and vale. The air is exhilarating as champagne, and there is no next-morning headache in it. At the hotel you can have the baths and the treatment, the electric light, and perfect peace, and the pension is only 8fr. a day. I have taken a room for the season there myself, and the entire staff have guaranteed that after a fortnight's treatment I shall never know a pang of dyspepsia again. Ye gods, what an angel I shall return to my native shores if it comes off!

The shades of night were falling fast ere we left the hospitable homes of the Val Gatti. Our drive back to Biasca in the darkness made us sit tight and clutch each other, and think now and then that we might have been better men had we tried; but we skirted the torrents and dodged the avalanches all right, and we were no sooner in the train than we all fell fast asleep, overcome with fatigue and the mountain air, and we should probably have slept and been taken on to Calais or Milan or Timbuctoo if Albert Edward had not snored so violently as to alarm the engine-driver and to cause him to pull up and hold a hurried conversation with the guard. They both listened, and felt certain that some terrible convulsion of nature was taking place in the mountains. They came to the carriages and begged the passengers to alight. 'We fear an earthquake or a landslip,' they said. 'This thunderous roaring betokens mischief.' But when they came to our carriage and found the great convulsion of nature was only Albert Edward snoring, they woke us up and apologized to the other passengers, and we resumed our journey. And so ended one of the most remarkable journeys it has ever been my lot to perform.

CHAPTER XX.

BERLIN EN PASSANT.

SNOW! Last night the moon shone with a steel-blue light in the cloudless heavens, and the sentinel stars stood out clear and bright, as on a frosty winter's evening. Never had I seen Berlin look more beautiful. Long after the good citizens had retired to their homes, I lingered under the lime-trees and gave myself up to the enchantment of the scene. It was five-and-twenty years almost to the day since I had set foot within the Prussian capital, and old memories crowded about me as I was lost in reverie. It was not until I turned my steps homeward that I found out how bitterly cold it was. I had not had time to think about the weather, or to remember what season of the year it was. But, walking home, it suddenly occurred to me that it was the merry month of May, and that in a few weeks it would be June. In Berlin it might have been a good old-fashioned Christmas Eve.

And to-day it is snowing—snowing in a way not to be mistaken. There is no half-hearted business about this snow. It doesn't change to rain just as it falls, like a snow that is ashamed of itself and endeavours to conceal its true character. Down it comes in flakes the size of shilling pieces, and the wayfarers' umbrellas are as white as their noses are red and their lips are blue.

Only forty-eight hours before, as I stepped gaily into the train at Victoria on the day of the Two Thousand Guineas, I said jokingly, 'When I travel I like to see Snow.' But I didn't mean the snow that fell upon me so unmercifully in Berlin. I meant the excellent Mr. Snow, who, promoted from the Club train to the management of the Sleeping Car Company's London office, still devotes himself to the comfort of Continental travellers, and makes the way pleasant before them. I had reason to be grateful to this most seasonable

Snow. Not only did he take the trouble to send me the winner of the Two Thousand to Dover, but when I arrived at Calais I found that he had ordered by telegraph an excellent dinner for me at the buffet, and had reserved me a compartment in the Cologne express, for all of which I felt exceedingly grateful. The snow that awaited me at Berlin was not nearly so agreeable. Still, as it is over, and the sun once more asserts its rights in the heavens, we may as well take the unseasonable downfall as a little practical joke on the part of the clerk of the weather, and say no more about it.

The sleeping cars which run between Calais and Cologne in connection with the Club train are excellent, but as I didn't go to sleep until midnight, and had to turn out at half-past two fully dressed at the frontier and fit obstinate keys into troublesome locks, and then had to undress again with the pleasant knowledge that at five a.m. I should be turned out at Cologne, I can't say that, taken as a whole, my night's rest was all that a selfish man could wish for himself. At half-past five, however, I had some excellent coffee at the Cologne buffet, and then went into the cathedral and assisted at a most interesting ceremony, in which a bishop was taking the leading part. I stayed in the cathedral till seven, and at twenty minutes to eight I found one of the nicest trains I ever saw in my life waiting to take me on to Berlin. It wasn't a special train of luxury due to private enterprise, with a premium of fifty or seventy-five per cent. to pay for the privilege of sitting in it, but a train provided by the Government for ordinary first and second class passengers.

A polite conductor, having inspected my ticket, begged me to do him the honour of seating myself, and ushered me into a comfortable compartment containing four easy-chairs and a small dining-table. At the same time he handed me a card containing a map of the route, the time of arrival at each station, and a list of various hot and cold delicacies and refreshing beverages which could be served *en route* to the traveller. The prices attached were most moderate. For instance, feeling hungry about eleven o'clock (remember, I breakfasted soon after five), I touched an electric bell, and instantly a waiter appeared bowing and smiling in front of my easy-chair. I ordered a beefsteak and potatoes and a bottle of Mosel wine. The steak was tenderness itself, and the potatoes were excellent. For this repast, including bread, butter, and cheese, I paid, according to the tariff, 1s. 6d., and the bottle of wine was

2s. Everything on the bill was as moderately priced. For instance, a plate of soup and bread is 4d.; a plate of cold meat, with the usual etceteras, 1s.; half a cold chicken and bread, 1s. 6d. The 'drinks' are quite as reasonable. A bottle of seltzer is 3d.; a lemonade, 3d.; a bottle of beer, 3d.; and the wines are proportionately cheap. When you think of these prices you must also remember that the entire train is on the corridor system, and is luxuriously fitted up in first and second class sitting-rooms, with every convenience for the toilet, and that there is a large staff of attendants. Whatever faults the German Government may have, it has made express railway travelling the comfort of the many instead of the luxury of the few.

In Berlin, when you arrive at a railway-station, an official gives you a huge brass plate with a number of a cab on it, and you can't have a cab without you have the brass plate. It is an excellent idea if you can get a porter to carry the plate; if you can't, it takes less out of you to walk to your destination.

Berlin cabs are first-class and second-class. The first-class cab is one in which the united ages of the driver, the horse, and the cab are under one hundred years. As soon as they are more than that they become second class.

Berlin is, I should fancy, now the cleanest and the best-lighted city in Europe. After months of darkest London, brightest Berlin is a distinct relief to me. From end to end in every street and in every shop it is a blaze of electric light and clean white colour.

I went to the steeplechases at Charlottenburg, where a few days previously our well-known gentleman rider, Mr. 'Charley Thompson,' had captured the hearts of the Berliners by his plucky riding in the race for the gold cup, which he won after being thrown heavily and having a can-can performed upon his chest by his horse. Berlin racing is a calm and serious affair. The officers (in uniform) ride their own horses, and all the soldiers on the course come to attention and salute as they pass by. No bookmakers are allowed, and you have to pay ten marks for a special ticket before you can even back a horse at the 'totalizer.' The object of this is to make it impossible for the working classes to gamble, and it is highly effective.

At one time anybody could patronize the Pari-Mutuel, but the working classes lost their money and then kicked up a row about it, and said they were ruined. The Kaiser heard of it, and stopped all racing at once. But after about six weeks he cooled down and gave permission for racing to be resumed again under certain conditions. The ten marks admission to the Pari-Mutuel enclosure is one of them. It is thus that a paternal Government protects the earnings of its workmen. With a view also of keeping the working classes from the racecourse, no racing is now permitted on Sunday. This is 'all on account of the 'Lizer'—the totalizer.

Kaiser Wilhelm, in spite of his eccentricities, which the Germans freely acknowledge, is undoubtedly immensely popular with his people. He is a German of Germans, and the Germany-for-the-Germans feeling was never so strong as it is at present. Our national motto is 'Made in Germany,' but the Vaterland does not return the compliment. 'Made in England' is not a common object of the seashore in the Kaiser's dominions.

They tell many amusing stories in Berlin of the strength of the 'national' feeling. When Queen Victoria sent the Kaiser's baby-boy a pair of shoes, knitted with her own royal and great-grandmotherly hands, the Emperor shook his head and laid them aside. 'A German prince,' he said, 'must wear German shoes.' And the baby's little feet were at once duly encased in the home-made article.

I was in a blissful condition of lazy don't-careism, enjoying myself in my own way, lounging in the sunshine (it turned suddenly warm after that snowstorm) 'unter den Linden,' sitting outside the confectioner's eating ices, smoking cigarettes, and drinking chocolate, when in an evil hour I came suddenly upon an old German friend, who has been long a resident in Berlin. He insisted at once upon being my guide, philosopher, and friend. He said that he would 'take me about' and show me everything. He has kept his word, and I have had to telegraph home for new boots.

I remember an old song which was in years gone by a great favourite with Italian prime donne during the London opera season. They used to take it as an encore in the middle of various centuries and under every variety of surrounding circumstances. I think it was called 'Home, Sweet Home.' There was a passage in it which, as far as I could gather from the singers' accent and 'variations,' ran somewhat after this fashion:

'Through places and palaces though I may roam,
Be it ever so humble, there's no place like home.'

Since my friend swooped down on me I have been roaming through nothing but places and palaces—especially palaces. Last Sunday, although I was dog tired, he banged at my bedroom-door at the unearthly hour of nine, and bore me off breakfastless to Potsdam and palaced me to such an extent that the sight of an ordinary middle-class dwelling would have been a positive relief.

He conducted me through Babelsburg, the charming summer palace of old Kaiser Wilhelm; he took me all over the Marble Palace, in which the Crown Princes of Prussia reside as soon as they are old enough; and he made me visit every nook and corner of Sans Souci, and gave off the life of Frederick the Great in chapters—a chapter in each room. I have always respected the memory of Frederick the Great because he was so kind to his dogs, and buried them in the palace grounds and put up stones to their memory. For that I long ago forgave him for playing the flute and painting ladies with two right feet and other anatomical eccentricities; but after three hours of Sans Souci I began to resent Frederick the Great as a personal injustice, and I wasn't in the least sympathetic when my friend explained to me that the great man was a martyr to the gout and suffered terribly with his nerves.

I was trotted over more Potsdam palaces after Sans Souci, and was graciously admitted to the private apartments of the imperial family, not usually shown to strangers. At any other time I should have felt flattered, but so thoroughly worn out was I that even the sight of the imperial nursery and the imperial clothes-horse, on which the imperial baby-linen is dried in front of the imperial fire, failed to put me in a good temper; and at last, as my friend was dragging me up the steps of another palace to show me a room in which everything was solid silver, I turned round and fled, and never halted until I had jumped into a train that was starting for Berlin, where I arrived just in time to put on a pair of carpet-slippers, and in these I had to rush off to Kroll's Theatre to see 'Die lustigen Weiber von Windsor' ('The Merry Wives of Windsor'), as the performance commenced at the unearthly hour of seven. I have gone through a great deal in my time, but I never expected to have to go through six palaces in one day. After that you will easily understand how the words of the poet who preferred his humble home to roaming through palaces came home to me.

CHAPTER XXI.

PRAGUE.

WHEN a man wakes up in the morning and can't quite make out where he is, and the first thing that catches his eyes as they wander inquiringly round an unfamiliar bedroom is an electric bell, and underneath it these words:

> '*Na sklepnika, rate 1 nou;*
> *Na panskou, rate 2 kráte;*
> *Na poshluhu, rate 3 kráte;*'

he may fairly be excused if he feels like a stranger in a strange land. It will probably dawn upon him that somewhere amid these printed specimens of an unknown tongue there is lurking a request that if he wants the waiter he will ring once; that if he requires the chambermaid he will ring twice; and that if he needs the services of the boots he will ring thrice. This is what gradually shaped itself in my mind when I woke up the other morning in Prague, and found myself face to face with the Bohemian or Czechish language.

My earliest recollections of Prague are associated with a piece of well-thumbed music which used to lie about on a piano, and was something to do with a battle. Later on it cropped up occasionally in the schoolroom in connection with a gentleman named Huss, who got into trouble early in the Fourteens; but the world-famous old town fairly burnt itself into my memory in the now almost forgotten lines of poor Prowse, 'Nicholas' of *Fun*:

> '*The longitude's rather uncertain,*
> *The latitude's equally vague;*
> *But that person I pity who knows not the city,*
> *The beautiful city of Prague.*'

It was not of the Bohemia over which Francis Josef reigns to-day that the young poet sang, but of that vaster Bohemia which in years gone by was the happy land of the children of art, of letters, and of song. 'La Vie de Bohème' exists no more. The old Bohemians have turned their backs upon their tents, and live in stucco villas. They have crushed the clay pipe under the heels of their patent-leather boots, and taken to cigarettes. They have ceased to herd together in the bonds of brotherhood; they go into Society and eye each other superciliously when they get crushed together on the staircases of the nobility.

But, though the old rhyme has lost its reason, it was the one that came back to me first when I found myself in the real Prague of the true Bohemians. These Bohemians, too, have their song, though I doubt if that, too, has not grown old and a little out of fashion. The old national ditty, *Kde domof mug*, began something like this:

> 'Where is my house—where is my home?
> Streams among the meadows creeping,
> Brooks from rock to rock are leaping;
> Everywhere bloom spring and flowers
> Within this paradise of ours;
> There—'tis there, the beauteous land,
> Bohemia, my fatherland!'

A beauteous land it undoubtedly is, but the language has peculiarities which are not calculated to make it grateful and comforting to the traveller who has to take it on after he is past his first youth.

When I arose and donned my clothes and oped my chamber-door in Prague to let in the 'sklepnik' with my coffee and *brödchen*, I had just two days to learn the language, see everything, and be off to Vienna. So, although my sklepnik was busy and the bells were ringing for him all over the house, I held on to him and insisted upon him giving me a short lesson in Czechish. But when I found that even his own name when you call him is not the same name as when you speak of him, and that he became in the course of five minutes' conversation sklepnick, sklepnickee, sklepnicka, sklepniko, etc., I let him go and take other people their breakfast, and got on with mine.

My panskou was so good-looking that I had serious thoughts of writing a song in her honour, entitled 'The Prettiest Panskou in Prague,' and getting somebody to put it into Czechish, that I might send it to her anonymously next Valentine's Day; but I heard that she was engaged to be married to the poshluhu on the third-floor, and so another example was added to my famous collection of 'Songs without Words.'

Before I went out to see the sights of Prague I gave myself just a few minutes further private instruction in the language of the land, and sat down with a dictionary and a pipe in front of the printed notice in my bedroom. This time I selected for study the following startling passage: 'Racte pouzy ucty kancelári stvrzone vyplácenti! Pokrmy a napoje v jidelne oderbrane buatez tamtez zaplaceny.' I worried at it with my German Czechish dictionary until I felt that if there was any insanity in my family history I should develop the latent Deemingism in my system, and possibly bury the sklepnik, the panskou, and the poshluhu under the same cement; and then I sent for my guide. My guide was a Bohemian who acquired English early in the sixties in the goldfields of California. He has lost a good deal of it since. 'Honyrabble zir!' he said, 'dat mean, your honour. Dat vat you eats and drinks underneath ze stairs pays for itself dere at ze times, honyrabble zir.' After a few minutes of serious reflection, I solved this further problem: Racte pouzy ucty kancelári, etc., meant that all meals taken in the restaurant should be paid for at the time, and not put on the bill.

When you have sufficiently admired Prague itself, and recognised the fact that it is 'picturesquely situated on the banks of the Moldau' (vide guide-books), the first thing you do is to explore the venerable Hradshin, or Capitol. High on the Hradshin Hill stands the Archbishop's Palace, the Schwarzenberg Palace, and the palace of the Emperor, and the famous cathedral dedicated to St. Vitus. On the hottest day of this present May, with thunder threatening and never a breath of air blowing, did I pant through palaces and crawl around cathedrals with the Californian-Bohemian. Many were the wonders that he showed me, and at least a hundred times that day did he call me 'honyrabble zir.' At last I became so worn out that it was almost with relief that I saw him suddenly slip up on a stone and turn his ankle. I am afraid he was in great pain; but his ardour and his pace were alike moderated after that, and I was saved from an apoplectic stroke following on over-exertion on a blazing hot day. After the accident, I offered him one arm and hired a native to give another; and between us we led him slowly around the Hradshin, and I allowed him to explain as much as I wanted to know, and then bore him away in triumph to something else. While he was a free agent his lectures were interminable, and he kept me for three-quarters of an hour looking at a brick wall in St. Vitus's because a Jew boy had been buried behind it some centuries previously.

There are two legends, or perhaps I should say historical facts, which follow you all over Prague—the story of St. John of Nepomuk and the story of Slavata and Martinitz. From the moment you land in Prague to the moment you leave it the names of these three gentlemen are dinned into your ears with damnable iteration. I happened to be in Prague on the eve of the great annual fête of St. John of Nepomuk, and so I had an extra dose of him.

Of course you know the story of the patron saint of Bohemia. You remember that Johanko von Nepomuk was a great preacher in Prague in the fourteenth century. He became almoner to King Wenzel or Venzeslaus IV., the great German Emperor, and King of Bohemia, and confessor to the Queen. The Queen soon afterwards began to look depressed, and tears were often in her eyes. King Wenzel was annoyed. 'Charlotte,' he said, 'why are you always in the blues? It gives me the hump. Cheer up, old lady, or tell me what is the matter.' The Queen only shook her head and sniffed. Then Wenzel swore several oaths of the period, and went off to the Rev. Mr. Johanko von Nepomuk and said to him, 'Look here, your reverence, the Queen confesses to you, so you know what is the matter with her, and why she is always snivelling and howling!' (He was a brutal fellow was Wenzel, and very coarse in his conversation.) 'Now, then, is it because I bully her, or has she got a love affair—eh, old chap? Own up!' The Rev. Johanko frowned and shook his head.

'The secrets of the confessional are sacred. Go to!'

The wicked Wenzel didn't go to, as you will presently see. He went nap. Soon afterwards, at a royal dinner-party, a capon came up, and the King got a slice from the breast that was slightly underdone. Whereupon, in a rage, he seized the capon, hurled it on the floor, and jumped upon it. (I fancy he suffered with his liver, this Wenzel, and was subject to neurotic blizzards.) Then he sent for the cook and had him spitted alive and roasted in front of his kitchen fire. 'And see that he is better done than this capon,' was the King's final instruction to the cookers of the cook.

The Rev. Mr. Nepomuk, when he heard of this, gave the King a piece of his mind, for which impertinence he was put into prison, and, while there, the King sent for him and said, 'Now, my friend, are you going to tell me what the Queen confessed?' 'Certainly not, sire,' replied Nepomuk, although, after what had happened to the cook, he guessed his refusal would get him into trouble. It did. Every effort of the King having failed to shake the determination of the rev. gentleman, he was one day seized by soldiers, bound hand and foot, and flung over the big bridge into the Moldau.

King Wenzel fancied no one would know what had become of Nepomuk; but a miracle happened. When the rev. gentleman fell into the water the water retired, and the bed of the river was dry for three days. The body was recovered, and to-day it is in a glass coffin enclosed in a solid silver one in the cathedral on the Hradshin. The saint has moreover in the cathedral a solid silver monument, and silver angels holding golden lamps of immense value hover over his shrine. I shall not forget that silver monument for many a long day. I was so entranced with it that I let the Californian-Bohemian tell me stories about Nepomuk that would have caused the Marines to shake their heads, and it wasn't until he had called me 'honyrabble zir' for the fourteenth time that at last I took his arm and led him limping away.

Ever since this occasion St. Nepomuk has been the patron saint of bridges (he was canonized by Benedict XIII.), and in Bohemia and some parts of Austria his fête-day is kept with the wildest rejoicings. Oddly enough, though the people of Prague always sing 'St. Nepomuk, protect me' when they cross a bridge, the bridge from which he was thrown—the glorious Karlsbrücke—- was broken down, and the middle of it carried away, by the great floods of 1890. A wooden bridge does duty while the grand old structure is being rebuilt. As I crossed the portion of the old stone bridge which is still standing I saw a huge gilt altar, erected almost at the point where the arches have been swept away. It was surrounded by hundreds of lamps, and mighty banks of flowers were piled around it. This was the altar to St. Nepomuk, which was being prepared for May 16. On that day thousands of pilgrims come from all parts of Bohemia to visit the bridge, and do honour to the saint. This year they found that the patron saint of bridges had allowed his own bridge to come to grief.

This St. Nepomuk Day in Prague is something you must see to understand. The streets are a dense mass of gay revellers and happy pilgrims from dawn till midnight. All the quaint national costumes of Bohemia light up the beflagged and beflowered thoroughfares. All day long the merry lads and lasses sing Bohemian songs, and dance Bohemian dances in the streets, the squares, and the parks. At night fireworks blaze up from all parts of the town, and a million extra lights make the glorious city on the Moldau a never-to-be-forgotten spectacle.

I lingered in Prague for the fête of St. Nepomuk, and I saw a sight which I shall remember all my days without referring either to notebook or diary. Good old St. Nepomuk! If he had not been thrown over the Karlsbrücke I should not have seen the Bohemian national fête. King Wenzel, I owe you one!

The National Theatre in Prague, where only plays and operas in the Czechish language are performed, is one of the finest in Europe. I saw there a Czechish opera entitled 'Prodaná Nevěsta,' or 'The Sold Bride.' At the 'Národni Divadlo,' or National Theatre, the operas are staged in a manner which excites the admiration even of our own Sir Augustus, and the chorus works as I have never seen a chorus work before. Everybody enters into the business of the scene, and fills it up, and the illusion is absolutely perfect.

As they thought it worth while to make an exhibition of theatrical programmes at the Vienna Exhibition, I may as well give you a little bit of a Prague programme (no charge), just to show you how it looks. Here is the one for which in a private box I paid ten kreuzers, and which an old lady obligingly stuck on to the velvet with a pin to prevent its falling over.

PRODANÁ NEVĚSTA.
Komická zpěvohra o třech jednáních. Hudbu složil
Bedřich Smetana. Slova od K. Sabiny.

Osoby:

Krušina, sedlák	p. ryt. Skramlík.
Ludmila, jeho manželka	sl. Vykoukalova.
Mařenka, jejich dcera	sl. Veselá.
Mícha, statkář	p. Viktorin.
Háta, jeho manželka	pí. Klánová-Panznerova.

Vašek, jejich syn	p. Krössing.
Jeník, selský hoch	p. Veselý.
Kecal, dohazovač	p. Heš.
Komediant, principál	p. Mošna.
Esmeralda, jeho dcera	sl. Cavallarova.
Ind án, komediant druhý	p. Pulc.
První —selský kluk—	p. Mušek
Druhý	sl. Vobořilova

Selská chasa, komedianti, kluci.
Děj v čas pouti na české vesnici.

Coming home from the Divadlo I lost myself, and had a bad quarter of an hour wandering around small back streets and trying to ask my way in Czechish. The theatres begin at half-past six in Prague, some of them as early as five, so that soon after ten there are very few people in the streets. It was half-past ten when I succeeded in getting out of a labyrinth of byways into what looked like a main thoroughfare, and then there was not a soul to be seen—not even a Prague policeman with ostrich feathers in his hat. I wondered how on earth I should get to my hotel, for I hadn't the faintest idea where it was, and one street was very like another to me. I wandered up and down for a quarter of an hour, hoping a belated wayfarer would come along, but I only met a couple of cats swearing at each other in Czechish, and they fled at my approach.

What was I to do? I didn't feel inclined to wander about Prague all night. Suddenly a brilliant idea occurred to me. I saw a red light over a door, and outside a bell, with the German for night bell written below it. A doctor lived there. I hesitated a moment, and then I rang it. Presently a gentleman put his head out of an upper window and addressed me in Czechish. I replied in German that I didn't understand the language. Then he asked me what I wanted in German. I replied, 'Advice; I am not well. Please come down and feel my pulse and look at my tongue.' He closed the window, came down and opened the front-door, and asked me to come in. 'No, thank you,' I said; 'I am in a hurry. Come under the lamp-post.' He came under the lamp-post, looked at my tongue, felt my pulse, and said that I was only a little bilious. I had better go to the chemist's and get some antibilious pills. 'Thank you, doctor,'

I said. 'What is your fee?' He told me his fee was three gulden for a night consultation. I paid the money, and then I said to him: 'And now, doctor, if you will kindly tell me which is my way to the Hôtel Royal, I shall be much obliged to you.' The doctor gave me minute directions, bowed, put my three gulden in the pocket of his dressing-gown, and went back to bed; and I went back to my hotel and did ditto.

It was rather an expensive method of asking your way, but what are you to do when you are lost in a town where everybody goes to bed at ten, and not a living soul reappears in the streets till the next morning? I don't know whether the policemen go to bed, but I didn't see one about. Perhaps they were all having pipes round a quiet corner.

Messrs. Slavata and Martinitz owe their immortality to their having been victims of that excellent Bohemian method of getting rid of an enemy which is called 'po starotshesku.' There is a splendid simplicity about the process. It merely consists of taking your enemy by the legs and throwing him out of the window. The higher the window the better for you and the worse for your enemy. Slavata and Martinitz were flung out of the window of a high tower in which the Council Chamber was situated. Although both fell actually on their heads, they figuratively fell on their feet, for a heap of manure received them safely and broke the news that they had arrived at their destination gently to them. They escaped and lived for some years afterwards, but the religious party in whose cause they had made themselves objectionable kept their memory green, and to-day in Prague, after you have honoured St. John of Nepomuk, you are expected to pay homage to the memory of Slavata and Martinitz.

After I had finished the Hradshin, and wandered through the royal palace, I had to lead my guide through the palace of Wallenstein, where he pointed out to me all the mementoes of the mighty general of the Thirty Years' War in the famous halls. By this time I was so dog-tired that I began to hate Bohemia, and almost to think unkind things about St. John of Nepomuk; and when my guide wanted me to take him over another church, I rose up and politely intimated to him that if he asked me to see anything else that day I would give him a chance of immortality by throwing him into the Moldau at the very spot where Nepomuk perished. I think he saw

I meant it, so he allowed me to put him in a carriage and take him home.

I have only hummed one air since I came into Austria, and that is, 'Oh, them gulden slippers.' They give you your gulden in a banknote, and a gulden is not quite two shillings. The astonishing rapidity with which those guldens became gulden slippers must be seen to be believed. Cabmen, railway porters, restaurant waiters, and the people generally who expect tips, never have any change, and it is cheaper to give the gulden than to wait while they go to the Bank of Austria to get it changed. If they have change it is of such a character that you are better without it. Eating cheap tinned peas, the colour of the O'Flaherty floral abomination, is a harmless amusement compared with keeping the small coin currency of the Austrian Empire in your pocket with chocolate creams, peppermints, cough lozenges, digestive tablets, and other delicacies of the season.

CHAPTER XXII.

VIENNA.

UNDER a domed roof, a green garden with flower-beds and gravel paths. In the centre a fountain. The outer circle built as a series of stages, each with a set scene—one a scene from a Russian play, another a scene from a German opera, another a scene from a Hungarian comedy, and so forth, until about a dozen set scenes have been set out. Around, in outer rings, with rooms branching off, various galleries containing old musical instruments, cases of theatrical costumes, portraits of actors and actresses, and working models of stages. Beyond, in the grounds, cafés, restaurants, and wooden theatres in which performances of various kinds are given; also 'Old Vienna,' after the manner of 'Old London.' That is the Vienna Musical and Dramatic Exhibition of 1892.

I spent two afternoons and one morning in this exhibition, not because I amused myself, but because I felt that it was my duty to see all that was to be seen. Naturally my first endeavour, after I had taken a scamper round, was to find the English department—or the section allotted to England—in order to see what sort of a show my fellow-countrymen had made. The catalogue which I purchased for seventy-five kreuzers informed me that the president of the English committee was Se. Königliche Hoheit Herzog von Edinburgh, and that among the committee were A. C. Macencie, W. G. Cusins, S. B. Bankroft, Sir George Grow, etc. The correct spelling of names is not a strong point, evidently, at the Vienna Exhibition.

There is a good old proverb which says, 'Blessed is he that expecteth little, for he shall not be disappointed.' After wandering wearily about for three-quarters of an hour and closely cross-examining every official I encountered, an obliging Austrian workman, who was doing something to a packing-case, volunteered to take me to the British Section. He led me to a huge vacant space, in which in disorderly array stood a number of dirty empty glass cases. 'This, sir, is the British Section,' he said, waving his hand around a few feet of bare wall, and then pointing to a battered old packing-case labelled 'This side up—with care.' That, gentle reader, was the British Section as I saw it on May 16, and that was all that there was to see. The British exhibits, I was told, had only just arrived, and they would not be unpacked for several days.

I am told that the British exhibits, when they are unpacked, will be exceedingly novel and interesting. There is a curious coffin-shaped case still at the Custom House, which is said to contain the skeleton of a dramatic critic who attended every *matinée* to which he was invited. There is a full-length portrait of Mr. William Archer felling the Examiner of Plays to earth with the manuscript of a Norwegian tragedy. There is a wax model of a lady sitting in the stalls at a *matinée* with a hat three feet high, and behind her are several gentlemen standing up and dividing the feathers and ribbons on the top of it in order to peep through them at the stage. There is a life-size figure of Mr. Horace Sedger sitting with the map of London in front of him, and pointing out Islington as a provincial town to Mr. W. S. Gilbert. There is the famous 'No Fee' banner which was lowered from the gallery of the Olympic as a welcome back to London to Mr. Wilson Barrett; and there is also a complete collection in a glass case of the costumes worn by sandwich-men as advertisements for the West End Theatres of London.

All these things, I am assured, will be exhibited in due time to the gaze of the wondering crowd that will flock to the Vienna Exhibition. That they will give the foreigner an excellent idea of the status of the drama in Great Britain I have not the slightest doubt.

Up to the present, unfortunately, so far as the British Section is concerned, 'there is nothing in it.'

When I found nothing in the English Section, and very little in any other section except the Bavarian and the Russian, I determined to see something, and so I asked for Frederick the Great's flute. Somebody had told me that it had been forwarded to Vienna from Berlin. The first day that I went to the exhibition I asked many officials where it was, and they directed me to various parts of the building. I found hundreds of flutes of all ages here. As none of them had anything but a number on, and the catalogue would not be ready for a fortnight, I was unable to pitch upon the particular instrument. (There is a catalogue published—the one to which I am indebted for the names of the English committee—but that is only a catalogue of the modern instruments.) On the second day of my visit I made further inquiries, and drove the officials to despair. I suppose I must have asked the same people over and over again without knowing it, for at last when they saw me coming they walked rapidly away and hid behind grand pianos. I heard one man say to another, 'Lieber Gott, here is this Englander again who wants Frederick the Great's flute!' And the pair disappeared as if by magic.

I was determined not to be beaten, so on the third day I tried again; but the first man I went to, instead of replying, took me to the room of the secretary of the exhibition. The secretary was extremely polite. 'Ah, sir,' he exclaimed, 'I am very pleased to see you. You have driven our people very nearly mad. One of them came to me yesterday with a telegram which he wished sent to Berlin, and the entire staff had subscribed to the expense of forwarding it. This was the telegram: "For Heaven's sake tell us where Frederick the Great's flute is. There is an Englishman who does nothing but ask us all day long." I sent that telegram, sir, and have received a reply. Frederick the Great's flute has not been sent. It is still in Germany.' Of course, I apologized for the trouble I had given, and blamed the person who had told me the famous instrument was among the German exhibits. Fancy an exhibition of famous musical instruments without Frederick the Great's flute! It is 'Hamlet' without the Prince of Denmark.

In the theatres of Austria, as in those of the German Empire, ladies are expected to remove their bonnets everywhere except in the private boxes. No hats or bonnets are allowed in the stalls, dress circle, pit, or gallery. The reason of this restriction is that hats have of late years assumed such gigantic proportions, that a front row of females would shut out a view of the stage from the rest of the house.

But the ladies—Heaven bless them!—have discovered a way of taking their revenge. They have invented a method of wearing the hair which makes the removal of the hat a mere farce. The authorities are now seriously discussing the question of making lady playgoers leave their hair in the cloak-room as well as their hats.

I have been peculiarly unfortunate in my attempts to see something of the German and Austrian stage. The fact which I am about to narrate will, I have no doubt, be taken with several grains of salt, but on my honour it *is* a fact nevertheless. I went to the theatre in Dresden—to the opera—and a lady sat in front of me. She was a charming American lady, with a mass of gray hair, but she wore it absolutely a foot high, after the manner of a pantaloon's wig. At Prague, when I went to the Czechish Theatre, to my intense astonishment this lady came in with her husband and again sat in front of me. Two days later, on the Sunday night, I went to the Vienna Opera House to see the 'Puppenfee' and 'L'Amico Fritz.' The seats in front of me were vacant, and I was just congratulating myself on at last getting a view of the stage during a performance, when in walked the lady with the Eiffel Tower hair!

That I should have sat behind the same person, an utter stranger to me, in three towns one after the other, is a coincidence so extraordinary that I think it worth mentioning. I don't know what the odds against such a treble event coming off are—something in trillions I should fancy—but it did come off. The hair unfortunately did not.

The Prater on Sunday was thronged, and a dozen bands were playing in the excellent coffee gardens scattered about it. But the great sight to me was the 'Punch and Judy, or People's Prater.' Here, among hundreds of merry-go-rounds, Richardson's shows, outdoor balls, and the general 'fun of the fair,' you could walk upon the people's heads. I should like to take Messrs. M'Dougall and Parkinson through the Punch and Judy Prater of Vienna one day and show them how the toiling masses of a great city can enjoy themselves when plenty of cheap amusement and good wholesome refreshment are provided for them.

There is one peculiar custom in certain parts of Austria, notably in Vienna, which it takes an Englishman some time to get accustomed to. When you are generous to anyone the recipient of your bounty makes a tremendous bow and 'kisses your hand.' Sometimes this phrase is a mere form of words, 'Ich küsse die hand' (the Viennese say, 'Ich kiss die hand), but frequently the actual performance takes place. A lady gives, say, to the chambermaid of her hotel a gulden, and instantly the chambermaid exclaims, 'I kiss your hand,' and does it. I have seen the English ladies thoroughly nonplussed at the unexpected homage.

The porter at the Vienna railway-station who put my portmanteau on a cab told me that he kissed my hand, and my cabman, to my complete discomfiture, actually did it. As soon as I discovered it was a custom of the country, I became rather nervous, and when I went to a little theatre and an old lady handed me a programme, fearing the possible salute, I only gave her a copper coin. She didn't 'kiss my hand,' but went off muttering in the Viennese dialect something which, fortunately for my self-esteem, I was unable to grasp.

I spent a pleasant week in Vienna, but felt rather the worse for wear when I left. The custom of the country is that you should consume a mid-day meal with several glasses of beer, have wine in the middle of it, and finish up with cognac or kummel. Then in the afternoon everybody goes to the Prater, and sits at the first, second, or third coffee-house and drinks more beer—sometimes six glasses, one after the other. The middle-day meal is a terrific one, consisting of six or seven courses; but towards four the Viennese get hungry again, and so at the Prater coffee-gardens a man walks about with a basket of enormous sausages in one hand and a pair of scales in the other, and about half a hundredweight of Gruyère cheese under his arm. You have rolls of bread on every little table where you drink your beer, so all you have to do is to cry 'salami,' which is sausage, and instantly the gentleman with the basket comes to your table, cuts you as many slices as you require, weighs them, and puts them in front of you on a piece of clean white paper. You then drink your beer and eat your sausage with your fingers, gnawing a piece of bread in between. And thus the happy hours glide away towards evening, and the best military bands of Vienna soothe you with the soft strains of music. It is only in Vienna that you can have Strauss and salami together.

At ten, after the theatres are over, eating begins again, and is of a most formidable character. The best restaurants are crowded. At Sacher's you cannot get a table, for all the elegant world from the opera is there. At Leidinger's there is scarcely room for you to pass between the crowd of feasters and find a place for your hat and umbrella, and at the Old Tobacco-pipe, where the Viennese kitchen proper (or improper if you prefer it) reigns supreme, you sometimes have to wait your turn and stand at the door eagerly watching for a supster to come out that you may go in.

Before I left Vienna, having exhausted the theatres, I did a round of the waxwork exhibitions. These delighted me hugely, many of the subjects being realistic enough to make M. Zola's hair stand on end. Our Chamber of Horrors at Madame Tussaud's is buttermilk compared with the chambers of horrors I saw in Vienna. The whole series of tortures inflicted by the Inquisition are realized in one establishment in the Kohl Market, and the wax figures roll their eyes and quiver with agony, and open their mouths and gasp in so lifelike a manner, that sometimes the country-folks grow indignant and want to get at the Grand Inquisitor and the executioner and lynch them.

The Schneiders, who systematically robbed and murdered servant-girls, are prominent features in all the waxworks of Austria; but they didn't interest me nearly so much as an elegantly-dressed young gentleman of aristocratic appearance, who won renown some time ago by committing a murder under rather novel circumstances. He was a young man of good family, and at one time had money; but he gambled and lost it, and, being hard up, conceived a highly original plan for replenishing his purse. It is the custom in Austrian as in many European towns for the postman to bring a registered letter up to the room of the person who is to receive it, and to take the signature for it there. As this causes considerable delay on a round, the registered letters are kept back from the ordinary delivery, and sent out by a special postman. Our hero addressed an envelope to himself, put some money in it, registered it, and then made his little arrangements. When the postman came up to his bachelor apartment on the fourth-floor of a big house, he stunned him with a sudden blow, then finished him off, and, taking his bag of registered letters, opened the lot, extracted the banknotes, jewellery, etc., and made tracks with them. He got a very large sum of money, but the postman's body was quickly discovered, and the aristocratic youth went through the dead-letter office.

But the most ghastly bit of realism of all is, I think, a representation of 'The Last Moments of Alexander II.' The Czar lies on a real bed, with his uniform and his linen saturated with blood. His shirt is open to the breast, and a horrible gaping wound is exposed to the eye of the spectator. As the figure breathes convulsively, the eyes roll up in the head, and *real blood* gushes up to the surface of the terrible wound. I have never been so horribly fascinated in my life as I was by that figure of the dying Cæsar, with his life-blood welling up before my eyes. It was shocking, it was brutal, it was hideous; but it held me spellbound by its intense reality. You forgot you were looking at a wax figure in a glass-case. You seemed to be watching a real man dying a horrible death. It was with the greatest difficulty that I prevented myself running for the nearest doctor.

CHAPTER XXIII.

BUDAPEST.

AFTER my nocturnal adventure in Prague, I made up my mind that if I wanted to do Austria thoroughly in a fortnight it was absolutely necessary I should have someone familiar with the tongues of Bohemia and Hungary, to say nothing of Bosnia, Herzegovina, and Montenegro. I met Herr Julius, cosmopolitan courier, promiscuously at a café in Vienna. We fell into conversation, and I secured him then and there to accompany me upon my Hungarian explorations. Herr Julius not only speaks German, French, English, Italian, and Spanish fluently, but is as a native when it comes to Czechish and Magyar and Croatian.

Herr Julius shares with Albert Edward a taste for good cigars and high-class cookery. In other matters he has a frugal mind. He delights in bargains, and points with pride to his success in various parts of the world. Herr Julius is an object-lesson in economy. He shows me his umbrella, and his face lights up with pride as he informs me that he has had it for some years, and that he bought it for eight shillings in Cairo. He takes off his hat, pats it lovingly, and tells me that he got it in the winter of 1889 in Naples for four shillings and sixpence. He asks me what I think of his boots. I admire them, and he explains that he purchased them of a waiter at Seville for two shillings, because they had been left behind by a German prince who died in the hotel. Charmed by these revelations, I venture to ask him what he paid for his suit, and instantly his face assumes an expression of triumph. He asks me to guess. I guess five pounds. 'No, sir,' he exclaims, with a grin that displays every tooth in his head, and he has an excellent set; 'for dis suit I give two pounds five in Tottenhams Court Road more two year ago. Ah, what a suit! I put him away every winter and he comes out die nexto sommer every year better he was before.'

The most picturesque way of going to Budapest from Vienna is naturally down the Danube. But there are slight difficulties in the way. The steamer leaves at seven in the morning, and that means getting up at four o'clock at your hotel. Four o'clock is not my usual hour of rising. It is nearer my usual time of going to bed, and, much as I wanted to take the Danube trip, I could not contemplate that early departure without a shudder. But Herr Julius came to the rescue. 'You shall go on board the night before, you see, sir,' he said, 'and there you shall sleep comfortable, and no get up till so you choose.' I agreed that this would be one way out of the difficulty, but as I was desirous to go to the Theater an der Wien in the evening, in order to see 'Heisses Blut,' a play which had gained considerable vogue in Vienna, I explained that I should have to come on board rather late. 'That shall not matter,' replied Herr Julius, 'you shall pack everythings, pay your bill, go to the theatre, and I shall take your everythings on board de shiff and make you secure one nice cabines. Is that good?'

We took a 'fiaker' that afternoon, and drove to the ship, which was lying alongside the quay. There was only one official on board, and he received us with a bow so low that his front hair swept a lot of coal-dust from the deck. This official was the second steward. We explained our needs, and he immediately placed the entire vessel at our disposal. It was rarely that passengers came on board at night, but we were welcome. A bed should be made up for the gentlemen in a cabin. The kitchen would be shut at eleven, but cold meat and bread and wine should be left out, and he (the under-steward) would remain ever at the gentlemen's service. The preliminary arrangements were made, the under-steward swept the deck again with his front hair, and Herr Julius and your humble servant drove back to the town.

I packed and saw my luggage loaded on a cab and taken to the quay, and then I went to the theatre and was hugely entertained by 'Heisses Blut,' a musical absurdity written around a well-known Hungarian actress, Fräulein Palma. At ten I left the theatre, made my way to the ship, found an excellent supper waiting for me, went to bed, and slept soundly. When I awoke the ship was well on her way down the Danube, and the excellent Herr Julius was knocking at my cabin-door with a cup of strong tea and the information that it was a fine day, and that there was nobody on board but ourselves, ten dwarfs, a giant, and a performing boarhound.

I soon made friends with the dwarfs. Four of them were the smallest little fellows I have ever seen. They had been all over France and Germany, and had been touring for two years in Spain. The giant also was affable, and an American travelling with them as lecturer favoured me with much curious information.

Budapest is, as the guide-books say, 'picturesquely situated' on both sides of the Danube; Buda is on one side, and Pest is on the other. It takes you a little time after you arrive in Hungary to find out where you actually are, because the Hungarians in their intense Magyarism have abolished all German names, signs, notices, and indications. A traveller, for instance, who wanted to get off the Danube steamer at Pressburg, the first big stopping-place in Hungary one gets to after leaving Vienna, would probably pass Pozsony by. But Pozsony is Pressburg, though there is nothing but your guide-book to let you know it. At one time in Hungary names of streets, etc., were put up in the two languages; now the German is all taken down and Magyar reigns supreme.

No national movement in Europe has of late years made such tremendous strides as Magyarism. The Hungarians have Home Rule, and mean to stick to it. The Emperor of Austria reigns only as King of Hungary. Hungary has its own Parliament, makes its own laws, and has its own postage-stamps. The Austrians are not so unpopular as they were in years gone by, when the Hungarians called them 'damned Germans;' but there is still a strong feeling against Austrian interference. As I write these lines all Budapest is bubbling over with excitement about the death of General Klapka, the hero of Komorn, one of the patriots of the former stormy days. Klapka died in one of the hotels here. The Austrian officials—so the Hungarians say—tried to get him buried quietly and at once, whereupon Budapest rose up, and the voice of the Magyar was heard in the land. 'Is he a drowned dog, this our hero,' the Hungarians said, 'that he should be flung into the earth at once? No! we—we his fellow-countrymen, his fellow-sufferers in days gone by, his fellow-patriots now, will honour him dead as we loved him living!' And so General Klapka had a grand Hungarian funeral, and thousands upon thousands of Hungarians flocked to the ceremony.

There are two things you never get away from in Budapest—red pepper, called páprïka, and czigani, or gipsy music. On every table you have dark red pepper in a salt-cellar, and in every hotel you find the gipsy band worrying away at the fiddlestrings.

The Hungarian ladies are famed for their beauty, and Budapest has a reputation which would not recommend it as a summer residence to Messrs. M'Dougall and Parkinson. The poet might here indulge in 'a dream of dark women' to his heart's content. The baths for which Budapest is renowned are conducted on principles not altogether in accordance with English ideas of morality, and are frequently meeting-places for affairs of gallantry. The modest Englishman with insular prejudices has all his work cut out to avoid blushing at the propositions which are made to him by the couriers and guides attached to the principal hotels, propositions made not with a grin and a whisper, but with a stately bow, and in the ordinary tone of general conversation.

The Hungarian or Magyar language is startling in its peculiarities. When you wish to bid anyone good-day you say 'Yonapol,' and if you meet anyone to whom you wish to be polite you say 'Alarzatos Szolgaya'—'I am your humble servant.' That is the 'Adieu' of Hungary, and takes the place of the Viennese 'I kiss the hand.' Everybody in Hungary is 'your humble servant.'

My favourite stroll in Budapest when I am tired of red pepper and the gipsies is the bridge which connects Buda and Pest and makes them one town. The Danube here is 1,800 feet broad, and until the bridge was built in 1849 the only means of connection was a bridge of barges, and in the winter, when the Danube was swollen, this was frequently unsafe, and all connection between the two towns was suspended. The English engineers, Clark and Tiernay, built this bridge, but the opposition of the Hungarian nobles was tremendous. They had the right of crossing the old bridge free by reason of their rank, but Baron Sma, of Vienna, who found the £500,000 necessary for the undertaking, claimed the right to levy toll for the space of eighty-five years, and so everyone has to pay toll at the present day. The Hungarian nobleman still feels that he is sacrificing himself to 'a d——d German' every time he pulls out the kreuzers demanded by the bridge-keepers.

The old Hungarian prejudices remain, but, alas! the old Hungarian costumes are rapidly disappearing. The young noblemen still drive four spanking horses in a mail-phaeton, and now and then one sees the Hungarian coachman in high boots, light blue coat and silver buttons, and the pork-pie hat with long ribbons hanging down behind it. But the bulk of the populace have abandoned high boots and frogged coats, and now and then one even sees a tall hat on a Hungarian head.

The high Wellington boots are still worn by the peasant women and the peasant men, but not by the better classes. The high hat is not so generally adopted as modern trousers and boots, because for many years it was the sign of a 'German.' Herr Julius can remember the day when a man in a high hat was yelled at by the roughs wherever he went, and many a luckless owner of a chimney-pot was bonneted in public amid the jeers of the bystanders. 'A Schwoab!' the people would cry directly they espied the obnoxious topper. 'A Schwoab' means a German, and sounds suspiciously like 'a swab.' 'Német' is another name for a German. I am assured this feeling has passed away, but I know better. 'The King of Hungary' comes to his palace at Buda now for three months in the year, and the Austrians talk their German language and wear their chimney-pots without being insulted; but the Hungarians still look upon all things Austrian askance, and it did not need the demonstration and the speeches which the recent attempt to bury Klapka György Tabornok quietly has called forth to prove that the patriotic Magyar still chafes beneath the Austrian yoke.

I am going to the theatre in Budapest to see a Magyar melodrama, entitled 'A Betyár Kendöje' ('The Brigand's Handkerchief'). They call the theatre a Szinház. That is a little startling, but when you have got accustomed to fogado for a hotel, and you have to tell the porter to look after your podgyars for luggage, and you learn that ó nö is an old woman, and that Vienna is Bécs, and bor is wine, and viz—not namely—is water, and Isten is God, you are prepared for anything.

I like fruit, but when the waiter asks me if I will take some 'gyümöics' I hesitate. (In parentheses, the most exquisite thing I have eaten in Hungary is the fogas, a Lower Danube fish. Cold, with sauce Tartare, it is delicious. The red-pepper dishes I have not fallen so violently in love with, although páprïka huhn and gulyás are by no means to be despised.)

I started to go to the theatre the other night, but I found that the play was 'Hamlet, Dankiralfy,' which is 'Hamlet, Prince of Denmark,' and I thought better of it. It may interest the general reader to know that the performance took place on Vasárnap (which is Sunday), Május 22-én, and was 'Eredeti népszinmü dalokkal 4 szakaszban. Irta Abonyi Lajos. Zenéjét Nikolics Sándor.'

The Magyar melodrama, entitled 'The Brigand's Handkerchief,' turned out to be a very old friend. It was only 'Falsely Accused' in a foreign language. A Hungarian brigand, having behaved badly to his young wife and attempted to murder her to slow music in the snow, she leaves him and enters the service of a dear old lady under an assumed name. The dear old lady's son falls in love with her, and asks her to marry him. But she says there are reasons which stand in the way, and, being the leading lady, has a long soliloquy all to herself in the centre of the stage. In the meantime the brigand has fallen into the toils of a gipsy girl, who dances Hungarian dances and sings Hungarian songs at a low Hungarian public-house. The brigand is made drunk with fourteen bottles of wine and fourteen lighted candles, and agrees to go out at night with the gipsy girl and do a little house-breaking. I can't tell you why, when the fourteen bottles are placed on the table for the brigand, a lighted candle is placed by each bottle. It seemed to me a fearful waste of tallow, but I presume it is a custom of the country.

The gipsy lady dresses herself up as a man, and puts pistols in her belt, and off she goes with the brigand straight to the house of the dear old lady at midnight. All is quiet, only the unhappy wife is about, and she has just packed up everything she has in the world in a small pocket-handkerchief, and is about to leave the house of her benefactress clandestinely, in order to avoid the pathetic love-making of her young master. The brigand and brigandess enter. The wife, who has returned to her bedroom for a pocket-handkerchief—one her husband gave her on her wedding-day—comes out, and is about to be shot by the brigandess, when the brigand starts, and exclaims in the Magyar language, 'Heaven, it is my long-lost wife!' and dashes the pistol from his fair (or, rather, dark) accomplice's hand, while the injured wife falls fainting on the floor. At that moment the young master, having heard a noise, rushes in; the brigandess escapes, but the brigand is seized after a violent struggle, thrust into an inner room, and the keys turned upon him. Then off rushes the young master to fetch a policeman. The wife recovers, says, 'O Isten' (Isten is the Magyar for the Deity), 'my husband will be executed if he is caught and recognised as the notorious brigand.' So she unlocks the door, and promptly bids him leave by the window, which he does, after giving off a short speech.

You can guess the rest. When the police enter and find the man gone and the girl trembling, they at once accuse her of being an accomplice, and of having let the robber in and also of having let him out. The man has dropped a pocket-handkerchief of a peculiar pattern. On searching the girl they find one of the same make in her pocket. Evidently they were accomplices. So the girl is arrested.

The last act takes place at the police-station. The heroine has a bad time and weeps, but refuses to clear herself. Enter the brigand husband, who says, 'I am here. I am So-and-so, the notorious brigand. I broke into the house. This woman released me because I was her husband. See, here are the other five handkerchiefs of half a dozen I inherited from my mother. The sixth I gave to Marie on our wedding-day, and that is how our handkerchiefs are of the same pattern.' The police at once arrest the husband, and the wife is free. The husband is dragged off. A shot is heard. He has killed himself. At that moment the young master rushes in, and exclaims, 'Marie, will you marry me now?' Marie falls into her young master's arms and says, 'Yes—if you will wait.' I think she added, 'Until after the funeral,' but I am not sufficiently master of Magyar to commit myself absolutely on the point.

Some years ago the crowded house which greeted this Magyar melodrama would have been impossible. Half the audience, though

Hungarian, would not have understood their own language. They would have wanted it translated into German.

To understand the immense strides which Magyarism has made one must look back a little. To-day hardly a German word is to be heard in the thoroughfares, and no German words disfigure the public announcements, the sign-posts, the playbills, or the street corners. There are many thousands of Hungarians who do not even understand German. Think of this, and then remember that in 1840 a movement for the reintroduction of the Magyar language at the University of Pest met with but scant encouragement outside the town. The police then spoke German, the army spoke German, the lectures of the University were delivered in Latin. Up to the year 1790 there was not even a professor at the University who *spoke* Magyar. To-day in the towns everything is Magyar and nothing is German.

To-day (it was 'to-day' when this was written), in the hotel at which I am staying, the patriots have a dinner. Their dining-room adjoins the writing-room in which I am penning (or rather pencilling) these lines. Great speeches are being made, and every now and then the room rings again with the Magyar cries of 'Elyen! Elyen!' (Bravo! bravo!) and 'Hayunk, hayunk!' (Hear, hear). There is in the room, writing, a young man with a coal-black beard, fierce gleaming eyes, and the milk-white teeth for which the Magyars are renowned. He listens to the speeches that come through the closed door, and presently, as one of the speakers makes a great point amid a roar of applause in the next room, he springs to his feet and shouts 'Elyen! Elyen!' too. Then, catching my astonished gaze, he smiles, begs me to excuse him, and explains that he is the son of a Hungarian exile, that he was born in Egypt, whither his father fled to escape imprisonment for his political opinions in the days of tyranny, and that he is thinking of those years of exile now, and the father who died in a far-off country for love of his native land.

I left Budapest on Monday morning by the Orient express for Munich, and Herr Julius, who saw me to the railway-station, wept on my breast and whiled away the time with anecdotes of his past career. Herr Julius had once saved a nice little fortune—many thousands of florins—and he wanted to invest it. He knew many of the financial barons of Vienna. He asked their advice, and, acting on it, he bought the 'obligations' of a local company. These obligations cost him five hundred florins each, and they were soon to be worth a thousand, and Herr Julius would make a fine thing of his investment. But the best laid schemes o' mice and men gang aft a-gley, and the great 'krach' came suddenly, and with it widespread ruin. Companies were scattered before the winds like chaff. Great financial houses came tumbling down as though they had been built of cards, and Vienna rang with the cries and curses of the ruined and undone. The 'obligations' which Herr Julius had bought rattled down in value till at last they became almost worthless. In despair the poor fellow was glad to take five florins each for the 'obligations' for which he had paid five hundred, and he was lucky to get that, for a day or two afterwards the bubble burst utterly, and the 'papers' he had held were not worth a kreuzer each!

'Ah, sir,' says Herr Julius, his eyes filling with tears, 'after that my little fortune was gone, not for months did I sleep. I beat my breast, I tore my hair, I could eat nothings; my life was to me one great burthen. At last I say to myself, Julius, old man, this does not do; your little fortune it has gone, but you must cheer yourself and begin again the battle of life. So one day I say to myself, I will forget, I will drown care, I will go out and enjoy myself, and laugh with the rest. The first day that I shake the sorrow from my mind I go to the Prater in the afternoon. I enter the third coffee-house; I sit in the garden and listen to the band. I drink my beer and feel hungry. The man come with salami; I say I will eat, and I buy for twopence halfpenny some salami.

'Well, sir,' continued Herr Julius, 'the man he weigh me out my salami, and he spread out a piece of paper, and he put upon it my six slices. I drink a good draught of beer. I pick up my salami, and I say, "Julius, after all life is good, still can you have your beer and salami." At that moment my eye it catches the piece of paper. I look at it. It has print on it. It has a number. Ach, leiber Gott! it is my "obligation" for which I have paid once five hundred florins. On that has the sausage man served me with twopennyworth of salami! That night again I sleep not.'

I express my sympathy with Herr Julius, and the Orient express steams into the station. In his excitement at bidding me farewell Herr Julius drops his overcoat, which he carries over his arm. Instantly the platform is spread as for a feast. Herr Julius has carefully collected the débris of dinners for which I have paid without availing myself of all the privileges to which I am entitled. Oranges roll about in every direction; sweet biscuits are crushed under the heels of hurrying porters; pink prawns and white radishes make the dull platform gay with colour; the wing of a fowl and the leg of a goose fall together on to the line. Here is a piece of cheese, there half a dozen lumps of sugar. Herr Julius gives a wild shriek, falls upon his hands and knees, and proceeds to gather up the fragments that remain. And while he is still collecting these remnants of our many feasts the engine whistles, and the Orient express bears me away. I thrust my head out of the window, and the last glimpse I get of Herr Julius shows me that remarkable man busily engaged in picking gravel and cinders from a small piece of Gruyère cheese. I paid for it, and he is determined that it shall not be wasted.

I only spent one day in Munich, and then I fled to the Bavarian Alps. The customs of the city were too much for me. From early morn till late at night the Munichers drink beer and eat radishes the size of turnips. I had great difficulty, not being Sandow, in lifting up the mug of beer which was brought to me at a beer-garden. Putting it down I found a sheer impossibility. But I sat at a table with a fine young Bavarian, who put away ten huge mugs of the national beverage in rapid succession. I was taken to one garden—the Lion Brewery Garden—where the average sale is 10,000 litres a day, and there are fifty such establishments in full swing in Munich.

CHAPTER XXIV.

A MAD KING'S PALACE.

NOT being able to drink beer and eat turnip radishes, and the theatres all being closed, I went off to the mountains and made for Herrenchiemsee, the lovely lake on which the wide world's wonder, King Ludwig's gorgeous palace, is situated. Weird and woful is the tale of Bavaria's mad monarch, Ludwig II. He was cursed with that form of insanity which is called 'la folie des grandeurs.' He rode about in carriages of eye-dazzling magnificence, the panels of which were hand-painted by great artists at a cost of a thousand pounds per panel, and his carriages were always drawn by eight cream-white horses. He dressed himself up as Lohengrin and sailed about the lonely lakes at midnight on the back of a mechanical swan. The palace that he built at Herrenchiemsee is a blaze of golden glory. His bed alone cost £20,000, and he ruined himself before the palace was half finished. The magnificence of the state apartments and the famous Hall of Mirrors beggars description. Only a madman afflicted with the 'folie des grandeurs' would have commenced such a dwelling-place. Everything in it is real gold, real silver, and real marble, and all of the most exquisite workmanship. A peacock (if ever a peacock brought ill-luck this one did) which stands in the vestibule cost £7,500. The interior decoration of one room alone cost £21,000. For a writing-table in the royal study the King paid £2,000, and throughout the entire palace the cost of everything is in proportion. No wonder the King found himself penniless at last, and his subjects unwilling to supply him with further funds for his mad extravagance. It was the building of this palace which led to the terrible tragedy on the Starnberg Lake which filled all the world with horror.

For some time previous to 1886 the King had exhibited strong symptoms of insanity. He had retired from active participation in affairs of state, and lived only for his marvellous private operatic performances and the building of his peerless palace. It was not exactly a sane thing for a king to dress himself up as the hero of a Wagner opera and sail about on a swan's back, and it was, to say the least of it, odd for him to come mysteriously at midnight on a golden steamer across the silent lake to his lonely palace and order all the hundred thousand candles to be lighted that he might march about it and fancy himself a god.

On the hottest day of a hot week I went to the Starnberg Lake to visit the scene of the tragedy. Just at the spot where Ludwig dragged the doctor into the lake on the evening of Whit Sunday and murdered him the Prince Regent has erected a memorial, and here there burns day and night a blood-red lamp. Long after night had fallen on the lonely island, and the dull red ray of that lamp fell upon the silent waters, I sat by the water's edge and brooded over the strange, sad story of the Starnberg Lake.

It was Baron von Lutz, the brother of our own Herr Meyer Lutz, that master of melody, who for many a long year wielded the merry bâton of Gaiety burlesque, who really put an end to the mad pranks of Ludwig of Bavaria. When the King could get no more money to finish his 'enchanted palace' with, he ordered Freiherr von Lutz, the Bavarian Minister-President, to find him the sum he needed at once. Herr Meyer Lutz's brother informed the King that the country was not in a position to comply with such a demand. Immediately the King wrote to the Baron to say that unless he sent the sum within twenty-four hours the eminent composer of 'Faust Up to Date' would have to go into mourning for him, as his head would be cut off. This letter Baron von Lutz at once brought before the Ministry, and the result was that a Commission sat, and declared the King to be insane and incapable of managing his own affairs.

Ludwig was at this time at his castle of Hohen Schwangau in the mountains. Thither the Commissioners, accompanied by Dr. Gudden, the Asylum director, repaired, directly Prince Luitpold, the King's uncle, had accepted the Regency and authorized the arrest of his nephew. The Commissioners informed the King he was a prisoner, but others learned the news also. These others were the men of the mountains, who worshipped their monarch almost as a god—many of them, indeed, believing him to be superhuman. These brave fellows, arming themselves with axes and choppers and guns, came pouring down the mountains, and swore that they would slaughter the Commissioners and set the King free.

The situation looked so threatening that the King was secretly conveyed that afternoon to a little castle on the Starnberg Lake, where he could be more effectually guarded. One night only did the poor mad King spend there. On the evening of the second day—Whit Sunday, 1886—he went for a walk with Dr. Gudden and the attendants. He talked so calmly and rationally that when he said pleasantly, 'Doctor, must these fellows follow us about everywhere? It isn't exactly what I care for,' the doctor sent the men back to the castle. The King and the doctor went on along the edge of the lake alone, and were partly hidden from sight by the trees. What happened after that no human being can say with certainty; but it is conjectured that the King, saying he was tired, sat down on a seat, and invited the doctor to sit beside him. Suddenly the King sprang up and rushed to the lake. The doctor ran after him and seized him. The King then gripped the doctor by the throat, gave him a fearful blow in the face which stunned him, and then held him under the water till he was drowned. Then, freeing himself from the dead man's grasp, he walked on and on into the deep blue lake—on and on until the quiet waters closed over his head, and his mad dream of splendour ended in the eternal sleep of death.

No one can look upon the spot where the poor mad King died, and think of that gorgeous palace which was his glory and his life, and which stands unfinished to this day, without a pang of pity. It would be easy to moralize upon it. 'The vanity of human wishes' writes itself large on the quiet waters that lave the foot of the lonely memorial to Bavaria's hapless King. I have no doubt I should have moralized had I had time. But my programme was not mapped out for that sort of thing, and so I turned sadly away from the melancholy shore, gave one last look at the dim red lamp and the dying Saviour on the cross, and went quietly to the landing-stage and took the last boat to the opposite shore, and thence made my way by train to Munich, where I arrived just in time to pack up, make a light supper, and catch the Paris-bound Orient express at 1.15 a.m.

CHAPTER XXV.

HOLLAND.

I CANNOT swim. It is a humiliating confession to make at the best of times, but the admission at the present moment is an absolutely painful one. I am staying in a place where I am in hourly fear of falling into the water. My present address is Amsterdam, and no one but a native can walk about Amsterdam without an uneasy feeling that sooner or later he will find himself in a canal. There is a canal in front of my door, my bedroom window at the back of the house opens on to a canal, and there is a canal round the corner.

To get to the post-office from my hotel you have to cross fourteen bridges and walk along the side of seven canals. Some of the bridges suddenly go up in the air just as you are about to step on them. This is to let the ships through. It is quite right that ships should pass down the principal streets of Amsterdam, but it is a little annoying to have to wait for a small fleet to go by when you are in a hurry to get home. There is, however, this advantage about the bridge going up suddenly on end ten feet in the air. It makes a wall between you and the water. Now, when you walk *along* the canal instead of going over it there is no wall, and as in the dark the water looks uncommonly like a roadway, and you see gentlemen and ladies sitting at their doors opposite, you have to keep on remembering where you are, or else you would go to step in the middle of the road out of the way of a crowd or a passing vehicle, and find yourself in an awkward predicament.

A week ago I never thought I should get to Holland. I was afraid I should have to spend the rest of my days at Bingen on the Rhine, waiting for a registered letter. Of all the awful things that can happen to a foreigner in Germany, there is nothing that can compare with the tortures and anxieties to which he is subjected while waiting for a registered letter. According to the law of the land, the postman must, after preliminary inquiries as to your birth, parentage, and habits, deliver the said letter personally to you in the room in which your luggage is, and must further take your receipt for the same in ink, and said receipt must be signed in the presence of the landlord of the hotel at which you are staying, and the said landlord is also required to countersign the document.

These stringent regulations are doubtless very wise precautions, and they can be fulfilled without any great mental or physical suffering, provided, when you are on a journey, you remain in your hotel all day long waiting for the postman. Unfortunately I was not able to do so, and fell a victim to a series of misfortunes probably unprecedented in the history of registered letter addresses.

On the day that I expected my registered letter I made a little excursion from Bingen to Wiesbaden, and returned from Wiesbaden at seven in the evening. As I entered the portals of my hotel the manager, who speaks German to me, stepped forward and informed me that the postman had been there 'mit einem eingeschriebenen Briefe' for me. The porter, who is a Swiss, and addresses me in Italian, came up beaming with smiles, and told me that during my absence there had been 'una lettera raccomandata' for me. The chambermaid met me on the landing (she is from Alsace, and likes to keep up her French), and whispered confidentially that the postman had 'une lettre chargée' for me; and the head waiter, who speaks English on principle, even to the Germans, who can't understand it, rushed at me when I came downstairs to dinner and exclaimed, 'Sare, sare, de postmans, he bin here with wretcheder letter for you. He come again seven o'clock to-morrow mornings.'

Now, if there is one thing I abhor and abominate on the Continent it is the custom of the early postman banging at my bedroom door when I am fast asleep. I wake with a start, and wonder where I am. I travel rapidly, and so am one day in France, the next in Holland, the next in Germany, and perhaps the next in Italy. Under these circumstances, when first you open your eyes in a strange bedroom it takes you a few seconds to remember where you are and in what language it is necessary to reply to the person who is rapping, 'rapping at your chamber door.' As a rule, I generally start up, and exclaim, 'Eh, what is it? Who are you? Come in! Entrez! Herein! Entrate!' and wait for the reply.

Although I was hungry, I was careful to eat sparingly at supper in order to sleep lightly, and I retired to rest early. At six o'clock I rose and dressed myself carefully, got the ink in a safe place, put a new pen in the penholder, spread a clean sheet of blotting-paper on the table, and, assuming a dignified attitude, waited for the postman. He was to come at seven. At 9.15 I had to leave by the express for Cologne, *en route* for Amsterdam. I sat at the table patiently till eight; no postman. Then I went downstairs, and made inquiries. 'Ah, the postman—yes,' exclaimed the porter; 'he came with your registered letter at seven; but he said you might be asleep, so he wouldn't disturb. He'll bring it with the second delivery, at ten.'

The remark that I made to that porter in reply conveyed a mixed feeling of rage and despair boiled down into a single word of four letters, of which the last is superfluous. All my preparations were made to depart from Bingen at 9.15. The postman was then about the town delivering letters. I sent after him in all directions to bid him return at once with my registered letter. Alas! my messengers found him not. I left word that the letter was to be sent on to Poste Restante, Amsterdam, and I went away without it.

At Amsterdam I went to the post-office and asked for my registered letter. 'There is not one for you,' was the reply. I fancied I had not given it time perhaps to get there, so I called again the next day. 'No letter.' I handed in my passport to show the name. The clerk looked in 'S' again. 'No letter.' I was in despair. At last an idea struck me. 'Look in "G," if you please,' I said. The clerk looked in 'G' and produced my registered letter at once—it had been in 'G' for three days.

The gentleman who attends to my correspondence during my absence has a playful habit of running the initials of my front names right into the initial of my surname, and hence the mistake at the post-office. After all I got my registered letter, but it was a week's hard work to obtain it. My earnest advice to travellers on the Continent is 'never have a registered letter'; it may detain you in one place for months. If you have notes sent to you, let them be cut in half, and sent in separate envelopes to two addresses—one set of halves to your hotel, and the other to the Poste Restante. Only those who have experience of registered letters on the Continent and postal eccentricities abroad will appreciate the value of my little bit of advice.

Holland is to me one of the most interesting countries in Europe. Apart from the excitement of having to do a bit of Blondin, with the edge of a canal for your tight-rope, at intervals of a few minutes all day long, the Dutch themselves furnish you with never-ending study. I love to see the little Dutch boy of six smoking his clay-pipe or his cigar as he clings to his mamma's skirts. There is something at once novel and startling in finding a Dutch cheese and a penny bun placed in front of every guest at the breakfast-table. In a land where a public company is a Maatschappij and nearly every house of restauration announces that the thirsty traveller can there obtain 'tapperij, slitterij, and slemp,' there is always something to amuse you. I had a wild desire to order 'slitterij and slemp,' but I couldn't make up my mind to try and pronounce them, and I didn't know what I should get.

Then, again, the names of the streets and the names over the shop-doors are eminently calculated to tie your eye up in a knot. You get puzzled when you turn down Wijk 1 and come to Wijk 2, and cross a canal and find yourself in Wijk 24, and you find some difficulty in telling the waiter that you want your 'otbijt' (breakfast), and your politeness is sorely tried by having to say 'Als' t'v beleft' whenever you want to say 'If you please.' To come suddenly upon a dog-show and find it called a Rashondententoonstelling, and upon an announcement which reads 'Rijnspoorwegmaalschappij aan den daartoe aangewesen vertegenwoordiger' is calculated to stagger one; but, apart from a language which is trying alike to the eye and the tongue, Holland is a delightful place, and the Dutch are a splendid people.

There is a tremendous lot of the English character about the Dutch. Hoogstraat, Rotterdam, on Sunday night might be High Street, Islington, at the same time. The boys yell, the girls scream and rush about, and a dense black crowd surges and shoves up and down and sings and walks arm-in-arm a dozen wide, and generally comports itself with high spirits and low habits. A Dutch crowd is English in its rough unconcern for the delicate shades of etiquette. But individually the Dutch are kind, hospitable, and most courteous to strangers. The key to the Dutch character is given in one of their popular ballads;

> '*Wij leven vrij, vij leven blij*
>   *Op Neerlands dierbren grond;*
> *Ontworsteld aan de slavernij,*
> *Zijn wij door eendragt groot en vrij;*
> *Hier duldt de grond geen dwinglandij*
>   *Waar vrijheld eeuwen stond.*'

Roughly translated, this is what the above means:

> '*We live blithe, we live free,*
>   *On Netherland's dear shore;*
> *Delivered from slavery,*
> *We are through concord free and great;*
> *The land suffers no tyranny*
>   *Where freedom has subsisted for ages.*'

And your Dutchman does as he jolly well likes wherever he goes, and he doesn't care a Rotter, an Amster, or a Schie for anybody.

The Hague! The largest village in the world, the residence of the Court of Holland. It looks quiet as we steam into the station, but the omnibus is soon filled. I arrive at the hotel I have chosen. The landlord bows to the ground; my portmanteau is taken in, and then I am offered a table in the reading-room to sleep upon. 'No!' I exclaim, 'I require a bedroom.' The landlord is desolated; but there is not a bedroom in the hotel. I will go to another. The landlord is desolated again; but all the hotels are full. Do I not know that the great Medical Congress commences to-day, that the town is crammed, and that rooms have been bespoken a month beforehand? I accept the Congress and the situation, and I pass the night on a sofa in the reading-room surrounded by the principal journals of the world.

Before I retired to rest, pillowing my head upon *L'Étoile Belge* and using as sheets and blanket and counterpane the *Times*, the *New York Herald*, the *Neue Freie Presse*, the *Gil Bias*, and the *Kolnische Zeitung*, I took a stroll through the town. You might have walked on the people's heads, as the saying is, though it seems to me the people might always urge very reasonable objections to your doing so. I didn't go very far, because I hate crowds, and because tomorrow I am going to do the Hague 'thoroughly' in six hours and a half. But I got as far as a very nice square, covered with trees, very Dutch and very pretty. 'I will sit down on this nice seat,' I said to myself, 'and revel in being so far away from the ordinary routine of English life.' At that moment a man came up, and thrust a bill into my hand, and on it I read: 'Heden Avona, Grand Café Chantant. Voor het eerst optreden van de beroemden Mis Maud Haigh en Ada Blanche, het grootste succes van de London Musicall.'

I have made up my mind to go to Scheveningen, the Dutch Brighton, and loll by the sea and watch the Mynheers and their good vrows bathe, and young Holland build castles on the sand. I get as far as the starting-place of the steam tramway, when a huge flaring bill dazzles me, half blinds me, and brings me to attention sharper than the voice of my officer ever did when I was in the rifle-corps. (That was years ago, when I was a good citizen and wanted to defend my country. My uniform was pepper-and-salt cloth, with scarlet facings, and I am told that I looked very well in it when I had it all on; but that I generally managed to go about with a collar, or a cap, or a pair of boots, or something that was not in keeping with a strictly military get-up. I remember once going out in a hurry with my uniform on, and in a fit of absence of mind putting on a tall chimneypot hat. I met the Duke of Cambridge at the corner of the street, and I shall never forget his face as long as I live. But this is a digression.)

The bill which brought me up to attention so smartly informs me in huge letters that 'Donderdag 21 Augustus,' at 'Zeebad Scheveningen,' there will be a 'Groot Zomer-Feest.' No wonder I start. This very day that I have made up my mind to escape the Congress at the Hague, it is the great summer fête of the season at Scheveningen.

I had a delightful week in Holland. Once again I explored the beauties of Amsterdam, Rotterdam, Scheveningen, and the Hague, and my great regret was that I had not time to accept an invitation given me to visit the pauper colonies of Frederiksoord, Wilhelminaoord, and Wilhelmsoord, where the Dutch have made a most successful attempt to solve one of the great questions of the day. There is very little mendicancy in Holland, and pauperism is dealt with in a rational manner. At these colonies each adult, if able-bodied and willing to work, is provided with a few acres of land, a cow, a pig, and a few sheep, and the majority of the pauper colonists are made (after the first outlay) self-supporting for the rest of their days. There is strict discipline, of course, and the places are never allowed to be tempting homes for the vagabond. At Veenhuisen there are also colonies which are more penal in their character. These are for the idle and disorderly and for beggars.

I wonder that the pauper colonies of Holland and the Dutch system of dealing with vagrancy have not attracted more attention, seeing how burning is the question in this country, 'What shall we do with our poor?' The subject is well worth study, and an English delegate or two sent to the pauper colonies might return with some valuable information.

The Dutch, like the English, do not possess the genius of outdoor refreshment. The cafés and beer-houses are mostly under cover, and in all but the larger establishments you sit close, and are not over-burthened with light; but the Dutch enjoy themselves, and cling to old customs and old costumes with a conservatism which is part and parcel of the national character. They have had to fight the ocean for every inch of Holland, and they are a brave and a grand people who have triumphed over difficulties which might have caused Hercules to throw up the sponge. Such a people does not wear its heart on its sleeve and frivol and indulge in outward show.

The only thing that can be urged against the Dutch is the excessive cleanliness of the Dutch housewife. She scrubs and cleans and polishes every day and all day. The streets are generally impassable on Saturday afternoon, because every window is being washed with water ejected from an enormous squirt. An army of buckets lines the footpath, an army of housemaids is kneeling scrubbing at the steps for dear life, auxiliaries are polishing up door-handles, and everywhere you hear the swish of the water and the rasp of the besom. You think this cleanliness is charming at first. After about a week of it, when your shins are black and blue from falling over buckets and you have rheumatism all over you from wading knee-deep through rivers of water in the narrow streets, you think you can do with a little less of it.

CHAPTER XXVI.

ANTWERP AND BRUSSELS.

LONDON was hot, and London was noisy. Everybody was leaving London, but the more the people poured out of it the noisier it seemed to get. Moreover, it was dull. So I said to myself, said I, 'I'll get out of it.'

Thus said I to myself, said I, and off I went; and on a hot Saturday afternoon I got into a train at Liverpool Street, and went down to the sea with three Dutchmen and two Belgians; and when for two mortal hours we had been baked and boiled and fried in a compartment that must have been specially heated by a private pipe from the kitchen of his Majesty King Pluto, we arrived at Harwich, and went, 'all that was left of us,' on board a vessel; and then the whistle blew, and the anchor was heaved, and the harbour lights grew faint and fainter on our lea, and presently a lovely little breeze sprang up, and we were out on the open sea cleaving the waves, and making the best of our way towards Flanders.

I had a berth in a cabin with four other gentlemen. The berth was excellent, the sheets were sweet and clean as snow, the pillow was soft, and all was there to tempt one to sleep as soundly as the cabin-boy mentioned by our grand William. But, alas! one of the gentlemen in my cabin snored as surely never mortal snored before, and another dreamed dreams, and dreamed them aloud. Now he was pursued by banditti, and vowed that he would only surrender his purse with his life; anon, he was on a precipice, and before being hurled over it, he begged a few minutes' respite that he might make his will. So much I gathered from his disjointed remarks. Towards two in the morning the will must have been made, and he must have been lying senseless at the foot of the precipice, for he broke the silence of the night no more. But the snoring gentleman snored louder than ever, and I lay and tossed, and grew hot, and longed for daylight, and when daylight came I went on deck and drank in the cool morning air and some hot coffee, and wondered whether at any time the country on both sides of the Scheldt had been rolled so beautifully level by a steam-roller. At half-past nine we were alongside the quay at Antwerp, and the sweet chimes of the cathedral rang out a dulcet welcome that promised rest and repose.

Rest and repose! Alas! it was fête-day at Antwerp. It was 'festa,' as they say in Italy, and there was no peace that day for the native or the stranger within the gates. All Antwerp and its wife, or its sweetheart, turned out for the Kermesse. Through the streets in the heat of the day there passed the great procession of the Church. Hundreds of waving banners, thousands of candles, brazen images held aloft, a band, a chorus of mellow voices chanting, and then, under a broad canopy of gold, a sacred symbol to which, as it passed, the mighty crowd reverently bared the head and bowed the knee. A fine sight, a magnificent spectacle! I saw it four times, doubling on it down side-streets as the boys double on the Lord Mayor's Show. And all the time the vertical rays of the sun poured down on the back of my neck, and I would have given all the circular notes in my pocket for a cabbage-leaf.

All day long the people stopped in the streets and sang songs and drank beer, and at night we had fireworks and 'a grand harmony,' and the tramcars were loaded with fifty or sixty people at a time, and only one little horse to draw the lot. Poor horses! how they must dread 'festa'! The drivers in most countries double their fares, but the horses fare worse than ever. It was midnight before Antwerp settled down into its usual calm, and the noisiest Sunday I have known for years came to an end.

If ever you want to see how closely a church can be made to resemble a theatre, go to Antwerp Cathedral about noon, when the strangers come to see the Rubens pictures, which are covered with green baize curtains during the hours of service lest those who come to worship should get a peep at the paintings for nothing.

About twelve, when the service is over, the poor and the devout are driven out, and the sacristan and the guides swoop down on the foreigners and drive them up into a corner; and then seats are brought, and one fancies one's self in the stalls or the pit of a theatre, especially when an attendant in uniform comes round and demands a franc from each spectator before the green baize curtain rises on the show.

Many Englishmen, I have no doubt, share with me an antipathy to being 'guided' through cathedrals, picture-galleries, and museums on the Continent. But no one should miss the Antwerp pictures. 'The Descent from the Cross' makes one forget the flippancy and bad English of the guide. One doffs one's hat reverently to Peter Paul Rubens, and yields one's imagination to him without a murmur.

When I entered the 'sacred edifice' the famous Rubens pictures were uncovered. A British tourist in a violent red and yellow tweed suit was staring at 'The Descent from the Cross' through a pair of race-glasses, while the raucous-voiced and grinning guide, who seems nowadays to be part and parcel of a cathedral, was explaining carefully to him that the fat female was the painter's wife. I wish I had never known that the well-developed and modern lady who constantly appears in Peter Paul's pictures was Mrs. Rubens. One can have too much even of this lady, whom I once heard an American irreverently describe as 'Mrs. R.' Rubens could no more keep the head of Mrs. R. (would that he had been satisfied with the head!) out of his pictures, than Mr. Dick could keep King Charles's head out of his memorials, and I can't help thinking that, had she been a Mrs. Jackson, instead of 'a model wife,' it would have been a distinct gain to art.

Irritated by the eternal Mrs. R., the tourist with the race-glasses, and the irreverent comments of the grinning guide, I turned from the Rubens picture, and seeing a crowd in the centre of the building, made my way towards it. I found myself in front of a beautifully-decorated 'May altar.' Evidently some ceremony was expected, for on both sides was a densely-packed mob of bareheaded women and girls. I asked what was expected, and someone told me at three o'clock was to take place 'the benediction of the children.' Wondering what this might mean, I waited patiently, and my patience was later on rewarded by a touching and beautiful spectacle.

Presently a priest came out of the gloomy recesses of the cathedral, clad in raiment of white and gold, and ascended the altar-steps and waited. Soon afterwards there came from the far corner of the cathedral, by the small entrance door, the faint sound of little children's voices singing. All that one could hear as the baby chorus rose and fell was 'Ave Maria.' Nearer and nearer came the sound, and every head was turned in one direction. Then there came into sight a long procession of baby girls and boys, walking bareheaded, two and two. There were some two hundred children, and not one of them was over seven. The little girls were perfect Rubens babies; chubby-faced and rosy-cheeked, and their fair hair was prettily tied with gay ribbons, pink and blue being the prevailing colours. The little baby-boys had each his right arm tied up with a light blue or pink bow, and every little boy and every little girl carried a candle as an offering to the Virgin. Slowly the sweet procession filed along, the children breaking out from time to time in their little hymn of praise. The procession passed between the crowd of mothers and sisters right up to the altar, and then the good priest took from each little hand the candle it bore aloft and laid it on the altar-steps. All the children passed to the chairs arranged for them, and then the sunshine streamed through the stained-glass windows on their little sea of golden curls, making a picture that will linger in my mind for many a year to come.

After the children had presented their candles, a few lame and sickly little ones were carried up to the altar by their mothers to give theirs. One baby-boy had to be coaxed to let his candle go. He had been playfully beating his nurse with it, after the manner of infants, and when he got to the priest he had succeeded in putting the candle into his mouth. Gently the priest unclosed the little fist, and, patting the baby on the head, took the candle and laid it with the rest, while all the mothers smiled.

The last candle had been given up, the last child had been quietly seated in its chair, and there was a deep silence. Then a little girl of about six—a pretty little mite, with long fair hair, dressed in a red-spotted frock and a white pinafore—was lifted on to a chair in front of the altar, and, raising her little hands, she began to speak. The whole proceedings were in Flemish, and the child's words hardly reached me, as I stood at the edge of the crowd, so I may be wrong in saying that it was a speech—it might have been a prayer. Whatever it was it was intensely dramatic, and yet sweetly simple. Amid the dead silence that reigned in the great cathedral, the little mite spoke for nearly five minutes, using her hands with the grace and skill of a baby Bernhardt. And the mothers—rough working women, coarse of frock, stern of feature, and innocent of headgear most of them—wept. Some of the fathers—artisans and dock-labourers—who had come to see their children take part in the ceremony, tugged at their moustaches for a bit and blew their noses defiantly, and then rubbed their knuckles in their eyes, and at last gave it up as a bad job and let the big tears come. I could see the tears in the good priest's eyes as he listened to the baby's speech, and when she sat down, and the women, overcome with emotion, sobbed, I had to yield to the influence of my surroundings, and I bit my lip hard and had a wild struggle with the apple in my throat, and then I had to let the salt drops have their way.

I would give a good deal to be able to paint that scene, to reproduce on canvas that beautiful May altar in Antwerp Cathedral, and the great congregation of fair-haired, blue-eyed Flemish babies, in their simple little frocks and their pretty ribbons, all sitting as still as mice while their little playmate, standing on a chair, lifted her baby hands to heaven and prayed her prayer. I would that I were even an artist in words that I might give you some faint idea of the simple grandeur, the quiet pathos, the gentle beauty of that 'children's service' in the great cathedral. Alas, that glorious privilege is not mine! I am but a journeyman labourer in the great field of literature. I can but bow my head and uncover when the Angelus rings out, and leave you to read upon my face the message that it carries to my soul. I only know that in Antwerp Cathedral that sunny afternoon the message of the children touched me as no words of man have ever touched me yet, and I stole softly away from the flower-laden altar of the Mother of God, and passed out into the busy world with a baby's voice whispering words of hope and comfort to my doubting and desponding heart.

In the evening the scene was changed. On the Place Verte I was stopped by a mighty procession, headed by a band, and bearing illuminated banners. It was a Liberal manifestation, and five thousand lusty Liberals were yelling, 'Down with the Jesuit schools!' Presently, in an opposite direction, came a Catholic demonstration several thousand strong. They also had a band, and a yell, and a battle-cry. I was in the middle of the two processions, and I stopped till they met.

Then the fun began, and the police rushed in, and sticks were whirled about, and feet and fists went busily to work. I had dropped in for a political riot. Heads were broken—thank goodness, not mine. I managed to scramble out of the crowd and get behind a tree. After a good fight the processions separated and marched in different directions, shouting, hooting, cheering, singing. The whole town was in an uproar. The row was deafening. Till long past midnight the rival bands promenaded, and twice again they met and fought, and the sticks came down like a rain of hail. In Antwerp the political feeling is fiercer than in any part of Belgium, and the enmity of Liberals and Catholics leads at times to considerable bloodshed. I followed the Liberals, as they looked the stronger, and I huzzaed and shouted 'Hear, hear!' when a stand was made and a speech delivered.

But directly the fighting began I retired to a convenient distance. It was past one in the morning when I withdrew from the battlefield of the Liberals and the Catholics, but the shouts of the rival factions rang in my ears until I fell asleep from sheer exhaustion. I shall have to try Holland. I have heard of a very nice quiet place there where the peaceful Dutch enjoy themselves, and only express their joy in a quiet grunt. I sincerely hope there won't be a fête or a riot on when I arrive at the next station of my journey in search of a day's repose.

Enough of Antwerp. I tear myself away from Rubens and Quentin Matsys, from the silver chimes and the little carts drawn by the poor docile dogs; I blush and pass by the shop-window that exhibits 'Borgia s'amuse,' and I put my luggage on a fly and drive to the station. I arrive at Antwerp station half an hour before the train starts, and I consume five-and-twenty minutes of that spare time in a process peculiarly Continental, known as registering the baggage. At last I am allowed to pay a fabulous price for the carriage of my portmanteau. I enter the train and I start.

I had said to myself, said I, 'I will go to Brussels. It is a hot day. There will be no one in the wide, clean streets. I will potter about the Galerie de la Reine; I will climb the Rue Montagne de la Cour, and I will sit on a ten centimes chair in the park, and watch the clean Brussels nurses and the pretty little Brussels babies. I love to contemplate innocence. It rests the jaded eye and improves the *blasé* mind. So to Brussels I went, and when I got out at the station I thought 'Bedlam' had broken loose. Thousands of men dressed in the usual fête-day costume of the 'braves Belges'—all black—were promenading the streets with tickets stuck in their hats. In their hands they had flags and dolls and long trumpets and Japanese parasols. Shouting and singing and pouring through the streets in lines of twenty arm-in-arm, they carried all before them, and I had to dart into shops, to climb lamp-posts, and to crawl under the tables outside the cafés, or over and over again I should have been borne along by the mighty procession. Once I snatched at a flag and a Japanese umbrella, and thought it would be better to fall in and shout and sing; but I felt that an Englishman might recognise me, and my character would be gone for ever. So I went up a very narrow street, where there was only room for one person at a time, and hid in a doorway and waited till a policeman came by. Then I asked him what was the matter. He told me that to-day was the fifty-fourth anniversary of the National Independence, and all Belgium had gone mad and come to Brussels. That I should have chosen this of all days in the year! I am indeed the victim of a relentless fate—I mean 'fête.'

In Brussels I went to the Wiertz Museum. Antoine Wiertz, the mad painter, the 'eccentric genius' who refused to sell his pictures and flung back to the 'patrons of art' their proffered gold at a time that he was almost starving, crying out that gold was the murderer of art, is slowly but surely earning the fame for which he pined during his lifetime. That Wiertz was mad I have not the slightest doubt, but his madness was that to which 'great genius is oft allied,' and the world owes much to its madmen. I would a million times rather be mad with Wiertz than sane with some of the gentlemen who cover the walls of the Academy with pictures of 'Eliza, Wife of Jeremiah Snooks, Esq.,' 'A Soldier Buying a Baked Potato,' 'The Dying Cabman's Farewell to his Badge,' 'Wandsworth Parish Pump by Moonlight,' 'A Roman Lady Taking an Eighteenpenny Bath,' or 'A Greek God Waiting for his Shirt to Come Home from the Wash.'

The story of the life of Wiertz, the mad painter of Brussels, is a romance which belongs to the heroic age. It is a romance which is as startling in these matter-of-fact and money-grubbing days as the Clitheroe case would have been in the days of Eros and Psyche.

Wiertz was born in 1806 in Dinant, on the banks of the Meuse, and he died in 1865 in Brussels. He wanted to be Rubens at fourteen, and he spent his life in trying to be Rubens. He began to paint in a granary, which was so low that as he grew he had to stoop in it to avoid hitting his head against the roof. He starved to paint, and he painted for a long time only to starve. He attracted attention at last, and then he was allowed to paint in empty factories and lofty unused warehouses, because these were the only places where he could put up the huge canvases he sought to cover. His picture of the Greeks and Trojans contending for the body of Patroclus is thirty feet high and twenty feet wide. It is his grandest work, and the one which will live on through the centuries. All through his life he endured the most terrible disappointments, but at last he secured a studio where he could carry out his gigantic ideas. The Government gave it him, and there in a side street in Brussels he lived and painted, and to-day his house and studio form the Wiertz Museum, and there you can see his life-work, for he was true to his convictions to the end, and sold nothing.

In his later years he gave the reins to his fiery, untamed imagination, and it reared up occasionally and eventually bolted with him. Some of the paintings which adorn the museum you would only expect to find in a lunatic asylum where they have had artists for patients. Many of them are madly horrible, and their horror is heightened by a method of arrangement which is only worthy of the murder department of a waxwork exhibition. And yet the genius of the man is sublime. A hundred years hence he will be world-famous. To-day, outside Belgium he is comparatively little known.

Next to his 'Patroclus' his finest works are 'The Triumph of Christ,' 'The Revolt of Hell,' and 'The Forge of Vulcan.' But for one person who goes to admire these magnificent creations, a hundred go to the museum to gaze on the horrible, the grotesque, and the fantastic specimens of his art. One of his pictures, 'The Thoughts and Visions of a Severed Head,' is enough to make a nervous man have a fit in the building. I have just read a story in a magazine which professes to be a true account of what a decapitated head saw. The author has probably seen Wiertz's picture, and worked up the details in connection with hypnotism. The picture shows what the head of a guillotined man sees and *thinks* the first moment, the second moment, and the third moment after decapitation. It might with great propriety be called 'The Nightmare of Jack the Ripper, after eating a whole cold sucking-pig for supper.'

You look through a peephole to see 'Hunger, Madness, Crime,' and you behold a remarkably realistic picture of a young mad mother cutting up her baby in order to have it for dinner. The bleeding body is in the mother's lap; the foot and leg of the child are sticking out of the saucepan which is on the kitchen fire. I have a photograph of this picture hanging in my study now. Every time I look at it, portions of my hair, beard, and moustache turn white.

You look through another peephole, and see your own face, and, by a clever contrivance, all the rest of the picture is 'Old Nick.' Startled, you turn away, and you come upon a mad dog. He is tearing at his chain. You spring back, for you think it is a real dog. It is a madman's trick, and is painted on the wall, and intended to frighten you. Near it is the picture of a gentleman who has been buried in cholera times. The interment has been 'a little too previous,' and you see a living man madly trying to get out of his coffin. But heavy coffins are on one half of his 'casket,' and amid the ghastly surroundings of the charnel-house you know he will have to die of slow starvation.

A Belgian lady struggling with a French soldier fires a revolver in his face. The face which you see is pleasantly described in the catalogue as 'shattered into an indistinguishable mass of agony and horror.' 'The Orphans' is an awful picture of a family of children fighting with the undertaker for their father's corpse. They don't want the strange man to take 'papa' from them. You turn away with a shudder, and your hair rises on end. A woman opposite you is dragging a shrieking blistered child from a cradle which has caught fire. The flesh seems to peel from the little body as the terrified woman drags it from the flaming bassinette. With your eyeballs starting from their sockets you shriek for somebody to give you an arm to lean on that you may totter out, and then you pause and burst into a roar of laughter. M. Wiertz has had a funny fit, and painted for you the wife who wished for a black-pudding, and the husband who wished that it might stick to the end of her nose.

I need not take you through the catalogue of the master's mad vagaries and sickening atrocities. Once out in the air and the sunlight again, you gradually forget them; but his noble and heroic works, his idyllic and beautiful works, once seen will never fade from your memory. You have only to look upon his 'Patroclus' and his 'Triumph of Christ,' and you know that you have been in the presence of 'one of the great ones of the earth'—an artistic giant, a mighty genius, born in an age which has no room for genius that is above the regulation standard.

Wiertz died as he had lived—a disappointed man. His body and mind both gave way at last. He had sworn to rival Rubens, and he came very near the master once; but the fatal taint in his blood overpowered him, and he descended to the ghastly horrors of the charnel-house and the guillotine, and to arranging cannibal mothers and buried-alive bodies as peep-shows. He was raving when he died. In his last delirium he shrieked for his brushes and his palette. 'Quick! quick!' he cried; 'bring them to me. Oh, the picture I shall paint! Oh, I will surpass Raphael!' And, shrieking out what mighty things he meant to do, he fell back motionless, and passed into the great silence.

The fame he longed for during his life has come, even after his death, but slowly. But it will increase, and it will last. And this is the best way for fame to come to any man who works not for his own little day, but for the long ages the world has yet to know.

THE END.

www.ingramcontent.com/pod-product-compliance
Lightning Source LLC
Chambersburg PA
CBHW011341090426
42743CB00018B/3406